AF815363

Test Maturity Model integration ***TMMi***

Guidelines for Test Process Improvement

Test Maturity Model integration TMMi

Guidelines for Test Process Improvement

Erik van Veenendaal

Brian Wells

UTN Publishers 's-Hertogenbosch 2012

Trademarks

The following registered trademarks and service marks are used in this book: CMM®, CMMI®, IDEAL℠, ISTQB®, PRISMA®, TMap®, TMap NEXT®, TPI®, TPI NEXT®, TMM℠ and TMMi®.

CMM and CMMI are registered in the U.S. Patent and Trademark Office by Carnegie Mellon University, USA.

IDEAL are service marks of Carnegie Mellon University, USA.

ISTQB is a registered trademark of the International Software Testing Qualification Board, Belgium.

PRISMA is a registered trademark of Improve Quality Services, The Netherlands.

TMap, TMap NEXT, TPI and TPI NEXT are registered trademarks of Sogeti, The Netherlands.

TMM is a registered service mark of Illinois Institute of Technology, USA.

TMMi is a registered trademark of TMMi Foundation, Ireland.

UTN Publishers
Willem van Oranjelaan 5
5211 CN 's-Hertogenbosch
The Netherlands
www.utn.nl

ISBN 9789490986100

Contents

Part 2

The Process Areas and Practices of the Test Maturity Model

Part 3

Annexes, Glossary and References

Recommendations

The benefits of TMMi cannot be overestimated. With the focus now more than ever being on a quality customer experience, the availability of a defined maturity process for testing across the whole of the testing and delivery lifecycle will continue to serve as a major benefit. TMMi has set the standard for us all now to follow.
James Boyle, Deloitte Touche Tohmatsu, Australia

As the organization that issued the world's first formal TMMi certificate, we definitely acknowledge the value of the TMMi model. It addresses, of course, many aspects of testing, but it especially encourages organizations to think of what they want to achieve with testing and how to achieve it.
Rob Hendriks, Improve Quality Services BV, The Netherlands

The TMMi reference model will boost the progress of the software testing industry and having the official TMMi book available will strongly support this. I recommend the TMMi book as a mandatory resource for all software testing professionals.
Osmar Higashi, RSI Inform‡tica, Brazil

I'm sure TMMi Model will make a great contribution to increase the capability of your test organization. I strongly recommend this book to testing specialists around the world who would like to apply TMMi and surely after reading they will succeed in getting a direction about that.
Hyunjung Jeong , LG CNS, South-Korea

Testing maturity is often lacking even in environments with mature software development practices. TMMi provides a way to evaluate and improve testing maturity, particularly if you are already using CMMI to guide the development practices. This book gives a clear and easily followed guideline to the steps needed to mature your testing processes.
Judy McKay, independent test consultant, USA

TMMi framework and its formal assessment and certification program is the best tool to promote software testing as an invaluable tool for top management. For test experts, it is one of the most powerful tools to practically assess and improve their test processes with enormous learning experiences.
Wonil Kwon, STA Testing Consulting, South-Korea

As we architected the Capability Maturity Model Integration versions, we sought to provide a readily adaptable structure for others to use in ways that suited continuous process improvement. The TMMi approach provided a powerful example that fulfills that expectation well for a critical role in quality excellence!
Mike Philips, Software Engineering Institute, USA

Level 4 TMMI certification has made it possible to optimize our testing process and standardize the way of working for the whole company. It has helped us to create a measurement program that gives us a quantitative vision of product quality along the software lifecycle, measures our testing activities and feeds our continuous process improvement towards excellence.
Javier de la Plaza, MTP, Spain

The testing world has moved from process towards context-driven. This requires a profound level of testing skills. TMMi provides the right foundation to achieve this.
Martin Pol, Polteq Test Services, The Netherlands

Accenture's global testing practice has adopted TMMi as our standard Test Process Improvement methodology, enabling Accenture's worldwide clients to begin their journey towards higher software engineering maturity by focusing on the quality aspects of products and software. With TMMi, testing is no longer an afterthought but finally seen as the central cornerstone for every software development and maintenance lifecycle.
Matthias Rasking, Accenture GmbH, Germany

The TMMi model, with its clear structure and links to other maturity models with comparable set-up, provided us with an excellent framework in setting a clear and challenging aspiration for the team, in achieving smooth alignment and cooperation with our colleagues in other disciplines, and – last but not least – in gaining full support of our (business) stakeholders.
Gunther van de Rijt, Philips Healthcare, The Netherlands

The testing industry has suffered for many years without an independent model that it can use to assess its maturity. TMMi provides the missing independent industry model. We have carried out over 100 TMMi assessments and have seen many significant customer benefits ranging from a 12% savings in overall project costs to up to 40% saved in testing alone, together with many qualitative savings. TMMi really works; we recommend it.
Geoff Thompson, Experimentus, UK

Foreword

When we initiated the TMMi development and started out on the journey of developing a standard reference model for test and quality, we had no idea how popular this would become. We were just a few consultants concerned that there was no standard, independent approach to test improvement and assessment and, therefore, clients were simply at the mercy of the quality and experience of the consultant they employed when they wanted to understand how good their test processes were. TMMi, owned and managed by the TMMi Foundation, now provides the first non-commercial, organization-independent test maturity model. TMMi is being applied in various domains and industries word-wide and is rapidly gaining recognition. By many test professionals it is already perceived as the de-facto standard for test improvement and assessment. With TMMi, organizations can have their test process objectively evaluated by certified assessors, improve their test processes and even have their test process and test organization formally accredited if it complies with the requirements. The main advantages of the TMMi over other improvement models are independence, the alignment with international standards, the business-orientation (objective-driven) and the perfect match with the CMMI-framework.

TMMi Foundation

The TMMi model has been developed by the TMMi Foundation, a non-profit organization based in Dublin (Ireland) that has as main objectives to develop and maintain the TMMi model, create a benchmark database and facilitate formal assessment by accredited lead assessors. Testers can (free of charge) become a member of the TMMi Foundation, and from that membership a board is being elected. Many international test experts have contributed to the current version of TMMi. It has already proven to be highly useful in practice. Many organizations world-wide are already using TMMi for their internal test improvement process. Other organizations already have formally achieved TMMi level 2, level 3 and even TMMi level 4.

Target Audience

The audience for this book includes anyone interested in test process improvement – whether one is familiar with the concept or whether one is seeking information to get started on test improvement. It is intended for those who want an assessment to see where they are, those who already know what they want to improve, and those who are just getting started and want to develop a general understanding of TMMi. Testers and test managers can use the TMMi book to evaluate and improve their processes. Test consultants can use this TMMi book during assessments of test improvement projects. Other stakeholders can use it to acquire testing knowledge in general and TMMi knowledge in particular. CMMI consultants and QA employees can by using this book become familiar with a test improvement model that is compliant with CMMI.

Content

The book contains a full and detailed description of TMMi release 1.0. The full TMMi model can also be found at the web site of the TMMi Foundation: *www.tmmi.org*. This book is organized into three main part.

Part one consists of three chapters:

- Chapter 1, *'Test Maturity Model integration'*, describes the background and history of the TMMi, it also addresses the main sources used during its development and the scope of the TMMi.
- Chapter 2, *'TMMi maturity levels'*, provides an overview and description of the 5 maturity levels, including the various process areas.
- Chapter 3, *'Structure of the TMMi'*, describes all components of the TMMi process areas, provides a detailed overview of the generic goals and generic practices and discusses the relationship between the CMMI and the TMMi.

Part two, *'The process areas and practices of the Test Maturity Model'*, consists of 16 sections, one for each of the TMMi process areas. The sections are organized by maturity level. Each section contains the description of the goals, practices and examples.

Part three consists of six information resources:

- Annex A, *'TMMi assessments and certification'* provides an overview of the TMMi assessment types, accreditation for assessment methods and describes how certification can be achieved.
- Annex B, *'The improvement process'* provides an overview of the process that can be used with TMMi to perform test process improvement.
- The *'Glossary'* defines the terms used in TMMi.
- The *'References'* contains references you can use to locate documented sources of information that are related to the TMMi and references in this book.
- *'About the TMMi Foundation'*.
- *'About the Authors'*.

Acknowledgments

It would not have been possible to develop the TMMi model and write this book without the involvement of a great many supporters. Supporters, often in the role of reviewers, came from many different organizations throughout the world. Some were already using earlier versions of the TMMi model and provided valuable practical feedback. There are a few people we feel need special recognition because of the support they provided. First of all, we'd like to thank the other founding members of the TMMi Foundation who were also especially involved in the development of the TMMi levels 2 and 3: Andrew Goslin, Mac Miller, Klaus Olsen, Fran O'Hara, and Geoff Thompson. We would also like to thank Matthias Hamburg, Jan Jaap Cannegieter, Thomas George and Hareton Leung for their contribution to the development of TMMi levels 4 and 5, Srivatsan Tiruvallur Thattai for all the work he did on coordinating the many internal and external reviews, and finally Judy McKay for the wonderful technical editing of the TMMi model. It has been a great pleasure working with all of you!

Erik van Veenendaal
Brian Wells

Part 1

The Test Maturity Model: Background, Concepts and Structure

1 Test Maturity Model integration

1.1 Introduction

Organizations face tougher business objectives every day, e.g., decreased time-to-market, requirements or higher quality levels and reliability and reduced costs. Systems in which software is a dominant factor are becoming more and more challenging to build. They are playing an increasingly important role in society. New methods, techniques, and tools are becoming available to support development and maintenance tasks. Because systems play such an important role in our lives both economically and socially, there is pressure for the software engineering discipline to focus on quality issues. Poor quality software is no longer acceptable to society. Software failures can result in catastrophic losses. In this context the importance of the testing discipline, as one of the quality measures that can be taken, is growing rapidly. Testing has become a key activity that directly influences not only the product quality but also the 'performance' of the entire development and manufacturing process.

For the past decade, the software industry has invested substantial effort to improve the quality of its products. This has been a difficult job since the size and complexity of software increases rapidly while customers and users are becoming more and more demanding. At the same time, software development is becoming an outsourced activity or is co-developed with other sites. Despite encouraging results from various quality improvement approaches, the software industry is still far from zero defects. To improve product quality, the software industry has often focused on improving its development processes. A guideline that has been widely used to improve the development processes is the Capability Maturity Model Integration (CMMI). The CMMI is often regarded as the industry standard for software process improvement. Despite the fact that testing often accounts for at least 30-40% of the total project costs, only limited attention is given to testing in the various software process improvement models such as the CMMI. As an answer, the testing community has created its own improvement models. This document describes the Test Maturity Model Integration (TMMi). The TMMi is a detailed model for test process improvement and is positioned as being complementary to the CMMI.

1.2 Background and History

The TMMi framework has been developed by the TMMi Foundation as a guideline and reference framework for test process improvement and is positioned as a complementary model to the CMMI Version 1.3 [CMMI] addressing those issues important to test managers, test engineers and software quality professionals. Testing as defined in the TMMi is applied in its broadest sense to encompass all software product quality-related activities.

> ***Testing**: The process consisting of all lifecycle activities, both static and dynamic, concerned with planning, preparation and evaluation of software products and related work products to determine that they satisfy specified requirements, to demonstrate that they are fit for purpose and to detect defects. [ISTQB]*

Just like the CMMI staged representation, the TMMi also uses the concept of maturity levels for process evaluation and improvement. Furthermore process areas, goals and practices are identified. Applying the TMMi maturity criteria will improve the test process and have a positive impact on product quality, test engineering productivity, and cycle-time effort. The TMMi has been developed to support organizations with evaluating and improving their test process. Within the TMMi, testing evolves from a chaotic, ill-defined process with a lack of resources, tools and well-educated testers to a mature and controlled process that has defect prevention as its main objective.

Practical experiences are positive and show that TMMi supports the process of establishing a more effective and efficient test process. Testing becomes a profession and a fully integrated part of the development process. As stated the focus of testing changes from defect detection to defect prevention.

1.3 Sources

The development of the TMMi has used the TMM framework as developed by the Illinois Institute of Technology as one of its major sources [Burnstein]. In addition to the TMM, it was largely guided by the work done on the Capability Maturity Model Integration (CMMI), a process improvement model that has widespread support in the IT industry. The CMMI has both a staged and continuous representation. Within the staged representation the CMMI architecture prescribes the stages that an organization must proceed through in an orderly fashion to improve its development process. Within the continuous representation there is no fixed set of levels or stages to proceed through. An organization applying the continuous representation can select areas for improvement from many different categories.

The TMMi has been developed as a staged model. The staged model uses predefined sets of process areas to define an improvement path for an organization. This improvement path is described by a model component called a maturity level. A maturity level is a well-defined evolutionary plateau towards achieving improved organizational processes. At a later stage a continuous representation of the TMMi may become available. This will most likely not influence the content of the TMMi. It will 'only' provide a different structure and representation.

Other sources to the TMMi development include the Gelperin and Hetzel's Evolution of Testing Model [Gelperin and Hetzel], which describes the evolution of the testing process over a 40-year period, Beizer's testing model, which describes the evolution of the individual tester's thinking [Beizer], research on the TMM carried out in the EU-funded MB-TMM project [V2M2], and international testing standards, e.g., IEEE 829 Standard for Software Test Documentation [IEEE 829]. The testing terminology used in the TMMi is derived from the ISTQB Standard Glossary of terms used in Software Testing [ISTQB].

As stated for defining the maturity levels, the evolutionary testing model of Gelperin and Hetzel has served as a foundation for historical-level differentiation in the TMMi. The Gelperin and Hetzel model describes phases and test goals for the 1950s through the 1990s. The initial period is described as 'debugging-oriented', during which most software development organizations had not clearly differentiated between testing and debugging. Testing was an ad hoc activity associated with debugging to remove bugs from programs. Testing has, according to Gelperin and Hetzel, since progressed to a 'prevention-oriented' period, which is associated with current best practices and reflects the highest maturity level of the TMMi.

Furthermore, various industry best practices, practical experience using the TMM and testing surveys have contributed to the TMMi development providing it with its necessary empirical foundation and required level of practicality. These illustrate the current best and worst testing practices in the IT industry, and have allowed the developers of the TMMi framework to extract realistic benchmarks by which to evaluate and improve testing practices.

1.4 Scope of the TMMi

1.4.1 Software and System Engineering

The TMMi is intended to support testing activities and test process improvement in both the systems engineering and software engineering disciplines. Systems engineering covers the development of total systems, which may or may not include software. Software engineering covers the development of software systems.

1.4.2 Test Levels

Whereas some models for test process improvement focus mainly on higher test levels, e.g., Test Process Improvement (TPI) [Koomen and Pol] and its successor TPI Next [Sogeti], or address only one aspect of structured testing e.g., the test organization, the TMMi addresses all test levels (including static testing) and aspects of structured testing. With respect to dynamic testing, both lower test level (e.g., component test, integration test) and higher test levels (e.g., system test, acceptance test) are within the scope of the TMMi. Studying the model more in detail one will learn that the model addresses all four cornerstones for structured testing (lifecycle, techniques, infrastructure and organization) [TMap].

1.4.3 TMMi and CMMI

It is also important to note that TMMi is positioned as a complementary model to the CMMI. In many cases a given TMMi level needs specific support from process areas at its corresponding CMMI level or from lower CMMI levels. In exceptional cases there is even a relationship to higher CMMI levels. Process areas and practices that are elaborated within the CMMI are mostly not repeated within TMMi; they are only referenced. For example the process area configuration management, which is also applicable to test (work) products / testware, is not elaborated upon in detail within the TMMi; the practices from CMMI are referenced and implicitly re-used.

1.4.4 Assessments

Many organizations find value in benchmarking their progress in test process improvement for both internal purposes and for external customers and suppliers. Test process assessments focus on identifying improvement opportunities and understanding the organization's position relative to the selected model or standard. The TMMi provides an excellent reference model to be used during such assessments. Assessment teams use TMMi to guide their identification and prioritization of findings. These findings, along with the guidance of TMMi practices, are used to plan improvements for the organization. The assessment framework itself is not part of the TMMi. Requirements for TMMi assessments are described by the TMMi Foundation in the document 'TMMi Assessment Method Application Requirements'

[TAMAR]. These requirements are based upon the ISO 15504 standard. The achievement of a specific maturity level must mean the same thing for different assessed organizations. Rules for ensuring this consistency are contained in the TMMi assessment method requirements. The TMMi assessment method requirements contain guidelines for various classes of assessments, e.g., formal assessments, quick scans and self-assessments. More details on TMMi assessment and accreditation are provided in Annex A.

As the TMMi can be used in conjunction with the CMMI (staged version), TMMi and CMMI assessments are often combined, evaluating both the development process and the testing process. Since the models are of similar structure, and the model vocabularies and goals overlap, parallel training and parallel assessments can be accomplished by an assessment team. The TMMi can also be used to address testing issues in conjunction with continuous models. Overlapping process areas that relate to testing can be assessed and improved using the TMMi, while other process areas fall under the umbrella of the broader-scope model.

1.4.5 Improvement Approach

The TMMi provides a full framework to be used as a reference model during test process improvement. It does not provide an approach for test process improvement such as the IDEAL (Initiating, Diagnosing, Establishing, Acting, and Learning) model [IDEAL]. Practical experiences have shown that the most powerful initial step to test process improvement is to build strong organizational sponsorship before investing in test process assessments. Given sufficient senior management sponsorship, establishing a specific, technically competent test process group that represents relevant stakeholders to guide test process improvement efforts has proven to be an effective approach. More details on the improvement approach are provided in annex B. Some other ideas and guidelines regarding an approach for test process improvement can be found in 'The little TMMi' [Veenendaal and Cannegieter].

2 TMMi Maturity Levels

2.1 Overview

TMMi has a staged architecture for process improvement. It contains stages or levels through which an organization passes as its testing process evolves from one that is ad hoc and unmanaged, to one that is managed, defined, measured, and optimized. Achieving each stage ensures that an adequate improvement has been laid as a foundation for the next stage. The internal structure of the TMMi is rich in testing practices that can be learned and applied in a systematic way to support a quality testing process that improves in incremental steps. There are five levels in the TMMi that prescribe a maturity hierarchy and an evolutionary path to test process improvement. Each level has a set of process areas that an organization needs to implement on to achieve maturity at that level. Experience has shown that organizations do their best when they focus their test process improvement efforts on a manageable number of process areas at a time, and that those areas require increasing sophistication as the organization improves. Because each maturity level forms a necessary foundation for the next level, trying to skip a maturity level is usually counter-productive. At the same time, you must recognize that test process improvement efforts should focus on the needs of the organization in the context of its business environment and the process areas at higher maturity levels may address the current needs of an organization or project. For example, organizations seeking to move from maturity level 1 to maturity level 2 are frequent encouraged to establish a test group, which is addressed by the Test Organization process area that resides at maturity level 3. Although the test group is not a necessary characteristic of a TMMi level 2 organization, it can be a useful part of the organization's approach to achieve TMMi maturity level 2.

The process areas for each maturity level of the TMMi are shown in figure 1. They are fully described later in other chapters and are also listed below along with a brief description of the characteristics of an organization at each TMMi level. The description will introduce the reader to the evolutionary path prescribed in the TMMi for test process improvement.

Note that the TMMi does not have a specific process area dedicated to test tools and/or test automation. Within TMMi test tools are treated as a supporting resource (practices) and are therefore part of the process area where they provide support, e.g., applying a test design tool is a supporting test practice within the process area Test Design and Execution at TMMi level 2 and applying a performance testing is tool is a

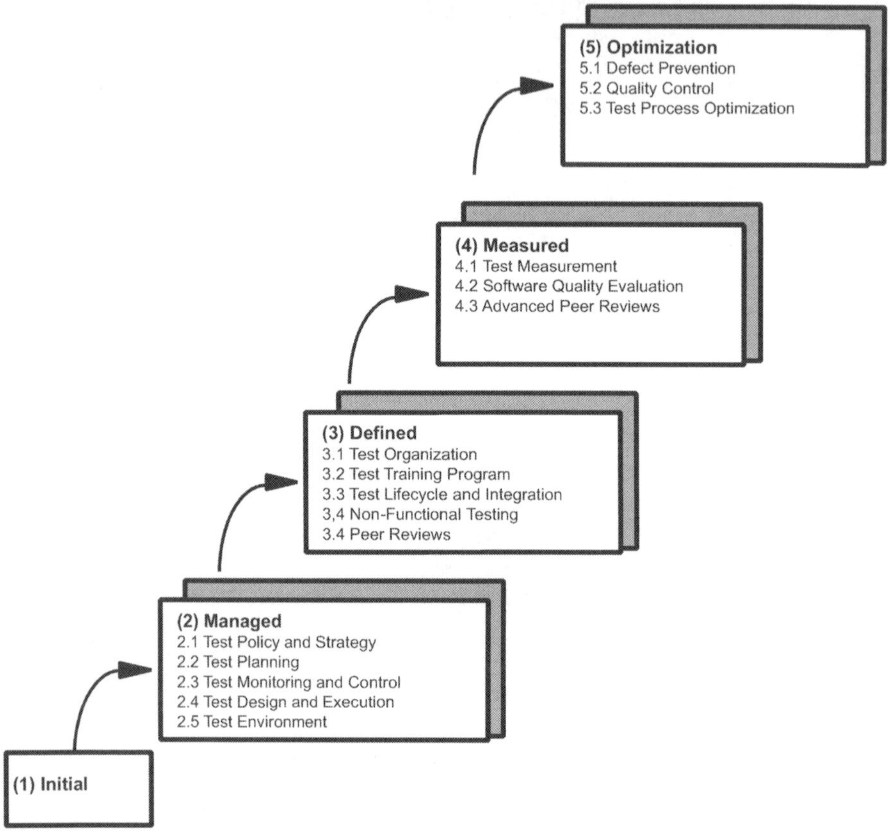

Figure 1: TMMi maturity levels and process areas

supporting test practice within the process area Non-functional Testing at TMMi level 3.

2.2 Level 1 Initial

At TMMi level 1, testing is a chaotic, undefined process and is often considered a part of debugging. The organization usually does not provide a stable environment to support the processes. Success in these organizations depends on the competence and heroics of the people in the organization and not the use of proven processes. Tests are developed in an ad hoc way after coding is completed. Testing and debugging are interleaved to get the bugs out of the system. The objective of testing at this level is to show that the software runs without major failures. Products are released without adequate visibility regarding quality and risks. In the field, the product often does not fulfill its needs, is not stable, and/or is too slow. Within testing there is a lack of resources, tools and well-educated staff. At TMMi level 1 there are no defined process areas. Maturity level 1 organizations are characterized by a tendency to over commit, abandonment of processes in a time of crises, and an inability to repeat their successes. In addition products tend not to be released on time, budgets are overrun and delivered quality is not according to expectations.

2.3 Level 2 Managed

At TMMi level 2, testing becomes a managed process and is clearly separated from debugging. The process discipline reflected by maturity level 2 helps to ensure that existing practices are retained during times of stress. However, testing is still perceived by many stakeholders as being a project phase that follows coding.

In the context of improving the test process, a company-wide or program-wide test strategy is established. Test plans are also developed. Within the test plan a test approach is defined, whereby the approach is based on the result of a product risk assessment. Risk management techniques are used to identify the product risks based on documented requirements. The test plan defines what testing is required, when, how and by whom. Commitments are established with stakeholders and revised as needed. Testing is monitored and controlled to ensure it is going according to plan and actions can be taken if deviations occur. The status of the work products and the delivery of testing services are visible to management. Test design techniques are applied for deriving and selecting test cases from specifications. However, testing may still start relatively late in the development lifecycle, e.g., during the design or even during the coding phase.

In TMMI level 2 testing is multi-leveled: there are component, integration, system and acceptance test levels. For each identified test level there are specific testing objectives defined in the organization-wide or program-wide test strategy. The processes of testing and debugging are differentiated.

The main objective of testing in a TMMi level 2 organization is to verify that the product satisfies the specified requirements. Many quality problems at this TMMi level occur because testing occurs late in the development lifecycle. Defects are propagated from the requirements and design into code. There are no formal review programs as yet to address this important issue. Post code, execution-based testing is still considered by many stakeholders the primary testing activity.

The process areas at TMMi level 2 are:
2.1 Test Policy and Strategy
2.2 Test Planning
2.3 Test Monitoring and Control
2.4 Test Design and Execution
2.5 Test Environment.

2.4 Level 3 Defined

At TMMi level 3, testing is no longer confined to a phase that follows coding. It is fully integrated into the development lifecycle and the associated milestones. Test planning is done at an early project stage, e.g., during the requirements phase, and is documented in a master test plan. The development of a master test plan builds on the test planning skills and commitments acquired at TMMi level 2. The organization's set of standard test processes, which is the basis for maturity level 3, is established and improved over time. A test organization and a specific test training program exist, and testing is perceived as being a profession. Test process improvement is fully institutionalized as part of the test organization's accepted practices.

Organizations at level 3 understand the importance of reviews in quality control; a formal review program is implemented although not yet fully linked to the dynamic testing process. Reviews take place across the lifecycle. Test professionals are involved in reviews of requirements specifications. Whereby the test designs at TMMi level 2 focus mainly on functionality testing, test designs and test techniques are expanded at level 3 to include non-functional testing, e.g., usability and/or reliability, depending the business objectives.

A critical distinction between TMMi maturity level 2 and 3 is the scope of the standards, process descriptions, and procedures. At maturity level 2 these may be quite different in each specific instance, e.g., on a particular project. At maturity level 3 these are tailored from the organization's set of standard processes to suit a particular project or organizational unit and therefore are more consistent except for the differences allowed by the tailoring guidelines. Another critical distinction is that at maturity level 3, processes are typically described more rigorously than at maturity level 2. As a consequence at maturity level 3, the organization must revisit the maturity level 2 process areas.

The process areas at TMMi level 3 are:
3.1 Test Organization
3.2 Test Training Program
3.3 Test Lifecycle and Integration
3.4 Non-functional Testing
3.5 Peer Reviews.

2.5 Level 4 Measured

Achieving the goals of TMMi level 2 and 3 has the benefits of putting into place a technical, managerial, and staffing infrastructure capable of thorough testing and providing support for test process improvement. With this infrastructure in place, testing can become a measured process to encourage further growth and accomplishment. In TMMi level 4 organizations, testing is a thoroughly defined, well-founded and measurable process. Testing is perceived as evaluation; it consists of all lifecycle activities concerned with checking products and related work products.

An organization-wide test measurement program will be put into place that can be used to evaluate the quality of the testing process, to assess productivity, and to monitor improvements. Measures are incorporated into the organization's measurement repository to support fact-based decision making. A test measurement program also supports predictions relating to test performance and cost.

With respect to product quality, the presence of a measurement program allows an organization to implement a product quality evaluation process by defining quality needs, quality attributes and quality metrics. (Work) products are evaluated using quantitative criteria for quality attributes such as reliability, usability and maintainability. Product quality is understood in quantitative terms and is managed to the defined objectives throughout the lifecycle.

Reviews and inspections are considered to be part of the test process and are used to measure product quality early in the lifecycle and to formally control quality gates. Peer reviews as a defect detection technique is transformed into a product quality measurement technique in line with the process area Product Quality Evaluation.

TMMi level 4 also covers establishing a coordinated test approach between peer reviews (static testing) and dynamic testing and the usage of peer reviews results and data to optimize the test approach with both aiming at making testing more effective and more efficient. Peer reviews are now fully integrated with the dynamic testing process, e.g. part of the test strategy, test plan and test approach.

The process areas at TMMi level 4 are:
4.1 Test Measurement
4.2 Product Quality Evaluation
4.3 Advanced Peer Reviews.

2.6 Level 5 Optimization

The achievement of all previous test improvement goals at levels 1 through 4 of TMMi has created an organizational infrastructure for testing that supports a completely defined and measured process. At TMMi maturity level 5, an organization is capable of continually improving its processes based on a quantitative understanding of statistically controlled processes. Improving test process performance is carried out through incremental and innovative process and technological improvements. The testing methods and techniques are optimized and there is a continuous focus on fine tuning and process improvement. An optimized test process, as defined by the TMMi is one that is:

- managed, defined, measured, efficient and effective
- statistically controlled and predictable
- focused on defect prevention
- supported by automation as much is deemed an effective use of resources
- able to support technology transfer from the industry to the organization
- able to support re-use of test assets
- focused on process change to achieve continuous improvement.

To support the continuous improvement of the test process infrastructure, and to identify, plan and implement test improvements, a permanent test process improvement group is formally established and is staffed by members who have received specialized training to increase the level of their skills and knowledge required for the success of the group. In many organizations this group is called a Test Process Group. Support for a Test Process Group formally begins at TMMi level 3 when the test organization is introduced. At TMMi level 4 and 5, the responsibilities grow as more high level practices are introduced, e.g., identifying reusable test (process) assets and developing and maintaining the test (process) asset library.

The Defect Prevention process area is established to identify and analyze common causes of defects across the development lifecycle and define actions to prevent similar defects from occurring in the future. Outliers to test process performance, as identified as part of process quality control, are analyzed to address their causes as part of Defect Prevention.

The test process is now statistically managed by means of the Quality Control process area. Statistical sampling, measurements of confidence levels, trustworthiness, and reliability drive the test process. The test process is characterized by sampling-based quality measurements.

At TMMi level 5, the Test Process Optimization process area introduces mechanisms to fine-tune and continuously improve testing. There is an established procedure to identify process enhancements as well as to select and evaluate new testing technologies. Tools support the test process as much as is effective during test design, test execution, regression testing, test case management, defect collection and analysis, etc. Process and testware re-use across the organization is also common practice and is supported by a test (process) asset library.

The three TMMi level 5 process areas, Defect Prevention, Quality Control and Test Process Optimization all provide support for continuous process improvement. In fact, the three process areas are highly interrelated. For example, Defect Prevention supports Quality Control, e.g., by analyzing outliers to process performance and by implementing practices for defect causal analysis and prevention of defect re-occurrence. Quality Control contributes to Test Process Optimization, and Test Process Optimization supports both Defect Prevention and Quality Control, for example by implementing the test improvement proposals. All of these process areas are, in turn, supported by the practices that were acquired when the lower-level process areas were implemented. At TMMi level 5, testing is a process with the objective of preventing defects.

The process areas at TMMi level 5 are:
5.1 Defect Prevention
5.2 Quality Control
5.3 Test Process Optimization.

3 Structure of the TMMi

The structure of the TMMi is largely based on the structure of the CMMI. This is a major benefit because many people/organizations are already familiar with the CMMI structure. The CMMI structure makes a clear distinction between practices that are required (goals) or recommended (specific practices, example work products, etc.) to implement. This aspect is also included in the TMMi. In this chapter, the components and structure of the TMMi are described. In addition the support provided by the CMMI to a TMMi implementation is described.

3.1 Required, Expected and Informative Components

The various components are grouped into three categories: required, expected and informative.

3.1.1 Required Components

Required components describe what an organization must achieve to satisfy a process area. This achievement must be visibly implemented in an organization's processes. The required components in TMMi are the specific and generic goals. Goal satisfaction is used in assessments as the basis for deciding if a process area has been achieved and satisfied.

3.1.2 Expected Components

Expected components describe what an organization will typically implement to achieve a required component. Expected components guide those who implement improvements or perform assessments. Expected components include both specific and generic practices. Either the practices as described or acceptable alternatives to the practices must be present in the planned and implemented processes of the organization, before goals can be considered satisfied.

3.1.3 Informative Components

Informative components provide details that help organizations get started in thinking about how to approach the required and expected components. Sub-practices, example work products, notes, examples, and references are all informative model components.

3.2 Components of the TMMi

The TMMi model required and expected components can be summarized to illustrate their relationship as in figure 2. The following sections provide a description of the components. Note that the TMMi also provides a specific glossary of terms. The terms used in the glossary are largely re-used from the international test terminology standard developed by the International Software Testing Qualifications Board (ISTQB): Standard glossary of terms used in Software Testing [ISTQB].

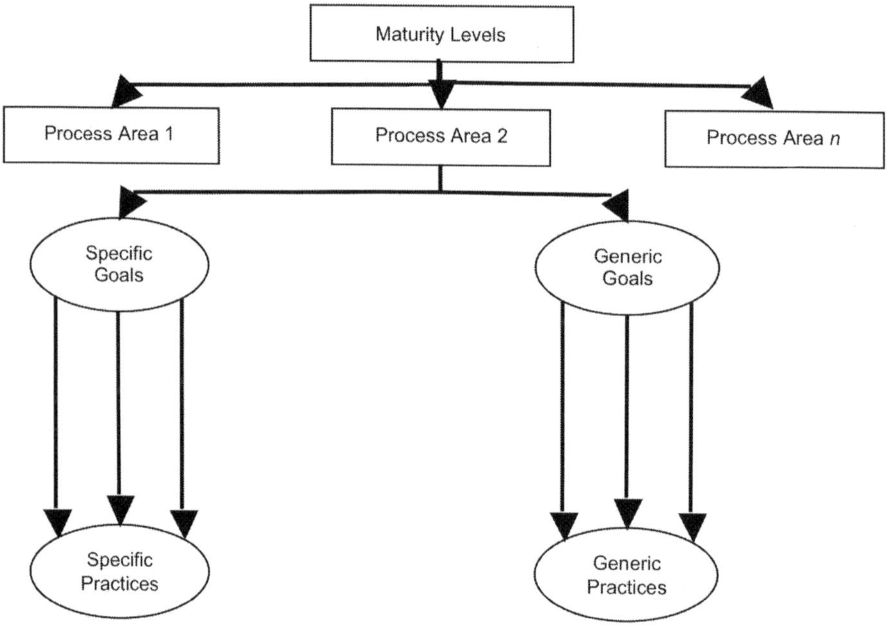

Figure 2: TMMi structure and components

Maturity Levels

A maturity level within the TMMi can be regarded as a degree of organizational test process quality. It is defined as an evolutionary plateau of test process improvement. Each level progressively develops an important part of the organization's test processes. There are five maturity levels within the TMMi. Each maturity level tells what to implement in order to achieve the given level. The higher the maturity level the organization achieves, the more mature the test process of the organization is. To reach a particular maturity level, an organization must satisfy all of the appropriate goals (both specific and generic) of the process areas at the specific level and also those at earlier maturity levels. Note that all organizations possess a minimum of TMMi level 1, as this level does not contain any goals that must be satisfied.

Process Areas

As stated with the exception of level 1, each maturity level consists of several process areas that indicate where an organization should focus to improve its test process. Process areas identify the issues that must be addressed to achieve a maturity level. Each process area identifies a cluster of test related activities. When the practices are all performed a significant improvement in activities related to that area will be made. In the TMMi, only those process areas that are considered to be key determinants of test process capability are identified. All process areas of the maturity level and the lower maturity levels must be satisfied to consider a maturity level to be achieved. For example, if an organization is at TMMi level 3, it has satisfied all of the process areas at both TMMi level 2 and TMMi level 3.

Purpose

The purpose statement describes the purpose of the process area and is an informative component. For example, the purpose statement of the test planning process area is 'define a test approach based on the identified risks and the defined test strategy, and to establish and maintain well-founded plans for performing and managing the testing activities'.

Introductory Notes

The introductory notes section of the process area describes the major concepts covered in the process area and is an informative component.

Scope

The scope section of the process area specifically identifies the test practices that are addressed by the process area, and if necessary test practices that are explicitly outside the scope of this process area.

Specific Goals

A specific goal describes the unique characteristic that must be present to satisfy the process area. A specific goal is a required model component and is used in assessments to help determine whether a process area is satisfied.

Generic Goals

Generic goals appear near the end of a process area and are called 'generic' because the same goal statement appears in multiple process areas. A generic goal describes the characteristics that must be present to institutionalize the processes that implement a process area. A generic goal is a required model component and is used in assessments to help determine whether a process area is satisfied.

Specific Practices

A specific practice is the description of an activity that is considered important in achieving the associated specific goal. The specific practice describes the activities expected to result in achievement of the specific goals of a process area. A specific practice is an expected model component.

Example Work Products

The example work products section lists sample outputs from a specific practice. These examples are called 'example work products' because there are often work products that are just as effective but are not listed. An example work product is an informative model component.

Sub-practices

A sub-practice is a detailed description that provides guidance for interpreting and implementing a specific practice. Sub-practices may be worded as if prescriptive, but are actually an informative component meant only to provide ideas that may be useful for test process improvement.

Generic Practices

Generic practices appear near the end of a process area and are called 'generic' because the same practice appears in multiple process areas. A generic practice is the description of an activity that is considered important in achieving the associated generic goal. A generic practice is an expected model component.

Generic Practices Elaborations

Generic practices elaboration appears after a generic practice in a process area to provide guidance on how the generic practice should be applied uniquely to the process area. A generic practice elaboration is an informative model component.

Supporting Informative Components

There are many places where further information is needed to describe a concept. This informative information is provided in terms of the following components:

Notes

A note is text that can accompany any other model component. It may provide detail, background, or rationale. A note is an informative model component.

Examples

An example is a component comprising text and often a list of items, usually in a box, that can accompany nearly any other component and provides one or more examples to clarify a concept or described activity. An example is an informative model component.

References

A reference is a pointer to additional or more detailed information in related process areas and can accompany nearly any other model component. A reference is an informative model component.

3.3 Generic Goals and Generic Practices

This section describes all of the generic goals and generic practices. The generic goals and generic practices are largely derived from the CMMI. The generic goals are organized in numeric order. The generic practices are also organized in numerical order under the generic goal they support. Note that the generic goal from the CMMI, GG1 'Achieve Specific Goals' is not taken into account since this only relates to the continuous representation of the CMMI and therefore has no relevance to the staged representation of the TMMi. Otherwise the numbering scheme of the CMMI is fully adopted to avoid confusion for organizations using both CMMI and TMMi.

The capability level you are targeting will determine which generic goals and practices are applicable. When trying to reach maturity level 2 the process areas at maturity level 2 as well as generic goal 2 and the accompanying generic practices are applicable. Generic goal 3 is only applicable when trying to reach maturity level 3 or higher. This means that when you have already achieved a maturity level 2 rating, to achieve a maturity level 3 rating you must return to maturity level 2 process areas and apply generic goal 3 and the accompanying practices to those process areas.

Institutionalization is an important concept in process improvement. When mentioned in the generic goal and generic practice descriptions, institutionalization implies that the process is ingrained in the way the work is performed and there is commitment and consistency to performing the process. An institutionalized process is more likely to be retained during times of stress. When the requirements and objectives for the process change, however, the implementation of the process may also need to change to ensure that it remains active. The generic practices describe activities that address these aspects of institutionalization.

The following is a list of all the generic goals and practices in the TMMi.

3.3.1 GG 2 Institutionalize a Managed Process

A managed process is a process that accomplishes the work necessary to produce work products. It is planned and executed in accordance with policy, employs skilled people and has adequate resources to produce controlled outputs. A managed process involves relevant stakeholders, is monitored and controlled, is subjected to reviews and is evaluated for adherence to its process descriptions. The process may be instantiated by a project, group, or organizational unit. The control provided by a managed process helps to ensure that the established process is retained during times of stress.

GP 2.1 Establish an organizational policy

The purpose of this generic practice is to define the organizational expectations for the process and make these expectations visible to those in the organization who are affected. In general, senior management is responsible for establishing and communicating guiding principles, direction, and expectations for the organization.

GP 2.2 Plan the process

The purpose of this generic practice is to determine what is needed to perform the process and to achieve the established objectives, to prepare a plan for performing the process, to prepare a process description, and to get agreement on the plan from relevant stakeholders by performing reviews.

GP 2.3 Provide resources
The purpose of this generic practice is to ensure that resources necessary to perform the process as defined by the plan are available when they are needed. Resources include adequate funding, appropriate physical facilities, skilled people, and appropriate tools.

GP 2.4 Assign responsibilities
The purpose of this generic practice is to ensure that there is accountability for performing the process and achieving the specified results throughout the life of the process. The people assigned must have the appropriate authority to perform the assigned responsibilities. Responsibilities can be assigned using detailed job descriptions or in living documents, such as the plan for performing the process.

GP 2.5 Train people
The purpose of this generic practice is to ensure that the people have the necessary skills and expertise to perform or support the process. Appropriate training is provided to the people who will perform the work. Overview training is provided to orient people who interact with those performing the work. Training supports the successful performance of the process by establishing a common understanding of the process, and by imparting the skills and knowledge needed to perform the process.

GP 2.6 Manage configurations
The purpose of this generic practice is to establish and maintain the integrity of the selected work products of the process throughout their useful life. The selected work products are specifically identified in the plan for performing the process, along with a specification of the level of configuration management, e.g., version control or formal configuration management using baselines. Examples of configuration management practices include version control, change history and control, status identification and usage of configuration management tools for storage. Refer to the Configuration Management process area within CMMI for more information on placing work products under configuration management.

GP 2.7 Identify and involve relevant stakeholders
The purpose of this generic practice is to establish and maintain the expected involvement of stakeholders during the execution of the process. Relevant stakeholders are involved in activities such as planning, decisions, commitments, communications, reviews and resolution of problems. Critical stakeholders in the testing process include managers and users/customer. The manager's role involves commitment and the ability to perform activities and tasks related to improving testing capability. The user's or customer's role involves co-operation, support and sometimes performing testing activities. Users/customers should be

involved in quality-related activities and tasks that concern user-oriented needs. The focus is on solicitation of user/customer support, consensus and participation in activities such as product risk analysis, acceptance testing and possibly usability testing. Depending on the test level the developer may also be a stakeholder, e.g., at unit testing the developer often performs the testing activities himself; however, at the acceptance test level the developer becomes a stakeholder for discussing incidents found, agreeing on entry criteria etc.

GP 2.8 Monitor and control the process
The purpose of this generic practice is to perform the direct day-to-day monitoring and controlling of the test process. Appropriate visibility into the test process is maintained so that appropriate corrective action can be taken when necessary. Monitoring and controlling the process involves measuring appropriate attributes of the test process and work products produced by the test process. Refer to the Measurement and Analysis process area in CMMI for more information on measurement.

GP 2.9 Objectively evaluate adherence
The purpose of this generic practice is to provide credible assurance that the process is implemented as planned and adheres to its process description, standard, and procedures. People not directly responsible for managing or performing the activities of the test process typically evaluate adherence. In many cases, adherence is evaluated by people within the organization, but external to the test process or project. Refer to the Process and Product Quality Assurance process area within CMMI for more information on objectively evaluating adherence.

GP 2.10 Review status with higher level management
The purpose of this generic practice is to provide higher level management with the appropriate visibility into the process. Higher level management includes those levels of management in the organization above the immediate level of management responsible for the process. These reviews are for managers who provide policy and overall guidance for the process, not for those who perform the direct day-to-day monitoring and controlling of the process.

3.3.2 GG 3 Institutionalize a Defined Process

A defined process is a managed process that is tailored from the organization's set of standard processes according to the organization's tailoring guidelines. A defined process has maintained process descriptions; and contributes work products, measures, and other process improvement information to the organizational process assets. A critical distinction between a managed process and a defined process is the scope of application of the process descriptions, standards, and procedures. For a managed process descriptions, standards, and procedures are applicable to a particular project, group, or organizational function. As a result, the managed processes of two projects in one organization may be different. A defined process is standardized as much as possible across the organization and adapted only when required for a specific project or organizational function based on the tailoring guidelines.

GP 3.1 Establish a defined process

The purpose of this generic practice is to establish and maintain a description of the process that is tailored from the organization's set of standard processes to address the needs of a specific instantiation. The organization should have standard processes that cover the process area, as well as have guidelines for tailoring these standard processes to meet the needs of a project or organizational function. With a defined process, variability in how the processes are performed across the organization is reduced and process assets, data, and learning can be effectively shared. Refer to the Organization Process Definition process area in CMMI for more information about the organization's set of standard processes and tailoring guidelines.

GP 3.2 Collect improvement information

The purpose of this generic practice is to collect information and artifacts derived from planning and performing the process to support future use and improvement of the organization's processes and process assets. The information and artifacts are stored and made available to those who are (or who will be) planning and performing the same or similar processes.

3.4 Supporting Process Areas for Generic Practices

While generic goals and generic practices are the model components that directly address the institutionalization of a process across the organization, many process areas either in TMMi or CMMI likewise address institutionalization by supporting the implementation of the generic practices. The table below provides an overview of the process areas that partly or fully support the implementation of a generic practice.

Generic Practice	Supporting Process Area
GP 2.2 Plan the process	**Test Planning** - the TMMi Test Planning process area can implement GP 2.2 in full for all project-related process areas (except for test planning itself). Test planning itself can be addressed as part of the CMMI process area Project Planning.

GP 2.5 Train people	**Test Training Program** - the TMMi Test Training Program process area supports the implementation of GP 2.5 for all process areas by making the organization-wide training program available to those who will perform or support the processes. In addition the TMMi Test Planning process area may support this generic practice by identifying and organizing the training needs that are needed for testing in the project and documenting those in the test plan.
GP 2.6 Manage configurations	**Configuration Management** - the CMMI Configuration Management process area can implement GP 2.6 in full for all project-related process areas as well as some of the organizational process areas.
GP 2.7 Identify and involve the relevant stakeholders	**Test Planning** - the TMMi Test Planning process area may support this generic practice for all project-related process areas by planning the involvement of identified stakeholders and documenting those in the test plan. Stakeholder involvement for test planning itself can be addressed as part of the CMMI process area Project Planning.
GP 2.8 Monitor and control the process	**Test Monitoring and Control** - the TMMi Test Monitoring and Control process area can implement GP 2.8 in full for all process areas.
GP 2.9 Objectively evaluate adherence	**Process and Product Quality Assurance** - the CMMI Process and Product Quality Assurance process can implement GP 2.9 in full for all process areas.
GP 3.1 Establish a defined process	**Organizational Process Definition** - the CMMI process area Organizational Process Definition can support the implementation of GP 3.1 by establishing the organizational process assets needed to implement GP 3.1. **Test Lifecycle and Integration** - this TMMi process area can support the implementation of GP 3.1 by establishing the organizational process assets needed to implement GP 3.1 based on its specific goal SG 1 Establish Organizational Test Process Assets.
GP 3.2 Collect improvement information	**Organizational Process Focus** - the CMMI process area Organizational Process Focus can provide support for the implementation of GP 3.2 since it establishes an organizational measurement repository. **Test Lifecycle and Integration** - this TMMi process area can provide similar support for the implementation of GP 3.2 since it establishes an organizational test process database. **Measurement and Analysis** - for all processes the CMMI Measurement and Analysis process area and the TMMi Test Measurement process areas provide general guidance about measuring, analyzing, and recording information that can be used in establishing measure

Table 1: Supporting process areas for generic practices

3.5 Supporting CMMI Process Areas for TMMi

Although TMMi can be used in isolation, it is also positioned as a complementary model to the CMMI. As a result in many cases a given TMMi level needs specific support from process areas at its corresponding CMMI level or from higher CMMI levels. Process areas and practices that are elaborated within the CMMI generally are not repeated within TMMi; they are only referenced. Tables 2 to 5 summarize the CMMI process areas that compliment and/or overlap with the TMMi process areas. Note that, as shown in tables 2 to 5, supporting process areas (S) and parallel process (P) areas are denoted. Supported process areas (S) encompasses those process areas and related practices that should ideally be in place to support achievement of the TMMi goals. Parallel process areas (P) are those that are similar in nature in TMMi and CMMI, and can be simultaneously pursued. of the CMM An overview of supporting CMMI process areas required for TMMi level 2 achievement is shown in table 2. Tables 3, 4, and 5 provide an overview of the supporting and parallel CMMI process areas required for respectively TMMI levels 3, 4 and 5. Note that some of these relationships were already identified, although from a different perspective, in the previous section.

TMMI	CMMI	Supporting CMMI process areas for TMMi level 2
2	2	**Configuration Management** (S) - as stated above, the CMMI Configuration Management process area can implement GP 2.6 Manage configurations in full for all project-related process areas as well as some of the organizational process areas. **Process and Product Quality Assurance** (S) - as stated above, the CMMI Process and Product Quality Assurance process area can implement GP 2.9 Objectively evaluate adherence in full for all process areas. **Project Control and Monitor** (S) - this CMMI process area provides support for the implementation of the TMMi process area Test Monitoring and Control. Project management practices can be re-used for test management. **Project Planning** (S) - this CMMI process area provides support for the implementation of the TMMi process area Test Planning. Project management practices can be re-used for test management. Project planning also specifically support the implementation of the generic practice GP 2.7 Identify and involve the relevant stakeholders for Test Planning. **Measurement and Analysis** (S) - this CMMI process area provides support for the implementation of the SG 3 Establish test performance indicators of the TMMi process area Test Policy and Strategy. **Requirements Management** (S) - the implementation of this CMMI process area is a constraint for managing derived (work) products, such as the product risk analysis and test designs, and keeping them up-to-date. The practices regarding maintaining traceability possibly can be re-used within the Test Design and Execution TMMi process area.
2	3	**Requirements Development** (S) - practices from this CMMI process area can be re-used when developing test environment requirements within the TMMi process area Test Environment. **Risk Management** (S) - practices from this CMMI process area can be re-used for identifying and controlling product risk and test project risks within the TMMi process areas Test Planning and Test Monitoring and Control.

Table 2: Support for TMMi maturity level 2 from CMMI process areas

TMMI	CMMI	Supporting CMMI process areas for TMMi level 3
3	2	**Configuration Management** (S) - the CMMI Configuration Management process area can implement GP 2.6 Manage configuration in full for all project-related process areas as well as some of the organizational process areas. **Measurement and Analysis** (S) - The CMMI process area Measurement and Analysis provides general guidance about measuring, analyzing, and recording information thereby supporting the implementation of TMMi generic practice GP 3.2 Collect improvement information. **Process and Product Quality Assurance** (S) - the CMMI Process and Product Quality Assurance process area can implement GP 2.9 Objectively evaluate adherence in full for all process areas. **Project Planning** (S) - this CMMI process area provides support for the implementation of the TMMi process area Test Lifecycle and Integration, especially SG 3 Establish a master test plan. Project management practices can be re-used for test management.
3	3	**Organizational Process Definition** (P) - this CMMI process area provides support for the implementation of the TMMi process area Test Lifecycle and Integration, especially for SG 1 Establish organizational test process assets. The CMMI process area **Organizational Process Definition** can also support the implementation of GP 3.1 Establish a defined process by establishing the organizational process assets needed to implement GP 3.1. **Organizational Process Focus** (P) - this CMMI process area provides support for the implementation of the TMMi process area Test Organization, especially for SG 4 Determine, plan and implement test process improvements and SG 5 Deploy organizational test processes and incorporate lessons learned. The CMMI process area **Organizational Process Focus** also provides support for the implementation of the TMMi generic practice GP 3.2 Collect improvement information since it establishes an organizational measurement repository. **Organizational Training** (S) - this CMMI process area provides support for the implementation of the TMMi process area Test Training Program. **Verification** (P) - the practices within SG 2 'Perform peer reviews' of this CMMI process area will provide support for the implementation of the TMMi process area Peer Reviews.

Table 3: Support for TMMi maturity level 3 from CMMI process areas

TMMI	CMMI	Supporting CMMI process areas for TMMi level 4
4	2	**Configuration Management** (S) - the CMMI Configuration Management process area can implement GP 2.6 Manage configurations in full for all project-related process areas as well as some of the organizational process areas. **Measurement and Analysis** (S,P) - this CMMI process area provides support for the implementation of the TMMi process area Test Measurement. The measurement infrastructure and practices can be re-used for test measurement. It may be practical to implement the test measurement program as a supplement to the general measurement program. The CMMI process area **Measurement and Analysis** also provides general guidance about measuring, analyzing, and recording information thereby supporting the implementation of TMMi generic practice GP 3.2 Collect improvement information. **Process and Product Quality Assurance** (S) - the CMMI Process and Product Quality Assurance process area can implement GP 2.9 Objectively evaluate adherence in full for all process areas.
4	3	**Organizational Process Definition** (S) - This CMMI process area supports the implementation of GP 3.1 Establish a defined process by establishing the organizational process assets needed to implement GP 3.1. **Organizational Process Focus** (S) – this CMMI process area provides support for the implementation of GP 3.2 Collect improvement information since it establishes an organizational measurement repository.
4	4	**Quantitative Project Management** (S) - this CMMI process area provides support for the implementation of the TMMi process area Product Quality Evaluation, both for SG 1 Measurable project goals for product quality and their priorities are established, and SG 2 Actual progress towards achieving product quality goals is quantified and managed.

Table 4: Support for TMMi maturity level 4 from CMMI process areas

TMMI	CMMI	Supporting CMMI process areas for TMMi level 5
5	2	**Configuration Management** (S) - the CMMI Configuration Management process area can implement GP 2.6 Manage configurations in full for all project-related process areas as well as some of the organizational process areas. The CMMI process area **Measurement and Analysis** (S) also provides general guidance about measuring, analyzing, and recording information thereby supporting the implementation of TMMi generic practice GP 3.2 Collect improvement information. **Process and Product Quality Assurance** (S) - the CMMI Process and Product Quality Assurance process area can implement GP 2.9 Objectively evaluate adherence in full for all process areas.
5	3	**Organizational Process Definition** (S) - This CMMI process area supports the implementation of GP 3.1 Establish a defined process by establishing the organizational process assets needed to implement GP 3.1. **Organizational Process Focus** (S) – this CMMI process area provides support for the implementation of GP 3.2 Collect improvement information since it establishes an organizational measurement repository.
5	4	**Organizational Process Performance** (S,P) – This CMMI process area provides support for the implementation of the TMMi process area Quality Control, especially for SG 1 Establish a Statistically Controlled Test Process
5	5	**Causal analysis and Resolution** (P) – This CMMI process area provides support for the implementation of the TMMi process area Defect Prevention, especially for SG 1 Determine common causes of defects. **Organizational Innovation and Deployment** (S) - This CMMI process area provides support for the implementation of the TMMi process area Test Process Optimization, especially for SG 1 Select Test Process Improvements, SG 2 New testing technologies are evaluated to determine their impact on the testing process and SG 3 Deploy Test Improvements.

Table 5: Support for TMMi maturity level 5 from CMMI process areas

3.6 CMMI process areas Verification and Validation

Note that the test specific process areas of the CMMI **Verification** and **Validation** are not listed as supporting or parallel process areas for the dynamic testing processes within TMMi. For these CMMI process areas the relationship is complementary. The TMMi process areas provide support and a more detailed specification of what is required to establish a defined verification and validation process. Practical experiences have shown that an organization that complies with the TMMi level 2 requirements will, at the same time, largely or fully fulfill the requirements for the CMMI process areas verification and validation. (With the exception of the peer review specific goal and related practices within the verification process area). This is a good example of how satisfying the goals and implementation of the practices in one model (TMMi) may lead to satisfactory implementation in the other (CMMI). It is also a good example of how the TMMI test specific improvement model complements the more generic software and system development improvement models (e.g., CMMI).

Part 2

The Process Areas and Practices of the Test Maturity Model

TMMi Level 2: Managed

At TMMi level 2, testing becomes a managed process and is clearly separated from debugging. The process discipline reflected by maturity level 2 helps to ensure that existing practices are retained during times of stress. However, testing is still perceived by many stakeholders as being a project phase that follows coding.

In the context of improving the test process, a company-wide or program-wide test strategy is established. Test plans are also developed. Within the test plan a test approach is defined, whereby the approach is based on the result of a product risk assessment. Risk management techniques are used to identify the product risks based on documented requirements. The test plan defines what testing is required, when, how and by whom. Commitments are established with stakeholders and revised as needed. Testing is monitored and controlled to ensure it is going according to plan and actions can be taken if deviations occur. The status of the work products and the delivery of testing services are visible to management. Test design techniques are applied for deriving and selecting test cases from specifications. However, testing may still start relatively late in the development lifecycle, e.g., during the design or even during the coding phase.

In TMMI level 2 testing is multi-leveled: there are component, integration, system and acceptance test levels. For each identified test level there are specific testing objectives defined in the organization-wide or program-wide test strategy. The processes of testing and debugging are differentiated.

The main objective of testing in a TMMi level 2 organization is to verify that the product satisfies the specified requirements. Many quality problems at this TMMi level occur because testing occurs late in the development lifecycle. Defects are propagated from the requirements and design into code. There are no formal review programs as yet to address this important issue. Post code, execution-based testing is still considered by many stakeholders the primary testing activity.

The process areas at TMMi level 2 are:
2.1 Test Policy and Strategy
2.2 Test Planning
2.3 Test Monitoring and Control
2.4 Test Design and Execution
2.5 Test Environment.

Each of these is discussed in more detail in the sections hereafter.

Process Area 2.1 Test Policy and Strategy

Purpose

The purpose of the Test Policy and Strategy process area is to develop and establish a test policy, and an organization-wide or program-wide test strategy in which the test levels are unambiguously defined. To measure test performance, test performance indicators are introduced.

Introductory Notes

When an organization wants to improve its test process, it should first clearly define a test policy. The test policy defines the organization's overall test objectives, goals and strategic views regarding testing. It is important for the test policy to be aligned with the overall business (quality) policy of the organization. A test policy is necessary to attain a common view of testing and its objectives between all stakeholders within an organization. This common view is required to align test (process improvement) activities throughout the organization. The test policy should address testing activities for both new development and maintenance projects. Within the test policy the objectives for test process improvement should be stated. These objectives will subsequently be translated into a set of key test performance indicators. The test policy and the accompanying performance indicators provide a clear direction, and a means to communicate expected and achieved levels of test performance. The performance indicators must show the value of testing and test process improvement to the stakeholders. The test performance indicate will provide quantitative indication whether the organization is improving and achieving the defined set of test (improvement) goals.

Based upon the test policy a test strategy will be defined. The test strategy covers the generic test requirements for an organization or program (one or more projects). The test strategy addresses the generic product risks and presents a process for mitigating those risks in accordance with the testing policy. Preparation of the test strategy starts by performing a generic product risk assessment analyzing the products being developed within a program or organization.

The test strategy serves as a starting point for the testing activities within projects. The projects are set up in accordance with the organization-wide or program-wide test strategy. A typical test strategy will include a description of the test levels that are to be applied, for example: unit, integration, system and acceptance test. For each test level, at a minimum, the objectives, responsibilities, main tasks and entry/exit criteria are defined. The test strategy serves as a starting point for the testing activities within projects. The projects are set up in accordance with the organization-wide or program-wide test strategy. When a test strategy is defined and followed, less overlap between the test levels is likely to occur, leading to a more efficient test process. Also, since the test objectives and approach of the various levels are aligned, fewer holes are likely to remain, leading to a more effective test process.

Note that test policy and test strategy modification is usually required as an organization's test process evolves and moves up the levels of the TMMi.

Scope

The process area Test Policy and Strategy involves the definition and deployment of a test policy and test strategy. Within the test strategy, test levels are identified. For each test level, at a minimum, test objectives, responsibilities, main tasks and entry/exit criteria are defined. To measure test performance and the accomplishment of test (improvement) objectives, test performance indicators are defined and implemented.

Specific Goal and Practice Summary

SG 1 Establish a Test Policy
- SP 1.1 Define test goals
- SP 1.2 Define test policy
- SP 1.3 Distribute the test policy to stakeholders

SG 2 Establish a Test Strategy
- SP 2.1 Perform a generic product risk assessment
- SP 2.2 Define test strategy
- SP 2.3 Distribute the test strategy to stakeholders

SG 3 Establish Test Performance Indicators
- SP 3.1 Define test performance indicators
- SP 3.2 Deploy test performance indicators

Specific Practices by Goals

SG 1 Establish a Test Policy

A test policy, aligned with the business (quality) policy, is established and agreed upon by the stakeholders.

SP 1.1 Define test goals

Define and maintain test goals based upon business needs and objectives.

Example work products

1. Test goals

Sub-practices

1. Study business needs and objectives

Examples of business needs and objectives to be studied include the following:

- Mission statement
- Business and user needs regarding the products
- Business drivers
- Main goals of a quality program
- Business (quality) policy
- Type of business, e.g., risk level of products being developed

2. Provide feedback for clarifying business needs and objectives as necessary
3. Define test goals traceable to business needs and objectives

Examples of test goals include the following:

- Validate products for 'fit-for-use'
- Prevent defects from occurring in operation
- Verify compliance to external standards
- Provide visibility regarding product quality
- Shorten test execution lead-time

4. Review the test goals with stakeholders
5. Revisit and revise the test goals as appropriate, e.g., on a yearly basis

SP 1.2 Define the test policy

A test policy, aligned with the business (quality) policy, is defined based on the test goals and agreed upon by the stakeholders.

Example work products

1. Test policy

Sub-practices

1. Define the test policy based on the defined test goals

Examples of typical statements to be part of a test policy include the following:

- A definition of testing
- A definition of debugging (fault localization and repair)
- Basic views regarding testing and the testing profession
- The objectives and added value of testing
- The quality levels to be achieved
- The level of independence of the test organization
- A high level test process definition
- The key responsibilities of testing
- The organizational approach to and objectives of test process improvement

2. Clearly separate testing from debugging within the test policy
3. Review the test policy with stakeholders
4. Define and establish ownership for test policy
5. Revisit and revise the test policy as appropriate, e.g., on a yearly basis

SP 1.3 Distribute the test policy to stakeholders

The test policy and test goals are presented and explained to stakeholders inside and outside testing.

Example work products

1. Deployment plan
2. Presentation test policy

Examples of distribution mechanisms include the following:

- Documenting it in a handbook (quality system)
- Presenting in project and/or departmental meetings
- Referencing it via posters on the wall
- Making it part of the departmental introduction program
- Providing access to it on a central web portal

SG 2 Establish a Test Strategy

An organization-wide or program-wide test strategy that identifies and defines the test levels to be performed is established and deployed.

SP 2.1 Perform a generic product risk assessment

A generic product risk assessment is performed to identify the typical critical areas for testing.

Example work products

1. Generic product risk list, with a category and priority assigned to each risk

Sub-practices

1. Identify and select stakeholders that need to contribute to the generic risk assessment
2. Identify generic product risks using input from stakeholders
3. Document the context and potential consequences of the generic product risk
4. Identify the relevant stakeholders associated with each generic product risk
5. Analyze the identified generic products risks using the predefined parameters, e.g., likelihood and impact
6. Categorize and group generic product risks according to the defined risk categories
7. Prioritize the generic product risks for mitigation
8. Review and obtain agreement with stakeholders on the completeness, category and priority level of the generic product risks
9. Revise the generic product risks as appropriate

Note that product risk categories and parameters as defined in the Test Planning process area (SP 1.1 Define product risk categories and parameters) are largely re-used within this specific practice.

Refer to SG 1 Perform a Product Risk Assessment from the process area Test Planning for more details on the practices for performing a product risk assessment.

SP 2.2 Define test strategy

The test strategy is defined that identifies and defines the test levels. For each level, the objectives, responsibilities, main tasks, entry/exit criteria and so forth are defined.

Example work products

1. Test strategy

Sub-practices

1. Study test policy and goals
2. Provide feedback for clarifying test policy and goals as necessary
3. Define the test strategy providing clear linkage to the defined test policy and goals

Examples of topics to be addressed as part of a test strategy include the following:

- Generics risks of the products being developed
- Overall test model (V-model, incremental lifecycle) to be employed as a way to mitigate the risks
- Test levels (e.g., unit, integration, system and acceptance test)
- Objectives, responsibilities and main tasks at each test level, for example:,
  - For unit testing
    - Verifying that the unit operates as specified in the unit design
    - Achieving a certain level of code coverage
  - For integration testing
    - Verifying that the units together operate as specified in the global design
    - Verifying that the interfaces operate as specified in the interface specification
  - For system testing
    - Verifying that the system operates as specified in the requirements specification
    - Achieving a certain level of system requirements coverage
  - For acceptance testing
    - Verifying that the system satisfies defined acceptance criteria
    - Validating whether the system is 'fit for use'
    - Achieving a certain level of user requirements coverage
- Test case design techniques to be used at each test level
- Test types to be carried out at each test level
- Entry and exit criteria for each test level
- Standards that must be adhered with
- Level of independence of testing
- Environment in which the tests will be executed
- Approach to automation at each test level
- Approach to regression testing

4. Review the test strategy with stakeholders
5. Define and establish ownership for test strategy
6. Revisit and revise the test strategy as appropriate, e.g., on a yearly basis

Note that the test strategy will serve as a starting point for testing to be performed in a project. However, each project can tailor the overall strategy to its needs according the tailoring policy established for the document. Any areas of non-compliance shall be clearly documented in the project's test plan.

SP 2.3 Distribute the test strategy to the stakeholders

The test strategy is presented to and discussed with stakeholders inside and outside testing.

Example work products

1. Deployment plan
2. Presentation test strategy

Examples of distribution mechanisms include the following:

- Documenting it in a handbook and/or quality system
- Presenting in project and/or departmental meetings
- Referencing it via posters on the wall
- Making it part of the departmental introduction program
- Providing access to it on a central web portal

SG 3 Establish Test Performance Indicators

A set of goal-oriented test process performance indicators to measure the quality of the test process is established and deployed.

SP 3.1 Define test performance indicators

The test performance indicators are defined based upon the test policy and goals, including a procedure for data collection, storage and analysis.

Example work products

1. Test performance indicators
2. Data collection, storage, analysis and reporting procedures

Sub-practices

1. Study test policy and goals, e.g., the objectives for test process improvement
2. Provide feedback for clarifying test policy and goals as necessary
3. Define the test performance indicators traceable to the test policy and goals

Examples of test performance indicators include the following:

- Test effort and cost
- Test lead time
- Number of defects found
- Defect detection percentage
- Test coverage
- Test maturity level

In general the defined test performance indicators should relate to the business value of testing.

4. Review the performance indicators with stakeholders
5. Define and establish ownership for test performance indicators
6. Specify how performance indicators will be obtained and stored
7. Specify how performance indicators will be analyzed and reported

SP 3.2 Deploy test performance indicators

Deploy the test performance indicators and provide measurement results for the identified test performance indicators to stakeholders.

Example work products

1. Test performance indicator data
2. Reports providing information regarding the test performance indicators

Sub-practices

1. Obtain specified performance indicator data
2. Analyze and interpret performance indicator data
3. Manage and store performance indicator data and analysis results
4. Report the performance indicator data to stakeholders on a periodic basis
5. Assist stakeholders in understanding the results

Examples of actions to assist in understanding the results include the following:

- Discussing the results with relevant stakeholders
- Provide contextual information that provides background and explanation

Generic Practices by Goals

GG 2 Institutionalize a Managed Process

GP 2.1 Establish an organizational policy

Establish and maintain an organizational policy for planning and performing the Test Policy and Strategy process.

Elaboration

Typically, at an organizational level, it is documented that on a periodic basis, e.g., yearly, the test policy and test strategy will be revisited and updated as necessary.

GP 2.2 Plan the process

Establish and maintain the plan for performing the Test Policy and Strategy process.

Elaboration

The plan for performing the test policy and strategy process can be included (or referenced by) the organization's quality plan or test process improvement plan.

GP 2.3 Provide resources

Provide adequate resources for performing the Test Policy and Strategy process, developing the test work products, and providing the services of the process.

GP 2.4 Assign responsibilities

Assign responsibility and authority for performing the Test Policy and Strategy process, developing the work products, and providing the services of the Test Policy and Strategy process.

Elaboration

A group with the authority and knowledge is designated to be responsible for defining a test policy, test strategy and test performance indicators. The group typically consists of the following stakeholders: resource management, business management, quality management, project management, operations, test management and test engineers.

GP 2.5 Train people

Train the people performing or supporting the Test Policy and Strategy process as needed.

Elaboration

People involved in the practices of defining and maintaining the test policy and test strategy are provided with basic knowledge regarding structured testing. Those involved in the practices around test performance indicators are trained on measurement practices.

GP 2.6 Manage configurations

Place selected work products of the Test Policy and Strategy process under appropriate levels of configuration control.

Elaboration

Examples of work products placed under configuration management include the following:

- Test policy
- Test strategy
- Definitions of test performance indicators
- Measurement data

GP 2.7 Identify and involve relevant stakeholders

Identify and involve relevant stakeholders of the Test Policy and Strategy process as planned.

GP 2.8 Monitor and control the process

Monitor and control the Test Policy and Strategy process against the plan for performing the process and take appropriate actions.

GP 2.9 Objectively Evaluate Adherence

Objectively evaluate adherence of the Test Policy and Strategy process and selected work products against the process description, standards, and procedures, and address non-compliances.

Elaboration

Examples of review and/or audit evaluation adherence topics include the following:

- Compliance of test plans to test policy and test strategy
- Level of familiarity by test professionals and other stakeholders with test policy, test strategy and test performance indicators
- Availability of test performance indicator data to the stakeholders

GP 2.10 Review status with higher level management

Review the activities, status and results of the Test Policy and Strategy process with higher level management and resolve issues.

GG 3 Institutionalize a Defined Process

Only applicable at TMMi level 3.

GP 3.1 Establish a defined process

Establish and maintain a description of a defined Test Policy and Strategy process

GP 3.2 Collect improvement information

Collect process related experiences derived from planning and performing the Test Policy and Strategy process to support the future use and improvement of the organization's processes and process assets.

Process Area 2.2 Test Planning

Purpose

The purpose of Test Planning is to define a test approach based on the identified risks and the defined test strategy, and to establish and maintain well-founded plans for performing and managing the testing activities.

Introductory Notes

After confirmation of the test assignment, an overall study is carried out regarding the product to be tested, the project organization, the requirements, and the development process. As part of Test Planning, the test approach is defined based on the outcome of a product risk assessment and the defined test strategy. Depending on the priority and category of risks, it is decided which requirements of the product will be tested, to what degree, how and when. The objective is to provide the best possible coverage to the parts of the system with the highest risk.

Based on the test approach the work to be done is estimated and as a result the proposed test approach is provided with clear cost information. The product risks, test approach and estimates are defined in close co-operation with the stakeholders rather than by the testing team alone. The test plan will comply, or explain non-compliances, with the test strategy.

Within Test Planning, the test deliverables that are to be provided are identified, the resources that are needed are determined, and aspects relating to infrastructure are defined. In addition, test project risks regarding testing are identified. As a result the test plan will define what testing is required, when, how and by whom.

Finally, the test plan document is developed and agreed to by the stakeholders. The test plan provides the basis for performing and controlling the testing activities. The test plan will usually need to be revised, using a formal change control process, as the project progresses to address changes in the requirements and commitments, inaccurate estimates, corrective actions, and (test) process changes.

Scope

The process area Test Planning involves performing a product risk assessment on the test object and defining a differentiated test approach based on the risks identified. It also involves developing estimates for the testing to be performed, establishing necessary commitments, and defining and maintaining the plan to guide and manage the testing. A test plan is required for each identified test level. At TMMi level 2 test plans are typically developed per test level. At TMMi level 3, within the process area Test Lifecycle and Integration, the master test plan is introduced as one of its goals.

Specific Goal and Practice Summary

SG 1 Perform a Product Risk Assessment
- SP 1.1 Define product risk categories and parameters
- SP 1.2 Identify product risks
- SP 1.3 Analyze product risks

SG 2 Establish a Test Approach
- SP 2.1 Identify items and features to be tested
- SP 2.2 Define the test approach
- SP 2.3 Define entry criteria
- SP 2.4 Define exit criteria
- SP 2.5 Define suspension and resumption criteria

SG 3 Establish Test Estimates
- SP 3.1 Establish a top-level work breakdown structure
- SP 3.2 Define test lifecycle
- SP 3.3 Determine estimates for test effort and cost

SG 4 Develop a Test Plan
- SP 4.1 Establish the test schedule
- SP 4.2 Plan for test staffing
- SP 4.3 Plan stakeholder involvement
- SP 4.4 Identify test project risks
- SP 4.5 Establish the test plan

SG 5 Obtain Commitment to the Test Plan
- SP 5.1 Review test plan
- SP 5.2 Reconcile work and resource levels
- SP 5.3 Obtain test plan commitments

Specific Practices by Goals

SG 1 Perform Product Risk Assessment

A product risk assessment is performed to identify the critical areas for testing.

SP 1.1 Define product risk categories and parameters

Product risk categories and parameters are defined that will be used during the product risk assessment.

Example work products

1. Product risk categories lists
2. Product risk evaluation and prioritization criteria

Sub-practices

1. Determine product risk categories
   A reason for identifying product risk categories is to help in the future consolidation of the test tasks into test types in the test plans.

> *Examples of product risk categories include the following:*
> - Functional risks
> - Architectural risks
> - Non-functional risks, e.g., usability, efficiency, portability, maintainability, reliability
> - Change related risks, e.g., regression

2. Define consistent criteria for evaluating and quantifying the product risk likelihood and impact levels
3. Define thresholds for each product risk level
   Risk level is defined as the importance of a risk as defined by its characteristics (impact and likelihood). For each risk level, thresholds can be established to determine the acceptability or unacceptability of a product risk, prioritization of product risks, or to set a trigger of for management action.

SP 1.2 Identify product risks

Product risks are identified and documented.

Example work products

1. Identified product risks

Sub-practices

1. Identify and select stakeholders that need to contribute to the risk assessment
2. Identify product risks using input from stakeholders and requirements documents

> *Examples of product risk identification techniques include the following:*
> - Risk workshops
> - Brainstorming
> - Expert interviews
> - Checklists
> - Lessons learned

3. Document the background and potential consequences of the risk
4. Identify the relevant stakeholders associated for each risk

5. Review the identified product risks against the test assignment

SP 1.3 Analyze product risks

Product risks are evaluated, categorized and prioritized using the predefined product risk categories and parameters.

Example work products

1. Product risk list, with a category and priority assigned to each risk

Sub-practices

1. Analyze the identified products risks using the predefined parameters, e.g., likelihood and impact
2. Categorize and group product risks according to the defined risk categories
3. Prioritize the product risks for mitigation
4. Establish a horizontal traceability between products risks and requirements to ensure that the source of product risks is documented
5. Generate a requirements / product risks traceability matrix
6. Review and obtain agreement with stakeholders on the completeness, category and priority level of the product risks
7. Revise the product risks as appropriate

Examples of when product risks may need to be revised include the following:

- New or changing requirements
- Change of the software development approach
- Lessons learned on quality issues in the project

SG 2 Establish a Test Approach

A test approach, based on identified product risks, is established and agreed upon.

SP 2.1 Identify items and features to be tested

The items and features to be tested, and not to be tested, are identified based on the product risks.

Example work products

1. List of items to be tested and not to be tested
2. List of features to be tested and not to be tested

Sub-practices

1. Breakdown the prioritized product risks into items to be tested and not to be tested
2. Document the risk level and source documentation (test basis) for each identified item to be tested
3. Breakdown the prioritized product risks into features to be tested and not to be tested
4. Document the risk level and source documentation (test basis) for each identified feature to be tested
5. Review with stakeholders the list of items and features to be tested and not to be tested

SP 2.2 Define the test approach

The test approach is defined to mitigate the identified and prioritized product risks.

Example work products

1. The approach, e.g., selected set of test design techniques, should be described in sufficient detail to support identification of major test tasks and estimation of the time required to do each one.

Sub-practices

1. Select the test design techniques to be used. Multiple test design techniques are defined to provide adequate test coverage based on the defined product risks

> *Criteria for selecting a test design technique include the following:*
>
> - Type of system
> - Regulatory standards
> - Customer or contractual requirements
> - Level of risk
> - Type of risk
> - Documentation available
> - Knowledge of the testers
> - Time and budget
> - Development lifecycle
> - Previous experience with types of defects found

2. Define the approach to review test work products
3. Define the approach for re-testing

Examples of approaches for re-testing include the following:
- For all high risk test items a full re-test will take place re-executing the full test procedure
- For all low risk test items the incidents are re-tested in isolation

4. Define the approach for regression testing

Examples of elements of a regression test approach include the following:
- Focus of the regression testing, e.g., which items and/or features
- Methods to select the test cases to be executed
- Type of testing to be performed
- Manual testing or using test automation tools

5. Identify the supporting test tools to be used
6. Identify significant constraints regarding the test approach

Examples of constraints regarding the test approach include the following:
- Test resource availability
- Test environment features
- Project deadlines

7. Align the test approach with the defined organization-wide or program-wide test strategy
8. Identify any non-compliance to the test strategy and its rationale
9. Review the test approach with stakeholders
10. Revise the test approach as appropriate

Examples of when the test approach may need to be revised include the following:
- New or changed priority level of product risks
- Lessons learned after applying the test approach in the project

SP 2.3 Define entry criteria

The entry criteria for testing are defined to prevent testing from starting under conditions that do not allow for a thorough test process.

Example work products

1. Entry criteria per identified test level

Sub-practices

1. Define a set of entry criteria related to the test process

> *Examples of entry criteria related to the test process include the following:*
> - The availability of a test summary report from the previous test level
> - The availability of a test environment according to requirements
> - The availability of documentation, e.g., test release notes, user manual, installation manual

2. Define a set of entry criteria related to product quality

> *Examples of entry criteria related to product quality include the following:*
> - A successful intake test
> - No outstanding defects (of priority level X)
> - All outstanding defects have been analyzed

3. Review the entry criteria with stakeholders, especially those responsible for meeting the entry criteria

SP 2.4 Define exit criteria

The exit criteria for testing are defined to determine when testing is complete.

Example work products

1. Exit criteria per identified test level

Sub-practices

1. Define a set of exit criteria related to the test process

> *Examples of exit criteria related to the test process include the following:*
> - Percentage of tests prepared that have been executed (successfully)
> - Percentage of coverage for each test item, e.g., code coverage or requirements coverage
> - The availability of an approved test summary report

2. Define a set of exit criteria related to product quality

> *Examples of exit criteria related to product quality include the following:*
> - All high priority product risks mitigated
> - Defect detection rate falls below a threshold
> - Number of outstanding defects (by priority level)
> - Percentage of software modules supported by an inspected design

3. Review the exit criteria with stakeholders

Note that the exit criteria of a test level should be aligned with the entry criteria of the subsequent test level.

SP 2.5 Define suspension and resumption criteria

Criteria are defined that will be used to suspend and resume all or a portion of the test tasks on the test items and/or features.

Example work products

1. Suspension criteria
2. Resumption criteria

Sub-practices

1. Specify the suspension criteria used to suspend all or a portion of the test tasks on the test items and/or features

> *Examples of suspension criteria include the following:*
> - Number of critical defects
> - Number of non-reproducible defects
> - Issues with test execution due to the test environments

2. Specify the resumption criteria used to specify the test tasks that must be repeated when the criteria that caused the suspension are removed

SG 3 Establish Test Estimates

Well-founded test estimates are established and maintained for use in discussing the test approach with stakeholders and in planning the testing activities.

SP 3.1 Establish a top-level work breakdown structure

Establish a top-level work breakdown structure (WBS) to clearly define the scope of the testing to be performed and, thereby, the scope for the test estimate.

Example work products

1. Test work products list
2. Test tasks to be performed
3. Work breakdown structure

Sub-practices

1. Identify test work products to be developed based on the defined test approach
2. Identify test work products that will be acquired externally
3. Identify test work products that will be re-used
4. Identify test tasks to be performed related to the test work products
5. Identify indirect test tasks to be performed such as test management, meetings, configuration management, etc.

Note that the WBS should also take into account tasks for implementing the test environment requirements. Refer to the Test Environment process area for more information on this topic.

SP 3.2 Define test lifecycle

Define the test lifecycle phases on which to scope the planning effort.

Example work products

1. Test lifecycle phases definition
2. Test milestones

Sub-practices

1. Define test lifecycle phases. At a minimum a test planning, test preparation and test execution phase are distinguished
2. Schedule the test preparation phase such that it starts immediately upon the completion of the test basis
3. Align the top-level work breakdown structure with the defined test lifecycle
4. Identify major milestones for each test lifecycle phase

Note that understanding the lifecycle is crucial in determining the scope of the test planning effort and the timing of the initial planning, as well as the timing and criteria (at critical milestones) for re-planning.

SP 3.3 Determine estimates for test effort and cost

Estimate the test effort and cost for the test work products to be created and testing tasks to be performed based on the estimation rationale.

Example work products

1. Attribute estimates of test work products and test tasks
2. Test effort estimates
3. Test cost estimates

Sub-practices

1. Determine and maintain estimates of the attributes of the test work products and test tasks

Examples of attributes used to estimate test work products and test tasks include the following:

- Size, e.g., number of test cases, number of pages, number of test points, volume of test data, number of requirements
- Complexity of related test item, e.g., cyclomatic number
- Level of re-use
- Priority level of related product risk

Note that appropriate methods (e.g., validated models or historical data) should be used to determine the attributes of the test work products and test tasks that will be used to estimate the resource requirements.

2. Study (technical) factors that can influence the test estimate

Examples of factors that can influence the test estimate include the following:

- Usage of test tools
- Quality of earlier test levels
- Quality of test basis
- Development environment
- Test environment
- Availability of re-usable testware from previous projects
- Knowledge and skill level of testers

3. Select models and/or historical data that will be used to transform the attributes of the test work products and test tasks into estimates of the effort and cost

Examples of models that can be used for test estimation include the following:

- Test Point Analysis [TMap]
- Three point estimate
- Wide Band Delphi [Veenendaal]
- Ratio of development effort versus test effort

4. Include supporting infrastructure needs when estimating test effort and cost

Examples of supporting infrastructure needs include the following:
- Test environment
- Critical computer resources
- Office environment
- Test tools

5. Estimate test effort and cost using models and/or historical data
6. Document assumptions made in deriving the estimates
7. Record the test estimation data, including the associated information needed to reconstruct the estimates

SG 4 Develop a Test Plan

A test plan is established and maintained as the basis for managing testing and communication to stakeholders.

SP 4.1 Establish the test schedule

The test schedule, with predefined stages of manageable size, is established and maintained based on the developed test estimate and defined test lifecycle.

Example work products

1. Test schedule

Sub-practices

1. Identify test scheduling constraints such as task duration, resources, and inputs needed
2. Identify test task dependencies
3. Define the test schedule (timing of testing activities, test lifecycle phases and test milestones)
4. Document assumptions made in defining the test schedule
5. Establish corrective action criteria for determining what constitutes a significant deviation from the test plan and may indicate a need for rescheduling.

SP 4.2 Plan for test staffing

A plan is created for the availability of the necessary test staff resources who have the required knowledge and skills to perform the testing.

Example work products

1. Staffing requirements
2. Inventory of skill needs

3. Staffing and new hire plan
4. Test training plan

Sub-practices

1. Determine staffing requirements based on the work breakdown structure, test estimate and test schedule
2. Identify knowledge and skills needed to perform the test tasks
3. Assess the knowledge and skills available
4. Select mechanisms for providing needed knowledge and skills

> *Examples of mechanisms include the following:*
> - In-house training
> - External training
> - Coaching
> - External skill acquisition

5. Incorporate selected mechanisms into the test plan

SP 4.3 Plan stakeholder involvement

A plan is created for the involvement of the identified stakeholders.

Stakeholders are identified from all phase of the test lifecycle by identifying the type of people and functions needing during the testing activities. Stakeholders are also identified by their relevance and the degree of interaction for the specific testing activities. A two-dimensional matrix with stakeholders along one axis and testing activities along the other axis is convenient for accomplishing this identification.

Example work products

1. Stakeholder involvement plan

SP 4.4 Identify test project risks

The test project risks associated with testing are identified, analyzed and documented.

Example work products

1. Identified test project risks
2. Prioritized test project risk list
3. Test project risk mitigation plans

Sub-practices

1. Identify test project risks

Examples of project risk identification techniques include the following:
- Brainstorming
- Expert interviews
- Checklists

2. Analyze the identified test project risks in terms of likelihood and impact
3. Prioritize the analyzed test project risks
4. Review and obtain agreement with stakeholders on the completeness and priority level of the documented test project risks
5. Define contingencies for the (high priority) test project risks
6. Revise the test project risks as appropriate

Examples of when test project risks may need to be revised include:
- When new test project risks are identified
- When the likelihood of a test project risk changes
- When test project risks are retired
- When testing circumstances change significantly

SP 4.5 Establish the test plan

The test plan is established and maintained as a basis for managing testing and guiding the communication with the stakeholders.

The results of previous practices are documented in an overall test plan, tying together the information in a logical manner.

Example work products

1. Test plan

Examples of elements of a test plan include the following [after IEEE 829]:

- Test plan identifier
- An overall introduction
- Non-compliances with the test strategy and the rationale
- Items to be tested (including priority level) and not to be tested
- Features to be tested (including priority level) and not to be tested
- Test approach (e.g., test design techniques)
- Entry and exit criteria
- Suspension and resumption criteria
- Test milestones and work products
- Test lifecycle and tasks
- Environmental needs and requirements (including office environment)
- Staffing and training needs
- Stakeholder involvement
- Test estimate
- Test schedule
- Test project risks and contingencies

Refer to the Test Environment process area for information on environmental needs and requirements.

SG 5 Obtain Commitment to the Test Plan

Commitments to the test plan are established and maintained.

SP 5.1 Review test plan

Review the test plan (and possibly other plans) that affect testing to achieve and understand test commitments.

Example work products

1. Test plan review log

Sub-practices

1. Organize reviews with stakeholders to facilitate their understanding of the test commitments.

SP 5.2 Reconcile work and resource levels

Adjust the test plan to reconcile available and estimated resources.

Example work products

1. Revised test approach and corresponding estimation parameters

2. Renegotiated test budgets
3. Revised test schedules
4. Revised product risk list
5. Renegotiated stakeholder agreements

Sub-practices

1. Discuss differences between estimates and available resources with stakeholders
2. Reconcile any differences between estimates and available resources

   Note that reconciliation is typically accomplished by lowering or deferring technical performance, negotiating more resources, finding ways to increase productivity, changing the scope of the project such as removing features, outsourcing, adjusting staff skill mix, or revising the schedule.

SP 5.3 Obtain test plan commitments

Obtain commitments from relevant stakeholders responsible for performing and supporting the execution of the test plan.

Example work products

1. Documented requests for commitments
2. Documented commitments

Sub-practices

1. Identify needed support and negotiate commitments for that support with relevant stakeholders

   Note that the WBS can be used as a checklist for ensuring that commitments are obtained for all tasks. The plan for stakeholders' interaction should identify all parties from whom commitments should be obtained.

2. Document all organizational commitments, both full and provisional
3. Review internal commitments with senior management as appropriate
4. Review external commitments with senior management as appropriate

Generic Practices by Goals

GG 2 Institutionalize a Managed Process

GP 2.1 Establish an organizational policy

Establish and maintain an organizational policy for planning and performing the Test Planning process.

Elaboration

The test planning policy typically specifies:

- Each project will define a test plan that includes a test approach and the accompanying test effort and estimates
- Each project's test approach will be derived from the test strategy
- Test plans shall be developed using a standard process and template
- Standard tools that will be used when performing test planning
- The requirements will be used as a basis for test planning activities
- The testing commitments will be negotiated with resource management, business management and project management
- Any involvement of other affected groups in the testing activities must be explicitly agreed upon by these groups
- Management will review all testing commitments made to groups external to the organization
- The test plan will be managed and controlled

GP 2.2 Plan the process

Establish and maintain the plan for performing the Test Planning process.

Elaboration

Typically, the plan for performing the test planning process is included in the project plan, which is described in the CMMI Project Planning process area.

GP 2.3 Provide resources

Provide adequate resources for performing the Test Planning process, developing the test work products, and providing the services defined by the process.

Elaboration

- A documented and approved assignment exists for testing. This assignment typically covers issues and expectation regarding goals and objectives, exit criteria, items and features to be tested and not to be tested, type of testing to be performed, imposed standards, cost, schedule and resource constraints.

- Adequate time is provided to test management to perform the test planning activities
- Experienced individuals, who have expertise in the application domain of the test object and those who have expertise with the development process are available to support the creation of the test plan
- Tools to support the test planning process are available

Examples of tools include the following:

- Project planning and scheduling tools
- Estimation tools
- Risk assessment tools
- Test management tools
- Configuration management

GP 2.4 Assign responsibilities

Assign responsibility and authority for performing the Test Planning process, developing the work products, and providing the services of the Test Planning process.

Elaboration

A test manager is typically designated to be responsible for negotiating commitments and developing the test plan. The test manager, either directly or by delegation, coordinates the project's test planning process.

GP 2.5 Train people

Train the people performing or supporting the Test Planning process as needed.

Elaboration

Test management and other individuals or groups, involved in test planning, are trained in test planning and the accompanying procedures and techniques.

Examples of training topics include the following:

- Planning principles
- Test strategy
- Product and project risk assessment process and techniques
- Defining a test approach
- Test plan templates and standards
- Test organization
- Test estimation and test scheduling
- Introduction to test design techniques
- Supporting test planning tools

GP 2.6 Manage configurations

Place selected work products of the Test Planning process under appropriate levels of configuration control.

Elaboration

Examples of work products placed under configuration management include the following:

- Work breakdown structure
- Test estimation data
- Product risk assessment data
- Test plan review report
- Test plan

GP 2.7 Identify and involve relevant stakeholders

Identify and involve relevant stakeholders in the Test Planning process as planned.

Elaboration

Select relevant stakeholders from customers, end users, developers, producers, testers, suppliers, marketers, maintainers, service personnel, and others who may be affected by, or may affect, the product as well as the test process.

Examples of activities for stakeholder involvement include the following:

- Selecting the product and product components to be tested
- Participating in the product risk assessment by identifying the risk level and risk types of the product and product components to be tested
- Providing input to test estimates
- Reviewing and resolving issues on test project risks
- Explicitly committing test resources as needed
- Reviewing and approving the test plan

GP 2.8 Monitor and control the process

Monitor and control the Test Planning process against the plan for performing the process and take appropriate actions.

Elaboration

Examples of measures used in monitoring and controlling the test planning process include the following:

- Number of revisions to the test plan
- Lead-time and actual effort spent compared to the lead-time and effort planned in the test plan
- Number of test items for which the risk level was changed per revision
- Cost, schedule and effort variance per revision of plan

GP 2.9 Objectively evaluate adherence

Objectively evaluate adherence of the Test Planning process and selected work products against the process description, standards and procedures, and address any non-compliances.

Elaboration

Examples of review and/or audit adherence topics for evaluation include the following:

- Compliance to the test strategy
- Compliance to standards (procedures and templates)
- The quality of the test plan
- The defined test approach
- The risk assessment process
- The test estimation process
- The activities for reviewing and making test commitments

GP 2.10 Review status with higher level management

Review the activities, status and results of the Test Planning process with higher level management and resolve issues.

GG 3 Institutionalize a Defined Process

Only applicable at TMMi level 3.

GP 3.1 Establish a defined process

Establish and maintain a description of a defined Test Planning process

GP 3.2 Collect improvement information

Collect process related experiences derived from planning and performing the Test Planning process to support the future use and improvement of the organization's processes and process assets.

Elaboration

Examples of measures include the following:

- Percentage of test plans established according to procedure and template
- Percentage of test plans that have documented product risk assessment results and a test approach
- Percentage of test plans formally reviewed and approved by management
- Test planning effort
- Test estimation accuracy

Process Area 2.3 Test Monitoring and Control

Purpose

The purpose of Test Monitoring and Control is to provide an understanding of test progress and product quality so that appropriate corrective actions can be taken when test progress deviates significantly from plan or product quality deviates significantly from expectations.

Introductory Notes

The progress of testing and the quality of the products should both be monitored and controlled. The progress of the testing is monitored by comparing the status of actual test (work) products, tasks (including their attributes), effort, cost, and schedule to what is identified in the test plan. The quality of the product is monitored by means of indicators such as product risks mitigated, the number of defects found, number of open defects, and status against test exit criteria.

Monitoring involves gathering the required (raw) data, e.g., from test log and test incidents reports, reviewing the raw data for their validity and calculating the defined progress and product quality measures. Test summary reports should be written on a periodic and event-driven basis as a means to provide a common understanding on test progress and product quality. Since 'testing is the measurement of product quality' [Hetzel], the practices around product quality reporting are key to the success of this process area.

Appropriate corrective actions should be taken when the test progress deviates from the plan or product quality deviates from expectations. These actions may require re-planning, which may include revising the original plan or additional mitigations activities based on the current plan. Corrective actions that influence the original committed plan should be agreed by the stakeholders.

An essential part of test monitoring and control is test project risk management. Test project risk management is performed to identify and solve as early as possible major problems that undermine the test plan. When performing project risk management, it is also important to identify problems that are beyond the responsibility of testing. For instance, organizational budget cuts, delay of development work products or changed/added functionality can all affect significantly the test process. By building on the test project risks already documented in the test plan, test project risks are monitored and controlled and corrective actions are initiated as needed.

Scope

The process area Test Monitoring and Control involves monitoring the test progress and product quality against documented estimates, commitments, plans and expectations, reporting on test progress and product quality to stakeholders, taking control measures, (e.g., corrective actions, when necessary) and managing the corrective actions to closure.

Specific Goal and Practice Summary

SG 1 Monitor Test Progress against Plan
- SP 1.1 Monitor test planning parameters
- SP 1.2 Monitor test environment resources provided and used
- SP 1.3 Monitor test commitments
- SP 1.4 Monitor test project risks
- SP 1.5 Monitor stakeholder involvement
- SP 1.6 Conduct test progress reviews
- SP 1.7 Conduct test progress milestone reviews

SG 2 Monitor Product Quality against Plan and Expectations
- SP 2.1 Check against entry criteria
- SP 2.2 Monitor defects
- SP 2.3 Monitor product risks
- SP 2.4 Monitor exit criteria
- SP 2.5 Monitor suspension and resumption criteria
- SP 2.6 Conduct product quality reviews
- SP 2.7 Conduct product quality milestone reviews

SG 3 Manage Corrective Action to Closure
- SP 3.1 Analyze issues
- SP 3.2 Take corrective action
- SP 3.3 Manage corrective action

Specific Practices by Goals

SG 1 Monitor Test Progress Against Plan

The actual progress and performance of testing is monitored and compare them against the values in the test plan.

SP 1.1 Monitor test planning parameters

Monitor the actual values of the test planning parameters against the test plan.

Example work products

1. Records of test performance
2. Records of significant deviations from plan

Sub-practices

1. Monitor test progress against the test schedule

Examples of progress monitoring typically include the following:

- Periodically measuring the actual completion of test tasks, test (work) products and test milestones
- Comparing actual completion of test tasks, test (work) products and test milestones against the test schedule documented in the test plan
- Identifying significant deviations from the test schedule estimates in the test plan

2. Monitor the test cost and expended test effort

Examples of cost and effort monitoring typically include the following:

- Periodically measuring the actual test costs and effort expended and staff assigned
- Comparing actual test cost, effort and staffing to the estimates documented in the test plan
- Identifying significant deviations from the test cost, effort and staffing in the test plan

3. Monitor the attributes of the test work products and test tasks
   Refer to SP 3.3 Determine estimates of test effort and cost from the Test Planning process area for information about the attributes of test work products and test tasks.

Examples of test work products and test task attributes monitoring typically include the following:

- Periodically measuring the actual attributes of the test work products and test tasks, such as size or complexity
- Comparing the actual attributes of the test work products and test tasks to the estimates documented in the test plan
- Identifying significant deviations from the estimates in the test plan

4. Monitor the knowledge and skills of test staff

Examples of knowledge and skills monitoring typically include the following:

- Periodically measuring the acquisition of knowledge and skills of test staff
- Comparing actual training obtained to that documented in the test plan
- Identifying significant deviations from estimates in the test plan
- The ratio of defects being solved versus defects being found

5. Document the significant deviations in the test planning parameters.

SP 1.2 Monitor test environment resources provided and used

Monitor the test environment resources provided and used against those defined in the plan.

Example work products

1. Records of test environment resources provided and used
2. Records of significant deviations from plan

Sub-practices

1. Monitor test environment resources provided against the plan
2. Monitor the actual usage of the provided test environment resources against the plan
3. Identify and document significant deviations from the estimates in the plan

SP 1.3 Monitor test commitments

Monitor test commitments achieved against those identified in the test plan.

Example work products

1. Records of commitment reviews

Sub-practices

1. Regularly review commitments (both internal and external)
2. Identify commitments that have not been satisfied or that are at significant risk of not being satisfied
3. Document the results of the commitment reviews.

SP 1.4 Monitor test project risks

Monitor test project risks against those identified in the test plan

Example work products

1. Updated test project risk list
2. Records of project risk monitoring

Sub-practices

1. Periodically review the documentation of the test project risks in the context of the current status and circumstances

2. Revise the documentation of the test project risks, as additional information becomes available, to incorporate any changes
3. Communicate test project risk status to relevant stakeholders

SP 1.5 Monitor stakeholder involvement

Monitor stakeholder involvement against expectations defined in the test plan.

Once the stakeholders are identified and the extent of their involvement within testing is specified in the test plan, that involvement must be monitored to ensure that the appropriate interactions are occurring.

Example work products

1. Records of stakeholder involvement

Sub-practices

1. Periodically review the status of stakeholder involvement
2. Identify and document significant issues and their impact
3. Document the results of the stakeholder involvement status reviews

SP 1.6 Conduct test progress reviews

Periodically review test progress, performance and issues

Progress reviews are reviews to keep stakeholders informed. Reviews are often held both internally with test team members and externally with stakeholders outside testing. These reviews are typically informal reviews held regularly, e.g., weekly, bi-weekly or monthly.

Example work products

1. Test progress report
2. Documented test progress review results, e.g. minutes of the progress meetings

Sub-practices

1. Collect and analyze test progress monitoring measures
2. Regularly communicate status on test progress and performance to stakeholders

Examples of stakeholders typically include the following:
- Project management
- Business management
- Test team members

3. Regularly organize test progress review meetings with stakeholders
4. Identify, document and discuss significant issues and deviations from the test plan
5. Document change requests on test work products and major problems identified in test progress and performance
6. Document the results of the reviews, e.g., decisions made

SP 1.7 Conduct test progress milestone reviews

Review the accomplishments and progress of testing at selected test milestones

Test progress milestone reviews are planned during test planning and are typically formal reviews.

Example work products

1. Test milestone report
2. Documented milestone review results, e.g., minutes of the review meeting

Sub-practices

1. Conduct test progress reviews at meaningful points in the test schedule, such as the completion of selected stages, with relevant stakeholders
2. Communicate accomplishments and test progress and performance status to stakeholders
3. Review the commitments, plan, status, and project risks of testing
4. Review the test environment resources
5. Identify, document and discuss significant test progress issues and their impacts
6. Document the results of the reviews, actions items, and decisions
7. Update the test plan to reflect accomplishments and latest status

SG 2 Monitor Product Quality against Plan and Expectations

Actual product quality is monitored against the quality measurements defined in the plan and the quality expectations, e.g., of the customer/user.

SP 2.1 Check against entry criteria

At the start of the test execution phase check the status against the entry criteria identified in the test plan.

Example work products

1. Records of entry check

Sub-practices

1. Check the status against the entry criteria identified in the test plan
2. Identify and document significant deviations in compliance to entry criteria and initiate corrective action

SP 2.2 Monitor defects

Monitor measures of defects found during testing against expectations.

Example work products

1. Records of defect monitoring

Sub-practices

1. Monitor measures on defects found and status against expectations

Examples of useful defect measures include the following [Burnstein]:

- Total number of defects (for a component, subsystem, system) outstanding at each defined priority level
- Total number of defects found during the most recent test run at each defined priority level
- Number of defects resolved/unresolved (for all levels of test)
- Number of defects found for each given type
- Number of defects causing failures of severity level greater than X
- Number of defects/KLOC ('incident volume')
- Actual number versus estimated number of defects (based on historical data)

2. Identify and document significant deviations from expectations for measures regarding defects found

SP 2.3 Monitor product risks

Monitor product risks against those identified in the test plan.

Example work products

1. Updated test product risk list
2. Records of product risk monitoring

Sub-practices

1. Periodically review the documentation of the product risks in the context of the current status and circumstances with a selected set of stakeholders
2. Monitor changes and additions to the requirements to identify new or changed products risks
3. Revise the documentation of the product risks as additional information becomes available to incorporate the change on likelihood, impact and/or priority status
4. Monitor the (number of) product risks mitigated by testing against the mitigation stated in the plan
5. Communicate product risk status to relevant stakeholders

SP 2.4 Monitor exit criteria

Monitor the status of the exit criteria against those identified in the test plan.

Example work products

1. Records of exit criteria monitoring

Sub-practices

1. Monitor the test process related exit criteria, e.g., test coverage against plan
2. Monitor the product quality related exit criteria against plan
3. Identify and document significant deviations in exit criteria status from plan

SP 2.5 Monitor suspension and resumption criteria

Monitor the status of the suspension and resumption criteria against those identified in the test plan.

Example work products

1. Records of suspension criteria monitoring
2. Records of resumption criteria monitoring

Sub-practices

1. Monitor suspension criteria against those documented in the test plan
2. Suspend testing if suspension criteria are met and initiate corrective action
3. Monitor resumption criteria against those documented in the test plan
4. Initiate the resumption of testing once the issues have been solved using the defined resumption criteria

SP 2.6 Conduct product quality reviews

Periodically review product quality.

Product quality reviews are reviews designed to keep stakeholders informed. Reviews are often held both internally with test team members and externally with stakeholders outside testing. These reviews are typically informal reviews held regularly, e.g., weekly, bi-weekly or monthly.

Example work products

1. Product quality report
2. Documented product quality review results, e.g., minutes of the product quality meetings

Sub-practices

1. Collect and analyze product quality monitoring measures
2. Regularly communicate status on product quality to stakeholders

> *Examples of stakeholders typically include the following:*
> - Project management
> - Business management
> - Test team members

3. Regularly organize product quality review meetings with stakeholders
4. Identify, document and discuss significant product quality issues and deviations from expectations and plan
5. Document the results of the reviews, e.g., decisions made

SP 2.7 Conduct product quality milestone reviews

Review product quality status at selected test milestones.

Product quality milestone reviews are planned during test planning and are typically formal reviews.

Example work products

1. Test milestone report
2. Documented milestone review results, e.g., minutes of the review meeting

Sub-practices

1. Conduct product quality reviews at meaningful points in the test schedule, such as the completion of selected stages, with relevant stakeholders
2. Communicate product quality status to stakeholders by means of a formal product quality report

Examples of elements of a product quality test report include the following [after IEEE 829]:

- Identifier (and reference to test plan)
- Management summary
- Variances (against plan)
- Comprehensive assessment
- Summary of results
- Evaluation
- Summary of activities
- Approvals

3. Review the status regarding incidents, product risks and exit criteria
4. Identify and document significant product quality issues and their impacts
5. Document the results of the reviews, actions items, and decisions
6. Update the test plan to reflect accomplishments and the latest status

SG 3 Manage Corrective Actions to Closure

Corrective actions are managed to closure when test progress or product quality deviate significantly from the test plan or expectations.

SP 3.1 Analyze issues

Collect and analyze the issues and determine corrective actions necessary to address them.

Example work products

1. List of issues needing corrective actions

Sub-practices

1. Gather issues for analysis

Examples of issues to be gathered include the following:

- Significant deviations in actual test planning parameters from estimates in the test plan
- Commitments that have not been satisfied
- Significant changes in test project risk status, e.g., possible late delivery and/or poor quality of test basis and/or test object
- Stakeholder representation or involvement issues
- Significant deviations in test environment implementation progress from plan
- Number, severity and priority level of incidents found
- Status regarding exit criteria
- Significant changes in product risks

2. Analyze issues to determine need for corrective action

   Note corrective action is required when the issue, if left unresolved, may prevent testing or even the project from meeting its objectives.

SP 3.2 Take corrective action

Take corrective action as appropriate for the identified issues.

Example work products

1. Corrective action plan

Sub-practices

1. Determine and document the appropriate actions needed to address the identified issues

Examples of potential actions include the following:

- Re-negotiating commitments
- Adding resources
- Changing the test approach
- Re-visiting the exit criteria
- Deferring release date
- Changing the scope of the project, e.g., delivering less functionality

   Note that many of the potential actions listed above will lead to a revised test plan.

2. Review and get agreement with relevant stakeholders on the actions to be taken
3. Re-negotiate commitments with stakeholders (both internally and externally)

SP 3.3 Manage corrective action

Manage the corrective action to closure.

Example work products

1. Corrective action results

Sub-practices

1. Monitor corrective actions for completion
2. Analyze results of corrective actions to determine the effectiveness of the corrective actions

Generic Practices by Goals

GG 2 Institutionalize a Managed Process

GP 2.1 Establish an organizational policy

Establish and maintain an organizational policy for planning and performing the Test Monitoring and Control process.

Elaboration

The test monitoring and control policy typically specifies:

- A documented test plan is used and maintained as the basis for monitoring the test progress
- Monitoring is performed on the basis of a set of test-related measurements
- Test project tasks, efforts and costs are monitored throughout the project
- Contingency plans are developed based on the project risks identified
- Management and other stakeholders are kept informed regarding test progress
- Management and other stakeholders are kept informed regarding product quality
- Corrective actions are taken and managed to closure when test progress deviates significantly from plan or product quality deviates significantly from expectations
- Major changes to the test plan are reviewed by management and other stakeholders

GP 2.2 Plan the process

Establish and maintain the plan for performing the Test Monitoring and Control process.

Elaboration

Typically, the plan for performing the test monitoring and control process is included in the test plan, which is described in the TMMi Test Planning process area.

GP 2.3 Provide resources

Provide adequate resources for performing the Test Monitoring and Control process, developing the test work products, and providing the services of the process.

Elaboration

- A test plan against which testing can be monitored and controlled
- Adequate time is provided to test management to perform the test monitoring and control activities
- Tools to support the test monitoring and control process are available

Examples of tools include the following:

- Project management and progress tracking tools
- Risk management tools
- Incident management tools
- Test management tools

GP 2.4 Assign responsibilities

Assign responsibility and authority for performing the Test Monitoring and Control process, developing the work products, and providing the services of the Test Monitoring and Control process.

Elaboration

A test manager is typically designated to be responsible for test monitoring and control. The test manager, directly or by delegation, coordinates the project's test process.

Examples of monitor and control responsibilities to be assigned include the following:

- Monitor and control the costs, effort and schedule of testing
- Monitor and control test project risks
- Monitor and control product risks and product quality
- Report on test progress and product quality
- Initiate corrective actions when test progress deviates significantly from test plan
- Initiate corrective actions when product quality deviates significantly from expectations

GP 2.5 Train people

Train the people performing or supporting the Test Monitoring and Control process as needed.

Elaboration

Test management, and other individuals or groups, involved in test monitoring and control, are trained in test monitoring and control and the accompanying procedures and techniques.

Examples of training topics include the following:

- Project management fundamentals
- Managing testing
- Tracking of product quality, effort, cost and schedule
- Risk management
- Test reporting
- Contingency planning

GP 2.6 Manage configurations

Place selected work products of the Test Monitoring and Control process under appropriate levels of configuration control.

Elaboration

Examples of work products placed under configuration management include the following:

- Test schedule with status
- Test measurement data and analysis
- Test reports

GP 2.7 Identify and involve relevant stakeholders

Identify and involve relevant stakeholders of the Test Monitoring and Control process as planned.

Elaboration

Examples of activities for stakeholder involvement include the following:

- Assessing the testing performance against the test plan
- Reviewing commitments and resolving issues
- Reviewing product and test project risks
- Reviewing test data management activities
- Reviewing test progress and product quality
- Managing corrective actions to closure

Note that this generic practice only covers the involvement of relevant stakeholders in test monitoring and controlling.

GP 2.8 Monitor and control the process

Monitor and control the Test Monitoring and Control process against the plan for performing the process and take appropriate actions.

Elaboration

Examples of measures used in monitoring and controlling the test monitoring and control process include the following:

- Number of open and closed corrective actions
- Number of types of peer reviews performed
- Review schedule (planned versus actual and slipped target dates)

Note that this generic practice only covers the monitoring and controlling of test monitoring and control activities.

GP 2.9 Objectively evaluate adherence

Objectively evaluate adherence of the Test Monitoring and Control process and selected work products against the process description, standards, and procedures, and address any non-compliances.

Elaboration

Examples of review and/or audit evaluation adherence topics include the following:

- The monitoring of test progress against the test plan
- Managing corrective actions to closure
- The performance of test project risk management
- Compliance to standards (procedures and templates)
- Test and quality reports
- Review results

GP 2.10 Review status with higher level management

Review the activities, status and results of the Test Monitoring and Control process with higher level management and resolve issues.

GG 3 Institutionalize a Defined Process

Only applicable at TMMi level 3.

GP 3.1 Establish a defined process

Establish and maintain a description of a defined Test Monitoring and Control process

GP 3.2 Collect improvement information

Collect process related experiences derived from planning and performing the Test Monitoring and Control process to support the future use and improvement of the organization's processes and process assets.

Elaboration

Examples of measures include the following:

- Percentage of projects using the test reporting template
- Percentage of test milestones passed by means of a formal review
- Percentage of corrective actions closed within X days

Process Area 2.4 Test Design and Execution

Purpose

The purpose of Test Design and Execution is to improve the test process capability during test design and execution by establishing test design specifications, using test design techniques, performing a structured test execution process and managing test incidents to closure.

Introductory Notes

Structured testing implies that test design techniques are applied, possibly supported by tools. Test design techniques are used to derive and select test conditions and design test cases from requirements and design specifications. The test conditions and test cases are documented in a test specification. A test case consists of the description of the input values, execution preconditions, expected results and execution post conditions. At a later stage, as more information becomes available regarding the implementation, the test cases are translated into test procedures. In a test procedure, also referred to as a manual test script, the specific test actions and checks are arranged in an executable sequence. Specific test data required to be able to run the test procedure is created. The tests will subsequently be executed using these test procedures.

The test design and execution activities follow the test approach as defined in the test plan. The specific test design techniques applied (e.g., black box, white box or experienced-based) are based on level and type of product risk identified during test planning.

During the test execution stage, incidents are found and incident reports are written. Incidents are logged using an incident management system and are communicated to the stakeholders per established protocols. A basic incident classification scheme is established for incident management, and a procedure is put in place to handle the incident lifecycle process including managing each incident to closure.

Scope

The process area Test Design and Execution addresses the test preparation phase including the application of test design techniques to derive and select test conditions and test cases. It also addresses the creation of specific test data, the execution of the tests using documented test procedures and incident management.

Specific Goal and Practice Summary

SG 1 Perform Test Analysis and Design using Test Design Techniques
- SP 1.1 Identify and prioritize test conditions
- SP 1.2 Identify and prioritize test cases
- SP 1.3 Identify necessary specific test data
- SP 1.4 Maintain horizontal traceability with requirements

SG 2 Perform Test Implementation
- SP 2.1 Develop and prioritize test procedures
- SP 2.2 Create specific test data
- SP 2.3 Specify intake test procedure
- SP 2.4 Develop test execution schedule

SG 3 Perform Test Execution
- SP 3.1 Perform intake test
- SP 3.2 Execute test cases
- SP 3.3 Report test incidents
- SP 3.4 Write test log

SG 4 Manage Test Incidents to Closure
- SP 4.1 Decide disposition of test incidents in configuration control board
- SP 4.2 Perform appropriate action to close the test incident
- SP 4.3 Track the status of test incidents

Specific Practices by Goals

SG 1 Perform Test Analysis and Design Using Test Design Techniques

During test analysis and design, the test approach is translated into tangible test conditions and test cases using test design techniques.

SP 1.1 Identify and prioritize test conditions

Test conditions are identified and prioritized using test design techniques, based on an analysis of the test items as specified in the test basis.

Example work products

1. Test basis issue log
2. Test conditions
3. Test design specifications

Sub-practices

1. Study and analyze the test basis (such as requirements, architecture, design and interface specifications)
2. Discuss issues regarding the test basis with the document owner
3. Select the most appropriate test design techniques in line with the documented test approach

Examples of black box test design techniques include the following:

- Equivalence Partitioning
- Boundary Value Analysis
- Decision Tables (Cause/Effect Graphing)
- State Transition Testing

Examples of white box test design techniques include the following:

- Statement Testing
- Decision (Branch) Testing
- Condition Testing

Note that in addition to black box and white box techniques, experienced-based techniques such as exploratory testing can also be used which results in documenting the test design specification by means of a test charter.

Typically more than one test design technique is selected per test level in order to be able to differentiate the intensity of testing, e.g., number of test cases, based on the level of risk of the test items. In addition to using the risk level to prioritize testing, other factors influence the selection of test design techniques such as development lifecycle, quality of the test basis, skills and knowledge of the testers, contractual requirements and imposed standards.

4. Derive the test conditions from the test basis using test design techniques
5. Prioritize the test conditions based on identified product risks
6. Document the test conditions in a test design specification, based on the test design specification standard

Examples of elements of a test design specification include the following [after IEEE 829]:

- Test design specification identifier
- Items and/or features to be tested
- Approach refinements
- Test conditions
- Pass/fail criteria

7. Review the test design specifications with stakeholders
8. Revise the test design specifications and test conditions as appropriate, e.g., whenever the requirements change.

SP 1.2 Identify and prioritize test cases

Test cases are identified and prioritized using test design techniques.

Example work products

1. Test cases
2. Test case specification

Sub-practices

1. Derive the test cases from the test conditions using test design techniques. A test case consists of a set of input values, execution preconditions, expected results and execution post conditions.
2. Prioritize the test cases based on identified product risks
3. Document the test cases in a test case specification, based on the test case specification standard

> *Examples of elements of a test case specification include the following [IEEE 829]:*
> - Test case specification identifier
> - Items and/or features to be tested
> - Input specifications
> - Output specifications
> - Environmental needs
> - Special procedural requirements
> - Inter-case dependencies

4. Review the test case specifications with stakeholders
5. Revise the test case specifications as appropriate

SP 1.3 Identify necessary specific test data

Specific test data necessary to support the test conditions and execution of test cases is identified.

Example work products

1. Test data specification

Sub-practices

1. Identify and specify the necessary specific test data required to implement and execute the test cases
2. Document the necessary specific test data, possibly as part of the test case specification

SP 1.4 Maintain horizontal traceability with requirements

Traceability between the requirements and the test conditions is established and maintained.

Example work products

1. Requirements / test conditions traceability matrix

Sub-practices

1. Maintain requirements traceability to ensure that the source of test conditions is documented
2. Generate a requirements / test conditions traceability matrix
3. Set up the traceability matrix such that monitoring of requirements coverage during test execution is facilitated

SG 2 Perform Test Implementation

During test implementation, the test procedures are developed and prioritized, including the intake test. Test data is created, and the test execution schedule is defined during this phase.

SP 2.1 Develop and prioritize test procedures

Test procedures are developed and prioritized.

Example work products

1. Test procedure specification
2. Automated test script

Sub-practices

1. Develop test procedures by combining the test cases in a particular order and including any other information needed for test execution
2. Prioritize the test procedures based on identified product risks
3. Document the test procedures in a test procedure specification, based on the test procedure specification standard

Examples of elements of a test procedure specification include the following [IEEE 829]:

- Test procedure specification identifier
- Purpose
- Special requirements (execution preconditions), e.g., dependencies on other test procedures
- Procedure steps (test actions and checks)

4. Review the test procedure specifications with stakeholders
5. Revise the test procedure specifications as appropriate
6. Optionally, the test procedures can be automated and translated into automated test scripts

SP 2.2 Create specific test data

Specific test data, as specified during the test analysis and design activity, is created.

Example work products

1. Specific test data

Sub-practices

1. Create specific test data required to perform the tests as specified in the test procedures
2. Archive the set of specific test data to allow a restore of the initial situation in the future
   Refer to SP 3.2 Perform test data management from the process area Test Environment for managing the created test data.

SP 2.3 Specify intake test procedure

The intake test is specified. This test, sometimes called the confidence or smoke test is used to decide at the beginning of test execution whether the test object is ready for detailed and further testing.

Example work products

1. Intake checklist
2. Intake test procedure specification

Sub-practices

1. Define a list of checks to be executed during the intake test using the entry criteria as defined in the test plan as an input

> *Examples of checks to be part of an intake test include the following:*
> - All necessary major functions are accessible
> - Representative functions are accessible and working at least for the positive path case
> - Interfaces with other components or systems that will be tested are working
> - The documentation is complete for the available functionality, e.g., test release note, user manual, installation manual

2. Develop the intake test procedure based on the checks identified by putting the checks (test cases) in an executable order and including any other information needed for test execution
3. Document the intake test procedures in a test procedure specification, based on the test procedure specification standard
4. Review the intake test procedure specification with stakeholders

SP 2.4 Develop *test execution schedule*

A test execution schedule is developed that describes the sequence in which the test procedures will be executed.

Example work products

1. Test execution schedule

Sub-practices

1. Investigate the dependencies between the test procedures
2. Schedule the test procedures using their priority level as a main driver
3. Assign a tester to perform the execution of a test procedure
4. Review the test execution schedule with stakeholders
5. Revise the test execution schedule as appropriate

SG 3 Perform Test Execution

Tests are executed according to the previously specified test procedures and test schedule. Incidents are reported and test logs are written.

SP 3.1 Perform intake test

Perform the intake test (confidence test) to decide whether the test object is ready for detailed and further testing.

Example work products

1. Intake test log
2. Incident reports

Sub-practices

1. Perform the intake test (confidence test) using the documented intake test procedure to decide if the test object is ready for detailed and further testing
2. Document the results of the intake test by means of a test log, based on the test log standard
3. Log incidents when a discrepancy is observed

Note that this practice is highly related to the practice SP 2.4 Perform test environment intake test from the process area Test Environment. The intake test on the test object and test environment can possibly be combined.

SP 3.2 Execute test cases

According to the defined execution schedule, the test cases are run either manually using documented test procedures and/or via test automation using pre-defined test scripts.

Example work products

1. Test results

Sub-practices

1. Execute the test cases using documented test procedures and/or test scripts
2. Record actual results
3. Compare actual results with expected results
4. Repeat test activities after the receipt of a fix or change by performing perform re-testing (confirmation testing)
5. Perform regression testing as appropriate.

Note that some testing will be carried out informally using no pre-defined detailed test procedures, e.g., during exploratory testing or error guessing.

SP 3.3 Report test incidents

Discrepancies between the actual and expected results are reported as test incidents.

Example work products

1. Test incident reports

Sub-practices

1. Log test incidents when a discrepancy is observed.
2. Analyze the test incident for further information on the problem
3. Establish the cause of the test incident, e.g., system under test, test documentation, test data or test execution mistake
4. Assign an initial priority and severity level to the test incident
5. Formally report the test incident using an incident classification scheme

> *Examples of elements of a test incident report include the following [IEEE 829]:*
>
> - Test incident report identifier
> - Summary
> - Incident description (input, expected results, actual results, anomalies, date and time, test procedure step, environment, attempts to repeat, testers, observers)
> - Priority level
> - Severity level

6. Review the test incident report with stakeholders
7. Store the test incidents in a central repository

SP 3.4 Write test log

Test logs are written to provide a chronological record of relevant details about the execution of the tests.

Example work products

1. Test logs

Sub-practices

1. Collect test execution data
2. Document the test execution data by means of a test log, based on the test log standard

> *Examples of elements of a test log include the following [IEEE 829]:*
>
> - Test log identifier
> - Description (items being tested, environment in which the testing has been executed)
> - Activity and event entries (execution description, test results, anomalous events, incident report identifiers)

3. Review the test log with stakeholders

SG 4 Manage Test Incidents to Closure

Test incidents are managed and resolved as appropriate.

SP 4.1 Decide disposition of incidents in configuration control board

Appropriate actions on test incidents are decided upon by a configuration control board (CCB).

Example work products

1. CCB meeting report, including a decision log regarding test incidents

2. Updated incident report

Sub-practices

1. Establish a CCB with participation of stakeholders, including testing
2. Review and analyze the incidents found
3. Revisit the priority and severity level of the test incident
4. Determine actions to be taken for the test incidents found

> *Examples of decisions that can be made include the following:*
> - Rejected, incident is not a defect
> - Deferred, incident is declined for repair but may be dealt with during a later stage
> - Fix, incident is accepted and shall be repaired

5. Record the decision and other relevant information in the incident database; the incident report is updated.
6. Assign the incident to engineering to perform appropriate actions

SP 4.2 Perform appropriate action to fix the test incidents

Appropriate actions are taken to fix, re-test and close the test incidents or defer the incident(s) to a future release.

Example work products

1. Test log (including test results)
2. Updated incident report

Sub-practices

1. Repair the incident which may involve updating documentation and/or software code.
2. Record information on the repair action in the incident database; the incident report is updated.
3. Perform re-testing, and possibly regression testing, to confirm the fix of the incident.
4. Record information on the re-testing action in the incident database; the incident report is updated.
5. Formally close the incident provided re-testing was successful.

SP 4.3 Track the status of test incidents

The status of the test incidents is tracked and appropriate actions are taken as needed.

Example work products

1. CCB meeting report
2. Incident status report

Sub-practices

1. Provide status reports on incidents to stakeholders

> *Examples of elements that are covered in an incident status report include the following:*
> - Incidents opened during period XXXX-XXXX
> - Incidents closed during period XXXX-XXXX
> - Incidents remaining open for X or more weeks

2. Discuss status reports in a CCB meeting
3. Take appropriate action if needed, e.g., if an incident that needs repair has the same status for a certain period of time

Generic Practices by Goals

GG 2 Institutionalize a Managed Process

GP 2.1 Establish an organizational policy

Establish and maintain an organizational policy for planning and performing the Test Design and Execution process.

Elaboration

The test design and execution policy typically specifies:

- A set of suitable test design techniques will be identified per test level
- Test specifications will be supported by templates and standards
- Test execution will be done using documented test procedures
- The level of test execution automation required
- Test incidents are documented and reported using an incident classification scheme
- Reported test incidents are evaluated, classified and processed according to a documented procedure
- A basic central test incident repository is put into place

GP 2.2 Plan the process

Establish and maintain the plan for performing the Test Design and Execution process.

Elaboration

Typically, the plan for performing the test design and execution process is included in the test plan, which is described in the Test Planning process area. The activities for test design and execution are explicitly scheduled as part of the test plan.

GP 2.3 Provide resources

Provide adequate resources for performing the Test Design and Execution process, developing the test work products, and providing the services of the process.

Elaboration

- Adequate time is provided to perform the test design and execution activities
- Experienced individuals, who have expertise in the application domain of the test object and those who have expertise in the development process are available to support the development of the test designs, e.g., participating during reviews
- Tools to support the test design and execution process are available

Examples of tools include the following:

- Dynamic analysis tools
- Coverage analysis tools
- Test design tools
- Test data preparation tools
- Test execution tools
- Incident management tools

GP 2.4 Assign responsibilities

Assign responsibility and authority for performing the Test Design and Execution process, developing the work products, and providing the services of the Test Design and Execution process.

GP 2.5 Train people

Train the people performing or supporting the Test Design and Execution process as needed.

Elaboration

Test engineers, and other individuals or groups, involved in test design and execution, are trained in test design and execution and the accompanying procedures and techniques.

Examples of training topics include the following:

- Formal and informal test design techniques
- Test specification process
- Deriving and prioritizing test conditions and developing test designs
- Development and prioritization of test cases
- Documenting and prioritizing of test procedures
- Test execution activities
- Test specification and test log templates and standards
- Test incident reporting
- Test incident management
- Supporting test design and execution tools

GP 2.6 Manage configurations

Place selected work products of the Test Design and Execution process under appropriate levels of configuration control.

Elaboration

Examples of work products placed under configuration management include the following:

- Test design specifications
- Test case specifications
- Test procedure specifications (and/or test scripts)
- Test execution schedule
- Test logs
- Automated test scripts

GP 2.7 Identify and involve relevant stakeholders

Identify and involve relevant stakeholders of the Test Design and Execution process as planned.

Elaboration

Examples of activities for stakeholder involvement include:

- Reviewing and approving of test designs and test cases
- Executing tests, e.g., for validation purposes by end users
- Participating in the incident management process, e.g., at CCB meetings

GP 2.8 Monitor and control the process

Monitor and control the Test Design and Execution process against the plan for performing the process and take appropriate actions.

Elaboration

Examples of measures used to monitor and control the test design and execution process include the following:

- Number of test specifications completed
- Number of tests executed
- Percentage of tests passed
- Number of outstanding incidents (per priority level)
- Incident trends

GP 2.9 Objectively evaluate adherence

Objectively evaluate adherence of the Test Design and Execution process and selected work products against the process description, standards, and procedures, and address any non-compliances.

Elaboration

Examples of review and/or audit evaluation adherence topics include the following:

- The effectiveness and efficiency of test design techniques
- The compliance of the test specifications (test design, test cases, test procedures) to templates and standards
- The quality of the test cases
- The existence and quality level of the test logs
- Compliance with the incident management process

GP 2.10 Review status with higher level management

Review the activities, status and results of the Test Design and Execution process with higher level management and resolve issues.

GG 3 Institutionalize a Defined Process

Only applicable at TMMi level 3.

GP 3.1 Establish a defined process

Establish and maintain a description of a defined Test Design and Execution process.

GP 3.2 Collect improvement information

Collect process related experiences derived from planning and performing the Test Design and Execution process to support the future use and improvement of the organization's processes and process assets.

Elaboration

Examples of measures include the following:

- Number of test designs established using test design techniques
- Time spent per test specification
- Incident reports by priority and severity
- Effectiveness of test design techniques, e.g., using Defect Detection Percentage (DDP)
- Percentage of test cases automated.

Process Area 2.5 Test Environment

Purpose

The purpose of Test Environment is to establish and maintain an adequate environment, including test data, in which it is possible to execute the tests in a manageable and repeatable way.

Introductory Notes

A managed and controlled test environment is indispensable for any testing. It is also needed to obtain test results under conditions which are as close as possible to the 'real-life' situation. This is especially true for higher level testing, e.g., at system and acceptance test level. Furthermore, at any test level the reproducibility of test results should not be endangered by undesired or unknown changes in the test environment.

Specification of test environment requirements is performed early in the project. The requirements specification is reviewed to ensure its correctness, suitability, feasibility and accurate representation of a 'real-life' operational environment. Early requirements specification has the advantage of providing more time to acquire and/or develop the required test environment and components such as simulators, stubs or drivers. The type of environment required will depend on the product to be tested and the test types, methods and techniques used.

Availability of a test environment encompasses a number of issues which need to be addressed. For example, is it necessary for testing to have an environment per test level? A separate test environment per test team or per test level can be very expensive. Maybe it is possible to have the same environment shared between testers and developers. If so, strict management and control is necessary as both testing and development activities are done in the same environment and can negatively impact progress. When poorly managed, this situation can cause many problems ranging from conflicting reservations to people finding the environment in an unknown or undesired state when starting their activities.

Finally test environment management also includes managing access to the test environment by providing log-in details, managing test data, providing and enforcing configuration management and providing technical support on progress disturbing issues during test execution.

As part of the Test Environment process area, the requirements regarding generic test data, and the creation and management of the test data are also addressed. Whereas specific test data is defined during the test design and analysis activity, more generic test data is often defined and created as a separate activity. Generic test data is re-used by many testers and provides overall background data that is needed to perform the system functions. Generic test data often consists of master data and some initial content for primary data. Sometimes timing requirements influence this activity.

Scope

The process area Test Environment addresses all activities for specifying test environment requirements, implementing the test environment and managing and controlling the test environment. Management and control of the test environment also includes aspects such as configuration management and ensuring availability. The Test Environment process area scope includes both the physical test environment and the test data.

Specific Goal and Practice Summary

SG 1 Develop Test Environment Requirements
- SP 1.1 Elicit test environment needs
- SP 1.2 Develop the test environment requirements
- SP 1.3 Analyze the test environment requirements

SG 2 Perform Test Environment Implementation
- SP 2.1 Implement the test environment
- SP 2.2 Create generic test data
- SP 2.3 Specify test environment intake test procedure
- SP 2.4 Perform test environment intake test

SG 3 Manage and Control Test Environments
- SP 3.1 Perform systems management
- SP 3.2 Perform test data management
- SP 3.3 Coordinate the availability and usage of the test environments
- SP 3.4 Report and manage test environment incidents

Specific Practices by Goals

SG 1 Develop Test Environment Requirements

Stakeholder needs, expectations and constraints are collected and translated into test environment requirements.

SP 1.1 Elicit test environment needs

Elicit test environment, including generic test data, needs, expectations and constraints.

Example work products

1. Test environment needs

Sub-practices

1. Study the test approach and test plan for test environment implications
2. Engage testing representatives for eliciting test environment needs, including generic test data, expectations and constraints

Examples of test environment needs include the following:

- Network components
- Software components, e.g., operating systems, firmware
- Simulators, stubs and drivers
- Supporting documentation, e.g., user guides, technical guides and installation manuals
- Interfacing components or products
- Tools to develop stubs and drivers
- Test equipment
- Requirements for multiple test environments
- Generic test databases
- Test data generators
- Test data storage needs
- Test data archive and restore facilities

3. Document the test environment needs, including generic test data, expectations and constraints

SP 1.2 Develop the test environment requirements

Transform the test environment needs into prioritized test environment requirements

Example work products

1. Prioritized test environment requirements
2. Requirements allocation sheet

Sub-practices

1. Translate the test environment needs, including generic test data, expectations and constraints into documented test environment requirements
2. Establish and maintain a prioritization of test environment requirements
   Having prioritized test environment requirements helps to determine scope. This prioritization ensures that requirements critical to the test environment are addressed quickly.
3. Allocate test environment requirements to test environment components

SP 1.3 Analyze the test environment requirements

Analyze the requirements to ensure they are necessary, sufficient and feasible.

Example work products

1. Test environment requirements analysis report
2. Test environment requirements review log
3. Test environment project risks

Sub-practices

1. Analyze test environment requirements to determine whether they fully support the test lifecycle and test approach

> *Examples of practices to support the analysis of the test environment requirements:*
>
> - Mapping of test environment requirements to test levels
> - Mapping of test environment requirements to test types

2. Identify key test environment requirements having a strong influence on cost, schedule or test performance
3. Identify test environment requirements that can be implemented using existing or modified resources.
4. Analyze test environment requirements to ensure that they are complete, feasible and realizable
5. Analyze test environment requirements to ensure that it sufficiently represents the 'real-life' situation, especially for higher test levels
6. Identify test project risks related to the test environment requirements
7. Review the test environment requirements specification with stakeholders

SG 2 Perform Test Environment Implementation

The test environment requirements are implemented and the test environment is made available to be used during test execution.

SP 2.1 Implement the test environment

Implement the test environment as specified in the test environment requirements specification and according to the defined plan.

Example work products

1. Operational test environment
2. Unit test results for test environment components

Sub-practices

1. Implement the test environment as specified and according to the defined plan
2. Adhere to applicable standards and criteria
3. Perform unit testing on test environment components as appropriate
4. Develop supporting documentation, e.g., installation, operation and maintenance documentation
5. Revise the test environment components as necessary

An example of when the test environment may need to be revised is when problems surface during implementation that could not be foreseen during requirements specification.

SP 2.2 Create generic test data

Generic test data as specified in the requirements specification is created.

Example work products

1. Generic test data

Sub-practices

1. Create generic test data required to support the execution of the tests
2. Anonymize sensitive data in line with the policy when 'real-life' data is used as a source
3. Archive the set of generic test data

SP 2.3 Specify test environment intake test procedure

The test environment intake test (confidence test), to be used to decide whether the test environment is ready for testing, is specified.

Example work products

1. Test environment intake checklist
2. Test environment intake test procedure specification
3. Test environment intake test procedure specification review log

Sub-practices

1. Define a list of checks to be carried out during the intake test of the test environment
2. Develop the test environment intake test procedure based on the checks identified by putting the checks (test cases) in a executable order and including any other information needed for performing the test environment intake test

3. Document the test environment intake test procedure in a test procedure specification, based on the test procedure specification standard
4. Review the test environment intake test procedure specification with stakeholders

Note that this practice is highly related to the practice SP 2.3 Specify intake test procedure from the process area Test Design and Execution and can possibly be combined.

SP 2.4 Perform test environment intake test

The test environment intake test (confidence test) is performed to determine whether the test environment is ready to be used for testing.

Example work products

1. Test environment intake test log
2. Incident reports

Sub-practices

1. Perform the intake test (confidence test) using the documented intake test procedure to decide if the test environment is ready to be used for testing.
2. Document the results of the test environment intake test by means of a test log, based on the test log standard
3. Log incidents if a discrepancy is observed
   Refer to SP 3.3 Report test incidents from the process area Test Design and Execution for more information on incident logging.

Note that this practice is highly related to the practice SP 3.1 Perform intake test from the process area Test Design and Execution and the intake test on the test object and test environment can possibly be combined.

SG 3 Manage and Control Test Environments

Test environments are managed and controlled to allow for uninterrupted test execution.

SP 3.1 Perform systems management

Systems management is performed on the test environments to effectively and efficiently support the test execution process.

Example work products

1. System management log file
2. Test logging

Sub-practices

1. Install components needed, e.g., for a specific test session
2. Manage access to the test environment by providing log-in details
3. Provide technical support on progress disturbing issues during test execution
4. Provide logging facilities, which can be used afterwards to analyze test results

SP 3.2 Perform test data management

Test data is managed and controlled to effectively and efficiently support the test execution process.

Example work products

1. Archived test data
2. Test data management log file

Sub-practices

1. Manage security and access to the test data
2. Manage test data, e.g., with respect to storage resources needed
3. Archive and restore test data and other files on a regular basis and if necessary related to a test session

SP 3.3 Coordinate the availability and usage of the test environments

The availability and usage of the test environment by multiple groups is coordinated to achieve maximum efficiency.

Example work products

1. Test environment reservation schedule

Sub-practices

1. Set up a procedure for managing the usage of test environments by multiple groups
2. Make documented reservations of the test environments in the reservation schedule
3. Identifying specific test environment components needed when making a reservation
4. Discuss conflicting reservation with involved groups and stakeholders
5. Define a test environment reservation schedule for the upcoming period
6. Use the test environment during the reserved and assigned time-slot

7. Shut down the test environment correctly after usage, e.g., by making sure it is in a known state and test files are removed.

SP 3.4 Report and manage test environment incidents

Problems that occur when using the test environment are formally reported as incidents and are managed to closure.

Example work products

1. Test environment incident reports
2. CCB meeting reports, including a decision log regarding test environment incidents

Sub-practices

1. Log the test environment incident when a problem is observed
2. Formally report the test environment incident using an incident classification scheme
3. Manage test environment incidents to closure
   Refer to Test Design and Execution process area for practices and sub-practices covering incident reporting and management.

Generic Practices by Goals

GG 2 Institutionalize a Managed Process

GP 2.1 Establish an organizational policy

Establish and maintain an organizational policy for planning and performing the Test Environment process.

Elaboration

The test environment policy typically specifies:

- Test environment requirements specification shall be done early in the lifecycle
- Higher levels tests will be carried out in a test environment that is representative of 'real-life'
- Management and control of test environments is performed according to documented procedures
- Lower test levels, e.g., unit and integration testing, shall apply stubs and drivers for testing
- Privacy and security rules regarding the use of real-life data to create test data

GP 2.2 Plan the process

Establish and maintain the plan for performing the Test Environment process.

Elaboration

Typically, the plan for performing the Test Environment process is included in the test plan, which is described in the Test Planning process area. In a project where the test environment is more complex, and therefore requires more resources, a specific test environment plan may be established. The plan typically describes the implementation process of the test environment requirements in detail.

GP 2.3 Provide resources

Provide adequate resources for performing the Test Environment process, developing the work products, and providing the services of the process.

Elaboration

- Experienced individuals, who have expertise and technical knowledge, are available to support the test environment requirements specification
- Adequate time and resources are provided to implement, manage and control the test environment
- Adequate time and resources are provided to create, manage and control the test data
- Adequate time and resources are provided to engineers to develop stubs and drivers needed for low level testing

GP 2.4 Assign responsibilities

Assign responsibility and authority for performing the Test Environment process, developing the work products, and providing the services of the Test Environment process.

Elaboration

Examples of test environment responsibilities to be assigned include the following:

- Specification of the test environment requirements
- Implementation of the test environment
- Configuration management of the test environment
- Solving technical problems related to the test environment
- Ensuring that tests are reproducible with respect to the test environment
- Supporting and consulting on test environment-related procedures and technical issues
- Ensuring the availability of the test environment
- Supporting projects in defining an approach for test data
- Creation of generic test data
- Managing and protecting test data

GP 2.5 Train people

Train the people performing or supporting the Test Environment process as needed.

GP 2.6 Manage configurations

Place selected work products of the Test Environment process under appropriate levels of configuration control.

Elaboration

Examples of work products placed under configuration management include:

- Test environment requirements specification
- Test environment plans
- Test environments
- Test data
- Configuration scripts
- Installation scripts

Note that configuration management for test environments and test data is key to any testing and is a requirement for test reproducibility.

GP 2.7 Identify and involve relevant stakeholders

Identify and involve relevant stakeholders of the Test Environment process as planned.

Elaboration

Examples of activities for stakeholder involvement include:

- Reviewing test environment requirements specification
- Providing resources and/or input for the implementation of the test environment, e.g., subcontractors that develop test environment components

GP 2.8 Monitor and control the process

Monitor and control the Test Environment process against the plan for performing the process and take appropriate actions.

Elaboration

This is sometimes forgotten, but it is of course important to monitor progress of the development of stubs and drivers needed for unit and integration testing so that these progress in a timely manner according to the schedule.

GP 2.9 Objectively evaluate adherence

Objectively evaluate adherence of the Test Environment process and selected work products against the process description, standards, and procedures, and address any non-compliances.

Elaboration

Examples of review and/or audit evaluation adherence topics include:

- A test environment requirements specification is written early in the project
- The test environment is, as much as possible, 'real-life', especially for higher test levels
- The availability of the test environment is at an adequate level
- The management and control of the test environment is effective and efficient
- The test data is adequate for 'real-life' testing

GP 2.10 Review status with higher level management

Review the activities, status and results of the Test Environment process with higher level management and resolve issues.

GG 3 Institutionalize a Defined Process

GP 3.1 Establish a defined process

Establish and maintain a description of a defined Test Environment process

GP 3.2 Collect improvement information

Collect process-related experiences derived from planning and performing the Test Environment process to support the future use and improvement of the organization's processes and process assets.

Elaboration

Examples of measures include the following:

- Number of conflicting test environment reservations
- Effort needed for maintenance, repair and updates
- Number of test case failures due to the test environment
- Average down-time of the test environment
- Number of test environment incidents reported
- Percentage of test environments available on time and according to specification
- Number of defects found in production that were not found during testing because of inadequate test environment or test data

TMMi Level 3 Defined

At TMMi level 3, testing is no longer confined to a phase that follows coding. It is fully integrated into the development lifecycle and the associated milestones. Test planning is done at an early project stage, e.g., during the requirements phase, and is documented in a master test plan. The development of a master test plan builds on the test planning skills and commitments acquired at TMMi level 2. The organization's set of standard test processes, which is the basis for maturity level 3, is established and improved over time. A test organization and a specific test training program exist, and testing is perceived as being a profession. Test process improvement is fully institutionalized as part of the test organization's accepted practices.

Organizations at level 3 understand the importance of reviews in quality control; a formal review program is implemented although not yet fully linked to the dynamic testing process. Reviews take place across the lifecycle. Test professionals are involved in reviews of requirements specifications. Whereas the test designs at TMMi level 2 focus mainly on functionality testing, test designs and test techniques are expanded at level 3 to include non-functional testing, e.g., usability and/or reliability, depending the business objectives.

A critical distinction between TMMi maturity level 2 and 3 is the scope of the standards, process descriptions, and procedures. At maturity level 2 these may be quite different in each specific instance, e.g., on a particular project. At maturity level 3 these are tailored from the organization's set of standard processes to suit a particular project or organizational unit and therefore are more consistent except for the differences allowed by the tailoring guidelines. Another critical distinction is that at maturity level 3, processes are typically described more rigorously than at maturity level 2. As a consequence, at maturity level 3 the organization must revisit the maturity level 2 process areas.

The process areas at TMMi level 3 are:
3.1 Test Organization
3.2 Test Training Program
3.3 Test Lifecycle and Integration
3.4 Non-functional Testing
3.5 Peer Reviews

Each of these is discussed in more detail in the sections hereafter.

Process Area 3.1 Test Organization

Purpose

The purpose of the Test Organization process area is to identify and organize a group of highly skilled people that is responsible for testing. In addition to testing, the test group also manages improvements to the organization's test process and test process assets based on a thorough understanding of the strengths and weaknesses of the organization's current test process and test process assets.

Introductory Notes

Establishing a test organization implies a commitment to better testing and higher-quality software. To initiate the process, upper management must support the decision to establish a test group and commit resources to the group. It also requires leadership in areas that relate to testing and quality issues. The staff members of such a group are called test specialists. A test organization (group) is the representation of effective relationships between test specialists, test facilities and project-related test activities in order to achieve a high standard in structured testing. Well-defined communication links from the test group to business, development, and quality assurance are established. The synergy between these elements creates a structure that is more than the sum of the parts.

It is important for an organization to have an independent test group. The group shall have a formalized position in the organizational hierarchy. The term independence is used generically, but each organization must develop its own interpretation and implementation of the right level of independence. A test organization can, for instance, be organized as a test competence center with a test resource pool. In this type of organization, group members are assigned to projects throughout the organizations where they do their testing work, or as an independent test group that performs acceptance testing before release. In the TMMi sense, independence for the test organization means that testers are recognized as engineering specialists. Testers are not considered to be developers, and most importantly they report to management independent of the development management. Test specialists are allowed to be objective and impartial, unhindered by development organization pressures.

Testing is regarded as a profession and the test group is recognized as a necessity. Detailed and specialized knowledge and skills regarding test engineering, test management and the application domain are characteristics of the motivated individuals assigned to the test group. Test functions and test career paths are defined and supported by a test training program. The group is staffed by people who have the skills and motivation to be good testers. They are assigned to a specific test function and are dedicated to establishing awareness of, and achieving, product quality goals. They measure quality characteristics, and have responsibilities for ensuring the system meets the customers' requirements. Also the test activities, roles and responsibilities for other staff members (non-test specialists) are specified. For each test function the typical tasks, responsibilities, authorities, required knowledge, skills and test training are specified. As a result, the process areas 'Test Organization' and 'Test Training Program' are closely related and interdependent. One of the principal objectives of the training program is to support the test organization in training of test specialists.

Whereas at TMMi level 2 test process improvement is sometimes an ad hoc project, it is now well-organized and structured within the test organization. The responsibility for facilitating and managing the test process improvement activities, including coordinating the participation of other disciplines, is typically assigned to a test technology manager supported by a management steering committee. Sometimes a test process improvement group, often called a Test Process Group,is already established and staffed. Candidates for process improvements are obtained from various sources, including measurements, lessons learned and assessment results. Careful planning is required to ensure that test process improvement efforts across the organization are adequately managed and implemented. The planning for test process improvement results in a process improvement plan. This plan will address assessment planning, process action planning, pilot planning and deployment planning. When the test improvement is to be deployed, the deployment plan is used. This plan describes when and how the improvement will be implemented across the organization.

Scope

The process area Test Organization defines the functioning (tasks, responsibilities, reporting structure) and the position of a test group in the overall organization. Test roles, functions, and career paths are defined to support the acceptance of testing as a professional discipline. Within the test organization, test process improvement is a key activity. Test process improvement encompasses assessing the current test process and using lessons learned to identify possible test improvements, implementing improvements and deploying them in testing activities in projects.

Specific Goal and Practice Summary

SG 1 Establish a Test Organization

- SP 1.1 Define the test organization
- SP 1.2 Obtain commitments for the test organization

SP 1.3 Implement the test organization

SG 2 Establish Test Functions for Test Specialists
SP 2.1 Identify test functions
SP 2.2 Develop job descriptions
SP 2.3 Assign staff members to test functions

SG 3 Establish Test Career Paths
SP 3.1 Establish test career paths
SP 3.2 Develop personal test career development plans

SG 4 Determine, Plan and Implement Test Process Improvements
SP 4.1 Assess the organization's test process
SP 4.2 Identify the organization's test process improvements
SP 4.3 Plan test process improvements
SP 4.4 Implement test process improvements

SG 5 Deploy the Organizational Test Process and Incorporate Lessons Learned
SP 5.1 Deploy standard test process and test process assets
SP 5.2 Monitor implementation
SP 5.3 Incorporate lessons learned into the organizational test process

Specific Practices by Goals

SG 1 Establish a Test Organization

A test organization, which supports the testing practices in projects and the organization, is defined and established.

SP 1.1 Define the test organization

A test organization is defined and agreed upon by the stakeholders.

Example work products

1. Test organization description

Sub-practices

1. Define the test organization, e.g., based on the defined business goals and policy, test goals and policy, and/or test strategy

> *Examples of topics to be addressed when defining a test organization typically include the following:*
> - Formal position in the overall organization
> - Organizational type
> - Level of independence in relation to development
> - Tasks, competences and responsibilities of the test organization
> - Reporting structure
> - Starting points regarding resources, e.g., number of test specialists

Note, that ideally the test organization should be a separate organizational entity or function. However, this is not always possible or practical given the size of the organization, risk level of the systems being developed and the resources available.

2. Review the test organization description with stakeholders

SP 1.2 Obtain commitments for the test organization

Commitments for implementing and supporting the test organization are established and maintained.

Example work products

1. Documented requests for commitments
2. Documented commitments

Sub-practices

1. Identify needed support and negotiate commitments regarding the test organization with relevant stakeholders
2. Document all organizational commitments, both full and provisional
3. Review internal commitments with senior management as appropriate
4. Review external commitments with senior management as appropriate

SP 1.3 Implement the test organization

The test organization is implemented in the organization, based on the committed test organization definition.

Example work products

1. Status and results of implementing the test organization

Sub-practices

1. Track implementation progress and commitments
2. Identify, document, and track to closure issues in implementing the test organization
3. Ensure that the results of implementing the test organization satisfy the organizational goals and objectives

SG 2 Establish Test Functions for Test Specialists

Test functions with accompanying job descriptions are established and assigned to the test specialists.

SP 2.1 Identify test functions

A set of test functions is identified, as appropriate.

Example work products

1. List of identified test functions

Sub-practices

1. Analyze the test policy, test strategy and standard test process for typical test roles
2. Identify a set of test functions that cover the typical test roles, as appropriate

Examples of test functions include the following:

- Test manager
- Test team leader
- Test designer
- Test engineer
- Test consultant
- Test environment engineer

3. Identify test functions for specialized areas, as appropriate

Examples of test functions for specialized areas include the following:

- Test automation architect
- Test automation engineer
- Performance test engineer
- Usability test engineer
- Test process improvement officer

SP 2.2 Develop job descriptions

For the test functions identified, job descriptions are developed. For non-test specialist functions, existing job descriptions are enhanced with typical test tasks and responsibilities, as appropriate.

Example work products

1. Job description for test functions
2. Enhanced job description for non-test specialists

Sub-practices

1. Define job description for each of the identified test functions

Job descriptions typically include the following:

- Name of the test function
- Short description
- Salary scale
- Qualifications
- Typical tasks to be performed
- Responsibilities and authorities
- Required knowledge and skills
- Educational requirements
- Training modules to be followed

2. Incorporate the job descriptions into the organization's Human Resource Management (HRM) framework
3. Extend job descriptions for other job categories (non-test specialist) to include the test tasks and responsibilities, as appropriate

Examples of non-test specialists' job categories that typically encompass test activities and responsibilities include the following:

- Software developer
- System engineer
- System integrator
- User representative

4. Use the organization's standard test process as a major input to define and enhance the job descriptions
5. Review the job descriptions with stakeholders

SP 2.3 Assign staff members to test functions

Members of the test organization are assigned to the identified test functions.

Example work products

1. Staff members assigned to test functions as their job title

Sub-practices

1. Assign staff members to the test functions
2. Perform job interviews to fill open test specialist positions, using questionnaires to determine the interviewee's technical background, his or her personal skills and motivation
3. Ensure that the test specialist positions (functions) are kept occupied
4. Periodically evaluate test organization member performance

5. Take appropriate action based on the evaluation, if necessary

SG 3 Establish Test Career Paths

Test career paths are established that allow testers to improve their knowledge, skills, status and rewards.

SP 3.1 Define test career paths

Test career paths are defined that will allow testers to advance their careers.

Example work products

1. Test career path framework

Sub-practices

1. Differentiate within the test functions by creating a junior, intermediate and senior role and provide job descriptions for each of them
2. Link required knowledge and skills, typical tasks and responsibilities, training modules and experience level to the junior, intermediate and senior test roles for each of the differentiated functions
3. Develop job description for each of the identified differentiated test functions
4. Position the defined and differentiated test functions in a (hierarchical) test career path framework
5. Define a typical time frame that states when one can progress to a next test career path step
6. Link the test career path framework to other career path frameworks available in the organization, e.g., how one can move from being a test manager to a project manager
7. Incorporate the test career framework into the organization's Human Resource Management (HRM) framework

SP 3.2 Develop personal test career development plans

A personal test career development plan is developed and maintained for every member of the test organization.

Example work products

1. Personal career development plans

Sub-practices

1. Create personal development plans based on the test career path framework

2. Periodically review the personal development plan with the test staff member
3. Identify and document actions that are needed to advance the career development of the staff member
4. Track the defined test career development actions to closure
5. Revise the personal development plan, as appropriate

SG 4 Determine, Plan and Implement Test Process Improvements

Strengths, weaknesses, and improvement opportunities for the organization's test process are identified periodically and as needed. Process changes that address the improvements are planned and implemented.

SP 4.1 Assess the organization's test process

The organization's test process periodically is assessed to maintain an understanding of its strengths and weaknesses.

Example work products

1. Test process assessment report

Sub-practices

1. Understand the organization's test process needs using the business goals and policy, test goals and policy, and test strategy
2. Obtain sponsorship for the test process assessments from senior management
3. Define the scope of the test process assessment
4. Plan, schedule and prepare for the test process assessment
5. Conduct the test process assessment
6. Document and present the test assessment report

SP 4.2 Identify the organization's test process improvements

Desirable improvements to the organization's test process and test process assets are identified.

Example work products

1. Prioritized list of test improvements

Sub-practices

1. Determine candidate test process improvements from test assessment report
2. Prioritize the candidate test process improvements

Examples of factors that may be helpful to determine the priority of the candidate test process improvements include the following:

- In synchronization with business and test goals
- According to the maturity model
- Most visible process improvements first to create awareness and acceptance
- Provide measurable and clear business benefits
- Estimated cost and effort involved
- Level of difficulty
- Degree of acceptance
- Risks mitigated

3. Discuss and review the prioritized list with key stakeholders
4. Identify and document the test process improvements that will be implemented
5. Revise the list of planned test process improvements to keep it current

SP 4.3 Plan test process improvements

Actions that are needed to address improvements to the organization's test process and test process assets are planned.

Example work products

1. Test process improvement plan

Sub-practices

1. Identify strategies, approaches, and actions to address the identified test process improvements, e.g., new, unproven, and major changes are piloted before they are incorporated into normal use
2. Establish process action teams to define and implement the test process improvements
3. Document the test process improvement plan

Examples of elements of a test process improvement plan include the following:

- Test process improvement objectives
- Test process improvement organization structure
- Test process improvements that will be implemented
- Procedures for monitoring and control
- Strategies for piloting and implementing test process improvements
- Responsibilities and authorities
- Resources and schedules
- Measurement for determining the effectiveness of the test process improvements
- Risk associated with the test process improvement plan

4. Review and negotiate the test process improvement plan with stakeholders (including members of process action teams)
5. Review and update the test process improvement plan as necessary

SP 4.4 Implement test process improvements

The test process improvements addressed by the test improvement plan are implemented.

Example work products

1. Status and results of implementing test process improvements
2. Plans for test process improvement pilots

Sub-practices

1. Track progress and commitments against test process improvement plan
2. Plan and run pilots as needed to test selected test process improvements
3. Evaluate results of pilots against plan and with stakeholders
4. Review the activities and work products of process action teams
5. Identify, document, and track to closure issues in implementing the test improvement plan
6. Ensure that the results of implementing test process improvements satisfy the test process improvement objectives

SG 5 Deploy the Organizational Test Process and Incorporate Lessons Learned

The organizational standard test process and test process assets are deployed across the organization and test process-related experiences are incorporated into the organizational test process and test process assets.

The specific practices within this specific goal describe ongoing activities. Deployment of the standard test process and other organizational test process assets must be continually supported within the organization, particularly for new projects at startup.

SP 5.1 Deploy standard test process and test process assets

The standard test process and test process assets are deployed across the organization, especially to projects at their startup, and changes are deployed as appropriate throughout the life of each project.

It is important that not only those who are or will be executing the test process are involved, but also other organizational functions such as (test) training and quality assurance are involved in the deployment as necessary.

Example work products

1. Deployment plan
2. Documentation of changes to the organizational standard test process and test process assets
3. Organization's list of projects and status of test process deployment on each project
4. Deployment guidelines and other supporting material for deployment, e.g., training
5. Records of any tailoring done to the organization's standard test process for a project

Sub-practices

1. Identify projects within the organization that are starting up
2. Identify active projects that would benefit from implementing the organization's (changes to the) standard test process and test process assets
3. Establish plans to deploy the organization's standard test process and test process assets on the identified projects
4. Document the changes to the organizational standard test process and test process assets to enable communication on the changes
5. Ensure that training is available for those who want to start using the standard test process and test process assets

6. Provide guidance and consultation on the use of the standard test process and test process assets
7. Assist projects in tailoring the organization's standard test process and test process assets to meet project needs
8. Maintain records of tailoring and implementing processes on the identified projects and ensure that results from test process tailoring are incorporated into the plan for process-compliance evaluations (see next specific practice)
9. As the organization's standard test process is updated, identify which project should implement the changes

Refer to the process area Test Lifecycle and Integration for more information about how the deployment of organizational test process assets is supported and enabled by the organization's test process asset library.

SP 5.2 Monitor implementation

The implementation of the organization's standard test process and the use of the test process assets on projects are monitored.

Example work products

1. Results of monitoring test process implementation on projects
2. Status and results of test process compliance evaluations
3. Results of reviewing selected test process artifacts created as part of process tailoring and implementation

Sub-practices

1. Monitor projects for their use of the organization's test process and test process assets and changes to them
2. Review selected test process artifacts created during a project to ensure compliance
3. Review the results of test process-compliance evaluations to determine how well the organization's standard test process and test process assets have been deployed
4. Identify, document, and track to closure issues related to implementing the organization's standard test process

SP 5.3 Incorporate lessons learned into organizational test process

Lessons learned from planning and performing the test process are incorporated into the organizational standard test process and test process assets.

Example work products

1. Review results regarding the effectiveness and suitability of the standard test process and related test process assets
2. Lessons learned documents (e.g., test evaluation reports)
3. Test process improvement proposals
4. Records of organizational test process improvement activities

Sub-practices

1. Conduct periodic reviews of the effectiveness and suitability of the organization's standard test process and related test process assets relative to the business objectives, test goals, test policy and test strategy
2. Obtain feedback about the use of the organization's standard test process and test process assets
3. Derive lessons learned from defining, piloting, deploying and applying the organization's standard test process and test process assets
4. Make lessons learned available to the people in the organization as appropriate
   Projects will typically document their lesson learned in a test evaluation report [TMap].
5. Identify possible best practices to be made available to other projects and to be stored in the organization's test process asset library for re-use by other projects
6. Analyze the organization's test performance indicators and common set of test measures
7. From the information gathered and analyzed, derive test process improvement proposals and software process improvement proposals
8. Submit software process improvement proposals
9. Manage test process improvement proposals

> *Examples of activities for managing test process improvement proposals include the following:*
>
> - Soliciting test process improvement proposals
> - Collecting test process improvement proposals
> - Reviewing test process improvement proposals
> - Selecting test process improvement proposals that will be implemented
> - Tracking the implementation of test process improvement proposals

10. Establish and maintain records of the organization's test process improvement activities

Generic Practices by Goals

GG 2 Institutionalize a Managed Process

GP 2.1 Establish an organizational policy

Establish and maintain an organizational policy for planning and performing the Test Organization process.

Elaboration

The test organization policy typically specifies:
- The test group is recognized as an organizational entity
- Tasks and responsibilities, and the position of the test group in the overall organization
- The level of independence of the test group within the overall organization and projects
- Testing is recognized as a profession
- Test functions and career paths are identified and institutionalized

Examples of test functions include:
- Test manager
- Test team leader
- Test designer
- Test engineer
- Test consultant
- Test environment engineer

- The standard test process (including templates) that is defined and maintained by the test organization and is consistently applied
- The approach to test metrics, test databases, test tools, and test re-use
- The test activities that the test organization facilitates and/or coordinates in projects
- The test evaluation report (lessons learned) that each (test) project will provide for use in improving the standard test process
- The objectives and organizational structure regarding test process improvement
- The approach for planning, implementing and deploying test process improvements across the organization

GP 2.2 Plan the process

Establish and maintain the plan for performing the Test Organization process.

Elaboration

The plan called for in this generic practice addresses the comprehensive organizational planning for all of the specific practices in this process area required to achieve the specific goals.

The 'test process improvement plan' is part of the specific practices within this process area and is therefore not the plan referred to by this generic practice.

GP 2.3 Provide resources

Provide adequate resources for performing the Test Organization process, developing the test work products, and providing the services of the process.

Elaboration

- An annual budget is available for test organizational activities, e.g., for test process improvement
- Appropriate facilities and tools are made available to perform the test organizational activities
- Fully operational office environment for the test organization is available

GP 2.4 Assign responsibilities

Assign responsibility and authority for performing the Test Organization process, developing the work products, and providing the services of the Test Organization process.

Elaboration

A resource manager is designated to be responsible for managing the test group. Managing the standard test process is often delegated to a test technology manager. In addition a management steering committee for test process improvement is established and assigned responsibility to provide management sponsorship.

> *Examples of test organization responsibilities to be assigned include the following:*
>
> - Representing the test group in the overall organization
> - Human resource management for the test specialists and their career paths
> - Test process management and improvement
> - Facilitating the testing activities carried out within the projects

GP 2.5 Train people

Train the people performing or supporting the Test Organization process as needed.

Elaboration

Examples of training topics include the following:

- Human resource management training
- Staff appraisal sessions
- Coaching test professionals
- TMMi and other test process improvement reference models
- Planning and managing test process improvement
- Change management

Note that training for (test) engineers and (test) managers on the standard test process and supporting test tools is addressed as part of the process area Test Training Program.

GP 2.6 Manage configurations

Place selected work products of the Test Organization process under appropriate levels of configuration control.

Elaboration

Examples of work products placed under configuration management include the following:

- Test organization description
- Job descriptions for test functions
- Test career paths descriptions
- Personal career development plans
- Test assessment reports
- Test process improvement plans
- Deployment plans

GP 2.7 Identify and involve relevant stakeholders

Identify and involve relevant stakeholders of the Test Organization process as planned.

Elaboration

Examples of stakeholder involvement include the following:

- Senior management for addressing commitment to a test organization
- Human Resource Management for support and alignment regarding test function descriptions and career development plans
- Process improvement officer for alignment to other process improvement initiatives, e.g., software process improvement

GP 2.8 Monitor and control the process

Monitor and control the Test Organization process against the plan for performing the process and take appropriate actions.

Elaboration

Examples of measures used in monitoring and control the Test Organization process include the following:

- Actual number of test specialists per test function versus planned number of test specialists per test function
- Percentage of test specialists for which a personal test career development plan exists
- Number of test process improvement proposals submitted, accepted and/or implemented
- Schedules for the deployment of organization test process assets
- Percentage of projects using the current organization's set of standard test processes (or tailored version of the same)

GP 2.9 Objectively evaluate adherence

Objectively evaluate adherence of the Test Organizational process and selected work products against the process description, standards, and procedures, and address any areas of non-compliance.

Elaboration

Examples of review and/or audit topics for evaluation and adherence include the following:

- Operational performance test organization
- Test staff members assigned to defined test function
- Career development plans
- Planning and coordinating test process improvement activities
- Deployment of the organization's set of standard test processes on projects
- Test process improvement plans
- Test process deployment plans

GP 2.10 Review status with higher level management

Review the activities, status and results of the Test Organization process with higher level management and resolve issues.

Elaboration

Examples of issues to be reviewed with higher level management include the following:

- Performance of the test organization
- Number of open test positions
- Status of improvements being developed by action teams
- Results of pilots and deployments

GG 3 Institutionalize a Defined Process

GP 3.1 Establish a defined process

Establish and maintain a description of the defined Test Organization process

GP 3.2 Collect improvement information

Collect process related experiences derived from planning and performing the Test Organization process to support the future use and improvement of the organization's processes and process assets.

Elaboration

Examples of measures include the following:

- Number of test specialists in the test organization
- Test employee turnover
- Level of application regarding the standard test process
- Assessment findings that address strengths and weaknesses of the organization's test process
- Status of improvement activities against schedule

Process Area 3.2 Test Training Program

Purpose

The purpose of the Test Training Program process area is to develop a training program which facilitates the development of knowledge and skills of people so that test tasks and roles can be performed effectively and efficiently.

Introductory Notes

Test Training Program includes training to support the organization's strategic business objectives and to meet the training needs that are common across projects. Specific training needs identified by individual projects are handled at project level. Test Training Program is closely related to and interdependent with the Test Organization process area. One of the main objectives of the Test Training Program is to support the test organization by training the test specialists and other stakeholders involved. A quality training program ensures that those involved in testing continue to improve their testing skills and update their domain knowledge and other knowledge related to testing. The training program may be organized and managed by means of a dedicated training group.

Establishing a test training program is an additional commitment by management to support high quality testing staff and to promote continuous test process improvement. In testing, a variety of skills is needed. The main categories are test principles, test techniques, test management, test tools, domain knowledge, IT knowledge, system engineering, software development and interpersonal skills. A test training program, consisting of several training modules, is developed to address these categories. Note at higher levels of TMMi other more advanced training categories will become important, e.g., defect prevention at TMMi level 5. Some skills are effectively and efficiently imparted through informal vehicles (e.g., training-on-the-job and mentoring) whereas other skills require formal training.

The term 'training' is used throughout this process area to include all of these learning options. The test training program is linked to the test functions and test roles, and will facilitate test career paths. Deploying the training program guarantees the appropriate knowledge and skill level for all people involved in testing. The implementation of the Test Training Program process area involves first identifying the organizational test training needs, developing or acquiring specific training modules, conducting training to address the identified needs as required and, finally, evaluating the effectiveness of the training program.

Scope

The process area Test Training Program addresses the establishment of an organizational test training plan and test training capability. It also addresses the actual delivery of the planned test training. Project specific training needs are not part of this process area. They are addressed in the process area Test Planning.

Specific Goal and Practice Summary

SG 1 Establish an Organizational Test Training Capability
- SP 1.1 Identify the strategic test training needs
- SP 1.2 Align the organizational and project test training needs
- SP 1.3 Establish an organizational test training plan
- SP 1.4 Establish test training capability

SG 2 Provide Test Training
- SP 2.1 Deliver test training
- SP 2.2 Establish test training records
- SP 2.3 Assess test training effectiveness

Specific Practices by Goals

SG 1 Establish an Organizational Test Training Capability

A training capability, which supports the organization's test roles, is established and maintained.

SP 1.1 Identify the strategic test training needs

The strategic test training needs of the organization are identified and maintained.

Example work products

1. Training needs
2. Assessment analysis

Sub-practices

1. Analyze the organization's strategic business objectives, test policy and strategy and (test) process improvement plan to identify current and potential future test training needs

Examples of categories of test training needs include the following:

- Test engineering and process (e.g., organizational standard test process, test principles, test lifecycle, static test techniques, dynamic test techniques, test tools and test automation)
- Test management (e.g., test estimation, tracking, and risk management)
- IT related training (e.g., requirements engineering, configuration management, project management, system engineering, software development, development lifecycle models)
- Interpersonal skills (e.g., communication, team building)
- Domain expertise

Note that the identification of test process training is primarily based on the skills that are required to perform the organization's set of standard test processes.

2. Periodically assess the test skill set of the people involved in testing
3. Document the strategic test training needs of the organization
4. Map the test training needs to the test functions (including test career paths) and test roles of the organization
5. Revise the organizations strategic test training needs as necessary

SP 1.2 Align the organizational and project test training needs

The organizational and project test training needs are aligned and it is determined which of the test training needs are the responsibility of the organization and which should be left to the individual projects.

The organization's training staff is responsible for addressing common cross-project test training needs. In some cases, however, the organization's training staff may address additional test training needs of projects within the context of the training resources and the organization's training priorities.

Example work products

1. Common project test training needs
2. Training commitments to projects

Sub-practices

1. Analyze the test training needs identified by various projects

Analysis of specific project needs is intended to identify common test training needs that can be most efficiently addressed organization-wide. This analysis activity can also be used to anticipate future test training needs that are first visible at the project level.

2. Determine whether the training needs identified by the various projects are project specific or common to the organization.

   Test training needs common to the organization are normally managed by means of the organizational test training program.

3. Negotiate with the various projects on how their specific training needs will be satisfied

Examples of training appropriately performed by the project include the following:

- Training in the application domain of the project
- Training in the unique tools and methods used by the project

4. Document the commitments for providing test training support to the projects

Refer to SP 4.2 Plan for test staffing from the process area Test Planning for more information on project specific plans for training.

SP 1.3 Establish an organizational test training plan

An organizational test training plan is established and maintained.

Note that in many organizations this planning is performed annually with a review each quarter.

Example work products

1. Test training plan
2. Test training commitments

Sub-practices

1. Establish test training plan content

Examples of elements of an organizational test training plan include the following:

- Test training topics
- Schedules based on test training activities and their dependencies
- Methods used for training
- Requirements and quality standards for training materials
- Training tasks, roles and responsibilities
- Required resources including tools, facilities, environments, and staffing
- Required skills and knowledge of the trainers
- Data to be collected for measuring training effectiveness

2. Review test training plan with affected groups and individuals, e.g., human resources, test resources and project management.
3. Establish commitment to the test training plan
4. Revise test training plan and commitments as necessary

SP 1.4 Establish test training capability

A test training capability is established and maintained to address the organizational training needs and to support the project-specific training needs.

Example work products

1. Test training materials and supporting artifacts

Sub-practices

1. Select the appropriate approaches to satisfy specific test training needs

Examples of training approaches include the following:

- Classroom training
- Computer-aided instruction
- Guided self-study
- Formal apprenticeship and mentoring programs
- Brown-bag lunch seminars
- Structured on-the-job training

2. Determine whether to develop test training materials internally or acquire them externally

Example criteria that can be used to determine the most effective mode of knowledge or skill acquisition include the following:

- Time available to prepare the training materials
- Availability of in-house expertise
- Availability of training (materials) from external sources
- Available budget
- Time required for maintenance of training material

3. Develop or obtain test training materials
4. Develop or obtain qualified instructors
5. Describe the training in the organization's test training curriculum

Examples of the information provided in the test training descriptions for each course include the following:

- Training objectives
- Topics covered in the training
- Intended audience
- Prerequisites, e.g., other training courses and practical experience
- Preparation for participating
- Length of the training
- Lesson plans
- Completion criteria for the course

6. Revise the test training materials and supporting artifacts as appropriate

Examples of situations in which the test training materials and supporting artifacts may need to be revised include the following:

- Test training needs change (e.g., when new technology associated with the training topic is available)
- When evaluation of the test training identifies the need for change (e.g., evaluations of training effectiveness surveys, training program performance assessments, or instructor evaluation forms)

SG 2 Provide Test Training

Training necessary to perform their role effectively is provided for testers and other individuals involved in testing.

In selecting people to be trained, also consider the need for managers to understand the basic testing principles and test strategy, developers to be able to perform unit and integration testing, users to be able to participate in acceptance testing, etc.

SP 2.1 Deliver test training

Training is delivered according to the organizational test training plan.

Example work products

1. Delivered training course
2. Completed course evaluation forms

Sub-practices

1. Select the people who will receive the training necessary to perform their test role effectively
   Note a waiver may be provided to those that already possess the knowledge and skills required to perform well in their designated roles. Care should be taken that training waivers are not abused.
2. Schedule the training including any required resources, as necessary (e.g., facilities and instructors)
3. Conduct the training
4. Gather the participant completed course evaluation forms
5. Track the delivery of training against the plan

SP 2.2 Establish test training records

Records showing the organizational test training that has been conducted are created and maintained.

Although strictly speaking the scope of this process area is for test training performed at the organizational level, to provide consistent and complete information on each employee, the training records preferably include all training, whether performed at the organizational level or at the project level.

Example work products

1. Test training records
2. Training updates to the organizational repository

Sub-practices

1. Keep records for all employees who successfully complete a training course or other training activity as well as those who have been unsuccessful
2. Keep records of all employees who have been waived from specific training including rationale and management approval
3. Make training records available to the appropriate people for consideration in assignments, e.g., by providing a skill matrix with a summary of experience and education of people

SP 2.3 Assess test training effectiveness

The effectiveness of the organization's test training program is assessed.

The results of the test training effectiveness assessments should be used to revise training materials as described in the 'Establish training capability' specific practice.

Example work products

1. Training effectiveness surveys
2. Training program performance assessments
3. Training examinations results

Sub-practices

1. Assess in-progress or completed projects to determine whether employee knowledge is adequate for performing project test tasks
2. Assess the effectiveness of each training course with respect to established organizational, project, or individual learning objectives
3. Obtain student evaluations of how well training activities met their needs

Generic Practices by Goals

GG 2 Institutionalize a Managed Process

GP 2.1 Establish an organizational policy

Establish and maintain an organizational policy for planning and performing the organizational Test Training Program process.

Elaboration

The test training policy typically specifies:

- The knowledge and skills needed for performing the test functions and roles
- Test training vehicles for imparting knowledge and skills
- Test training is provided to build a knowledge and skill base for testing, to fulfill the needs of projects and to develop the skills of the individuals
- An in-house training group is established
- Test training is developed within the organization or obtained from outside the organization when appropriate
- Test training is also applicable for business representatives, software engineers, integrators and architects that fulfill a test role within a project

GP 2.2 Plan the process

Establish and maintain the plan for performing the organizational Test Training Program process.

Elaboration

This plan for performing the Test Training Program process differs from the test training plan described in a specific practice in this process area. The plan for this generic practice would address the comprehensive planning for all of the specific practices in this process area, from the establishment of strategic test training needs all the way through the assessment of the effectiveness of the test training effort. In contrast the test training plan would address the periodic planning for the delivery of individual training offerings.

GP 2.3 Provide resources

Provide adequate resources for performing the organizational Test Training Program process, developing the test work products, and providing the services of the process.

Elaboration

- An annual budget is available for test training
- People, e.g., the organizational training staff, with the appropriate skills are available

> *Examples of people (full or part time, internal or external), and skills include the following:*
>
> - Testing experts
> - Domain experts
> - Curriculum designers
> - Course designers
> - Instructors
> - Training administrators

- Appropriate facilities and tools are made available to perform training

> *Examples of training facilities and tools include the following:*
>
> - Classroom training facilities
> - Workstations to be used for training
> - Computer-based training packages
> - Packages for developing presentation materials

GP 2.4 Assign responsibilities

Assign responsibility and authority for performing the organizational Test Training Program process, developing the work products, and providing the services of the Test Training Program process.

Elaboration

A group (or person) is designated to be responsible for developing, managing and coordinating the test training program, e.g., organizational training department/coordinator, human resources, etc.

GP 2.5 Train people

Train the people performing or supporting the organizational Test Training Program process as needed.

Elaboration

Examples of training topics include the following:

- Knowledge and skill needs analysis
- Course design
- Training delivery techniques/methods
- Refreshing training on subject matter

GP 2.6 Manage configurations

Place selected work products of the organizational Test Training Program process under appropriate levels of configuration control.

Elaboration

Examples of work products placed under configuration management include the following:

- Test training plan
- Training records
- Training materials and supporting artifacts
- Evaluation forms

GP 2.7 Identify and involve relevant stakeholders

Identify and involve relevant stakeholders of the organizational Test Training Program process as planned.

Elaboration

Examples of activities for stakeholder involvement include the following:

- Identifying test training needs
- Reviewing the test training plan
- Assessing test training effectiveness

GP 2.8 Monitor and control the process

Monitor and control the organizational Test Training Program process against the plan for performing the process and take appropriate actions.

Elaboration

Examples of measures used in monitoring and control of the Test Training Program process include the following:

- Number of training courses delivered (e.g., planned versus actual)
- Actual attendance at each training course compared to the projected attendance
- Schedule for delivery of training
- Schedule for development of courses
- Training costs against allocated budget
- Progress in developing and providing training courses compared to the documented test training needs

GP 2.9 Objectively evaluate adherence

Objectively evaluate adherence of the organizational Test Training Program process and selected work products against the process description, standards, and procedures, and address any areas of non-compliance.

Elaboration

Examples of review and/or audit topics for evaluation and adherence include the following:

- Process for developing and revising the training plan
- Process for developing and revising training courses
- Providing necessary test training
- Test training plan
- Test training records
- Training materials and supporting artifacts
- Instructor evaluation forms

GP 2.10 Review status with higher level management

Review the activities, status and results of the organizational Test Training Program process with higher level management and resolve issues.

Elaboration

Examples of issues to be reviewed with higher level management include the following:

- The effectiveness of the test training program
- Progress regarding test training activities
- Test training costs
- The performance of subcontracted training organizations

GG 3 Institutionalize a Defined Process

GP 3.1 Establish a defined process

Establish and maintain a description of a defined organizational Test Training Program process

GP 3.2 Collect improvement information

Collect process related experiences derived from planning and performing the organizational Test Training Program process to support the future use and improvement of the organization's processes and process assets.

Elaboration

Examples of measures include the following:

- Number of training courses delivered (e.g., planned versus actual)
- Post-training evaluation ratings
- Training program quality survey ratings

Process Area 3.3 Test Lifecycle and Integration

Purpose

The purpose of Test Lifecycle and Integration is to establish and maintain a usable set of organizational test process assets (e.g., a standard test lifecycle) and work environment standards and to integrate and synchronize the test lifecycle with the development lifecycle. The integrated lifecycle ensures early involvement of testing in a project. The purpose of Test Lifecycle and Integration is also to define a coherent test approach across multiple test levels, based on the identified risks and the defined test strategy, and to provide an overall test plan, based on the defined test lifecycle.

Introductory Notes

An important responsibility of the test organization is to define, document and maintain a standard test process, in line with the organization's test policy and goals. Organizational test process assets enable consistent test process performance across the organization and provide a basis for cumulative, long-term benefits to the organization. The organization's test process asset library is a collection of items maintained for use by the people and projects of the organization. The collection of items include descriptions of test processes, descriptions of test lifecycle models (including supporting templates and guidelines for the test deliverables), supporting test tools, process tailoring guidelines and a test process database. The organization's test process asset library supports organizational learning and process improvement by sharing best practices and lessons learned across the organization.

The standard test lifecycle models define the main phases, activities and deliverables for the various test levels. The testing activities will subsequently be performed in projects according to these models. Standards and guidelines are developed for test related (work) products. The standard test lifecycle models are aligned with the development lifecycle models to integrate the testing activities in terms of phasing, milestones, deliverables, and activities. Lifecycle integration is done in such a way that early involvement of testing in projects is ensured, e.g., test planning starts during the requirements specification phase, integration and unit test planning are initiated at detailed design time. Testers will review the test basis documents to determine testability and development planning may be influenced by the test approach. The organization's set of standard test processes can be tailored by projects to create their specific defined processes. The work environment standards are used to guide creation of project work environments.

At TMMi level 3, test management is concerned with master test planning which addresses the coordination of testing tasks, responsibilities and test approach over multiple test levels. This prevents unnecessary redundancy or omissions of tests between the various test levels and can significantly increase the efficiency and quality of the overall test process. The information resulting from project test planning is documented in a project test plan, which governs the detailed level test plans to be written specifically for an individual test level. The master test plan describes the application of the test strategy for a particular project, including the particular levels to be carried out and the relationship between those levels. The master test plan should be consistent with the test policy and strategy, and, in specific areas where it is not, should explain those deviations and exceptions. The master test plan will complement the project plan or operations guide which describes the overall test effort as part of the larger project or operation. The master test plan provides an overall test planning and test management document for multiple levels of test (either within one project or across multiple projects). On smaller projects or operations (e.g., where only one level of testing is formalized) the master test plan and the level test plan will often be combined into one document.

Scope

The process area Test Lifecycle and Integration addresses all practices to establish and maintain a usable set of organizational test process assets (e.g., a standard test lifecycle) and work environment standards, and to integrate and synchronize the test lifecycle with the development lifecycle. Test Lifecycle and Integration also addresses the master test planning practices. The master test plan at TMMi level 3 defines a coherent test approach across multiple test levels.

Specific Goal and Practice Summary

SG 1 Establish Organizational Test Process Assets
- SP 1.1 Establish standard test processes
- SP 1.2 Establish test lifecycle model descriptions addressing all test levels
- SP 1.3 Establish tailoring criteria and guidelines
- SP 1.4 Establish the organization's test process database
- SP 1.5 Establish the organization's test process asset library
- SP 1.6 Establish work environment standards

SG 2 Integrate the Test Lifecycle Models with the Development Models
- SP 2.1 Establish integrated lifecycle models
- SP 2.2 Review integrated lifecycle models
- SP 2.3 Obtain commitments on the role of testing within the integrated lifecycle models

SG 3 Establish a Master Test Plan
- SP 3.1 Perform product risk assessment

SP 3.2 Establish the test approach
SP 3.3 Establish test estimates
SP 3.4 Define the organization for testing
SP 3.5 Develop the master test plan
SP 3.6 Obtain commitment to the master test plan

Specific Practices by Goals

SG 1 Establish Organizational Test Process Assets

A set of organizational test process assets is established and maintained.

SP 1.1 Establish standard test processes

The organization's set of standard test processes is established and maintained.

Multiple standard test processes may be needed to address the needs of different application domains, test levels, lifecycle models, methodologies, and tools. The organization's set of standard test processes typically focuses on technical processes. However, as needed by management, administrative, support and organizational processes can also be part of the standard test process framework. The organization's set of test processes should collectively cover all processes needed by the organization and projects, including those processes addressed at maturity level 2.

Example work products

1. Organization's set of standard test processes

Sub-practices

1. Decompose each standard test process into constituent process elements to the detail needed to understand and describe the process
2. Specify the critical attributes of each process element

Examples of critical elements include the following:

- Process roles and responsibilities
- Applicable standards
- Applicable procedures, methods, and tools
- Entry criteria
- Inputs
- Product and process measures to be collected
- Verification points (e.g., reviews)
- Outputs
- Interfaces
- Exit criteria

3. Specify the relationships of the process elements

Examples of relationships include the following:

- Sequence of process elements
- Interfaces between the process elements
- Interfaces with processes external to testing
- Interdependencies among process elements

4. Ensure that the organization's set of standard test processes adheres to organizational policies, standards, and models
   Adherence to applicable standards and models is typically demonstrated by developing a mapping from the organization's set of standard test processes to the relevant standards and models.
5. Ensure the organization's set of standard test processes satisfies the test process needs and objectives of the test organization
6. Document the organization's set of standard test processes
7. Conduct peer reviews on the organization's set of standard test processes
8. Revise the organization's set of standard test processes as necessary

SP 1.2 Establish test lifecycle model descriptions addressing all test levels

Descriptions of the test lifecycle models (including supporting templates and guidelines for the test deliverables) that are approved for use in the organization are established and maintained, ensuring coverage of all identified test levels.

Example work products

1. Description of test lifecycle models

Sub-practices

1. Select test lifecycle models based on the needs of the projects and the organization
2. Document the descriptions of the test lifecycle models

A test lifecycle model description typically includes the following:

- Test strategy, e.g., test levels and their objectives
- Test lifecycle phases, e.g., planning and control, test analysis and design, test implementation and execution, evaluating exit criteria and reporting, and test closure activities
- Entry and exit criteria for each phase
- Testing activities per phase
- Responsibilities
- Deliverables
- Milestones

3. Develop supporting templates and guidelines for the deliverables identified within the test lifecycle models

Examples of test deliverables that are supported by means of templates and guidelines typically include the following:

- Master test plan
- Level test plan
- Test design specification
- Test case specification
- Test procedure specification
- Test log
- Incident report
- Test summary report
- Test evaluation report

4. Conduct peer reviews on the test lifecycle models, and supporting templates and guidelines
5. Revise the description of the test lifecycle models, and supporting templates and guidelines, as necessary

SP 1.3 Establish tailoring criteria and guidelines

The tailoring criteria and guidelines for the organization's set of standard test processes are established and maintained.

Example work products

1. Tailoring criteria and guidelines for the organization's set of standard test processes

Tailoring criteria and guidelines typically include the following:

- How the organization's set of standard test processes and organizational test process assets are used to create tailored defined test processes
- Mandatory requirements that must be satisfied by the tailored defined processes
- Options that may be exercised and criteria for selecting among the options
- Procedures that must be followed in performing and documenting test process tailoring

Sub-practices

1. Specify the selection criteria and procedures for tailoring the organization's set of standard test processes

Examples of tailoring actions include the following:

- Modifying a test lifecycle model
- Combining elements of different test lifecycle models
- Modifying test process elements
- Replacing test process elements
- Deleting test process elements
- Reordering test process elements

2. Specify the standards for documenting the tailored test processes
3. Specify the procedures for submitting and obtaining approval of waivers from requirements of the organization's set of standard test processes
4. Document the tailoring guidelines for the organization's set of standard test processes
5. Conduct peer reviews on the tailoring guidelines
6. Revise the tailoring guidelines as necessary

SP 1.4 Establish the organization's test process database

The organization's test process database is established and maintained.

Example work products

1. Definition of the common set of test process elements and product data for the organization's set of standard test processes
2. Organization's test process database repository (i.e., the repository structure and support environment)
3. Organization's test process database

Sub-practices

1. The test process database is established to collect and make data available on the test processes and resulting work products

> *Examples of test process and work product data typically include the following:*
>
> - Test estimates and actual data, e.g., on size, effort and cost
> - Quality measures, e.g., number of defects found by priority level
> - Peer review coverage
> - Test coverage
> - Reliability measures

2. The data entered into the test process database is reviewed to ensure the integrity of the database content
   The test process database also contains or references the actual measurement data and related information and data needed to understand and interpret the measurement data and access it for reasonableness and applicability.
3. The test process database is managed and controlled
   User access to the test process database contents is controlled to ensure completeness, integrity, security and accuracy of the data

SP 1.5 Establish the organization's test process asset library

The organization's test process asset library is established and maintained.

Example work products

1. Organization's test process asset library
2. Catalog of items in the organization's test process asset library

Sub-practices

1. Design and implement the organization's test process asset library, including the library structure and support environment
2. Specify the criteria for including items in the library, e.g., primarily based on their relationship to the organization's set of standard test processes
3. Specify the procedures for storing and retrieving items
4. Enter the selected items into the library and catalog them for easy reference and retrieval

Examples of items to be stored in the organization's test process asset library typically include the following:

- Test policy and test strategy
- Defined test process descriptions
- Procedures (e.g., test estimation procedure)
- Templates
- Best practices test process assets
- Completed test plans
- Training materials
- Process aids (e.g., checklists)
- Lesson learned documents (e.g., test evaluation reports)

5. Make the items available for use in projects
6. Periodically review the use of each item and use the results to maintain the library contents
7. Revise the organization's test process assets library as necessary

SP 1.6 Establish work environment standards

The work environment standards are established and maintained.

Example work products

1. Work environment standards

Examples of work environment standards include the following:

- Procedures for operation, safety and security of the work environment
- Standard workstation hardware and software
- Standard application software

Sub-practices

1. Evaluate commercially-available work environment standards appropriate for the organization
2. Adopt existing work environment standards and develop new ones to fill gaps based on the organization's test process needs and objectives

SG 2 Integrate the Test Lifecycle with the Development Models

The test lifecycle is integrated, ensuring early test involvement, with the development lifecycle in terms of phasing, milestones, deliverables and activities.

SP 2.1 Establish integrated lifecycle models

Descriptions of the integrated test and development lifecycle models that are approved for use in the organization are established and maintained.

Example work products

1. Description of integrated lifecycle models

Sub-practices

1. Synchronize the phases of the test lifecycle models with the phases of the development lifecycle models
2. Ensure testing is involved early in the development lifecycle, e.g., during requirements development
3. Define mutual dependencies with respect to testing and development activities
4. Define mutual dependencies with respect to testing and development deliverables and lifecycle milestones
5. Document the descriptions of the integrated lifecycle models
6. Revise the description of the integrated lifecycle models, as necessary

SP 2.2 Review integrated lifecycle models

The integrated lifecycle models are reviewed with the stakeholders to promote their understanding of the role of testing within the integrated test and development lifecycle models.

Example work products

1. Integrated lifecycle review log

Sub-practices

1. Organize reviews with stakeholders to help them understand the role of testing within the integrated test and development lifecycle models.

SP 2.3 Obtain commitments on the role of testing within the integrated lifecycle models

Commitments are obtained regarding the role of testing within the integrated lifecycle models from the relevant stakeholders who are responsible for managing, performing and supporting project activities based on the integrated lifecycle models.

Example work products

1. Documented requests for commitments
2. Documented commitments

Sub-practices

1. Identify needed support and negotiate commitments with relevant stakeholders
2. Document all organizational commitments, both full and provisional
3. Review internal commitments with senior management as appropriate
4. Review external commitments with senior management as appropriate

SG 3 Establish a Master Test Plan

A master test plan is established to define a coherent test approach across multiple test levels and an overall test planning.

SP 3.1 Perform product risk assessment

A product risk assessment is performed to identify the typical critical areas for testing.

Example work products

1. Product risk list, with a category and priority assigned to each risk

Sub-practices

1. Identify and select stakeholders that need to contribute to the product risk assessment
2. Identify generic product risks using input from stakeholders
3. Document the context and potential effects of the product risk
4. Identify the relevant stakeholders for each product risk
5. Review the identified product risks against the test assignments
6. Analyze the identified product risks using the predefined parameters, e.g., likelihood and impact
7. Categorize and group product risks according to the defined risk categories
8. Prioritize the product risks for mitigation
9. Review and obtain agreement with stakeholders on the completeness, category and priority level of the product risks
10. Revise the product risks as appropriate

Refer to SG 1 Perform a Product Risk Assessment from the process area Test Planning for more details on the (sub) practices for performing the product risk assessment.

SP 3.2 Establish the test approach

The test approach is established and agreed upon to mitigate the identified and prioritized product risks.

Example work products

1. Test approach
2. List of items to be tested and not to be tested
3. List of features to be tested and not to be tested
4. Identified set of test levels
5. Allocation table of test items/test features/product risk to test levels
6. Entry criteria per test level
7. Exit criteria per test level

Sub-practices

1. Identify and document the items and features to be tested, and not to be tested, based on the product risks.

   Note that the level of aggregation of the test items and test features is likely to be higher during master test planning than at planning for an individual test level.

2. Identify the test levels that are needed to mitigate the product risks
3. Allocate the items and features to be tested as well as the product risks to the identified test levels
4. Select the test design techniques to be used at various test levels; multiple test design techniques are defined to achieve appropriate test coverage based on the defined product risks
5. Define the approach to review test work products
6. Define the approach for re-testing and regression testing
7. Identify the supporting test tools to be used
8. Identify significant constraints regarding the test approach
9. Define a set of entry criteria related to the test process and to product quality for each identified test level
10. Define a set of exit criteria related to the test process and to product quality for each identified test level
11. Align the test approach with the defined organization-wide or program-wide test strategy
12. Identify any non-compliances with the test strategy and the rationale for the variance
13. Review the test approach with stakeholders
14. Revise the test approach as appropriate

Refer to SG 2 Establish a Test Approach from the process area Test Planning for more details on the (sub) practices for establishing the test approach.

SP 3.3 Establish test estimates

Well-founded test estimates are established and maintained for use in discussing the test approach with stakeholders and in planning the testing activities.

Note that early in the development lifecycle, the required information may not all be available to establish a firm test estimate. As a consequence, the accuracy of the test estimate is limited. It is important for the test manager to make it clear to the stakeholders that the test estimate will have to be finalized, and possibly adapted, later on in the lifecycle when more information is available.

Example work products

1. Work breakdown structure (WBS)
2. Selected test lifecycle model
3. Test effort estimates
4. Test cost estimates

Sub-practices

1. Select a test lifecycle model from the organization's standard set on which to scope the planning effort
2. Establish a top-level work breakdown structure based on the defined test approach to clearly define the scope of the test estimate.
3. Estimate the test effort and cost for the test work products and tasks based on estimation rationale, e.g., test metrics from the test process database
4. Align the estimated test effort and costs with the overall estimated project effort and costs

Refer to SG 3 Establish Test Estimates from the process area Test Planning for more details on the (sub) practices for establishing test estimates.

SP 3.4 Define the organization for testing

The organization of the testing at the various levels is defined, including the interfaces to other processes, and a clear overview of what is expected from the various parties involved is established.

The relationship of testing to other processes such as development, project management, quality assurance, and configuration management is determined and described. This includes the lines of communication within the test organization, the authority for resolving issues raised by testing, and the authority for approving test products and processes. This may include a visual representation, e.g., an organizational chart.

Example work products

1. Description of the test organization

Sub-practices

1. Determine the test roles at various test levels to ensure alignment between the various test levels
2. Define authorities and responsibilities for the various test roles, products and processes
3. Define the organizational structure, e.g., the relationship between the various roles, the identified test levels and the other stakeholders within the development process
4. Define the communication structure (e.g., meetings and reports), both within testing and with external stakeholders

SP 3.5 Develop the master test plan

The master test plan is established to define a coherent test approach across multiple test levels.

Example work products

1. Master test plan

Sub-practices

1. Establish the master test schedule with predefined stages of manageable size for the identified test levels based on the defined test estimate and selected test lifecycle
2. Align the master test schedule with the overall project schedule
3. Plan for necessary test staffing resources with the required knowledge and skills to perform the testing
4. Plan the involvement of identified stakeholders
5. Identify, analyze and document the project risks associated with testing
6. Establish and maintain the master test plan

Examples of elements of a master test plan include the following [after IEEE 829]:

- Test plan identifier
- Overall introduction (scope, references, system overview and test overview)
- Organization, including roles and responsibilities
- Non-compliances with the test strategy and the rationale
- Items to be tested (including risk level) and not to be tested
- Features to be tested (including risk level) and not to be tested
- Identification of test levels and test types
- Test approach (e.g., test design techniques) per test level
- Entry and exit criteria per test level
- Test milestones and work products
- Test lifecycle and tasks
- Environmental needs and requirements (including office environment)
- Staffing and training needs
- Stakeholder involvement
- Test estimate
- Master test schedule
- Test project risks and contingencies

Refer to SG 4 Develop a Test Plan from the process area Test Planning for more details on the (sub) practices for developing a master test plan.

Refer to the process area Test Environment for more information on environment needs and requirements.

SP 3.6 Obtain commitment to the master test plan

Commitments to the master test plan are established and maintained.

Example work products

1. Documented requests for commitments
2. Master test plan review log
3. Revised and re-negotiated master test plan, including changes to test budgets, test schedule, product risk list and stakeholder agreements
4. Documented commitments

Sub-practices

1. Organize reviews with stakeholders to help them understand test commitments
2. Discuss differences between estimates and available resources with stakeholders

3. Reconcile any differences between estimates and available resources
4. Identify needed support and negotiate commitments with relevant stakeholders
5. Document all organizational commitments, both full and provisional
6. Review internal commitments with senior management as appropriate
7. Review external commitments with senior management as appropriate

Refer to SG 5 Obtain Commitment to the Test Plan from the process area Test Planning for more details on the (sub) practices for obtaining commitment to the master test plan.

Generic Practices by Goals

GG 2 Institutionalize a Managed Process

GP 2.1 Establish an organizational policy

Establish and maintain an organizational policy for planning and performing the Test Lifecycle and Integration process.

Elaboration

The policy for test lifecycle and integration typically specifies:

- A set of standard test processes for use in the organization is established and maintained
- The organization test process assets are made available across the organization
- A standard test lifecycle is defined for each test level
- Standards and guidelines are available for test (work) products at each lifecycle phase
- The defined test lifecycle is integrated with the development lifecycle
- Mater test planning coordinates test activities over multiple test levels
- The test levels that are governed by means of a master test plan
- Master test planning is aligned with the organization-wide or program-wide test strategy
- Testing is involved at an early stage of development

GP 2.2 Plan the process

Establish and maintain the plan for performing the Test Lifecycle and Integration process.

Elaboration

The plan for establishing and maintaining the organization's standard test processes and test process assets can be part of (or referenced by) the organization's test process improvement plan.

Typically, the plan for establishing the master test plan is included in the project plan, which is described in the CMMI process area Project Planning.

GP 2.3 Provide resources

Provide adequate resources for performing the Test Lifecycle and Integration process, developing the test work products, and providing the services of the process.

Elaboration

A test technology manager, supported by a test process group, manages the definition of organization's standard test processes. The test process group is typically staffed by a core of test professionals. The test process group is supported by test process owners, a process improvement manager and people with expertise in various testing and other disciplines.

Examples of other resources provided for defining and maintaining the organization's standard test processes include the following tools:

- Database management tools
- Process modeling tools
- Web page builders

Examples of resources for establishing the master test plan include the following:

- For the master test plan a documented and approved assignment exists for testing typically covering issues and expectation regarding goals and objectives, exit criteria, items and features to be tested and not to be tested, type of testing to be performed, imposed standards, cost, schedule and resource constraints
- Adequate time is provided to test management to perform the master test planning activities
- Experienced individuals, who have expertise in the application domain of the test object and those who have expertise on the development process are available to support the development of the master test plan
- Tools to support the master test planning process are available, e.g., project planning and scheduling tools, estimation tools, risk assessment tools, test management tools and configuration management tools.

GP 2.4 Assign responsibilities

Assign responsibility and authority for performing the Test Lifecycle and Integration process, developing the work products, and providing the services of the Test Lifecycle and Integration process.

Elaboration

A test technology manager, supported by a test process group, is often designated to be responsible for managing the definition of the organization's standard test processes. The test process group is typically staffed by a core of test professionals. The test process group is supported by test process owners, a process improvement manager and people with expertise in various testing and other disciplines.

A test manager is typically designated to be responsible for negotiating commitments and developing the master test plan. The test manager, either directly or by delegation, coordinates the project's master test planning process.

GP 2.5 Train people

Train the people performing or supporting the Test Lifecycle and Integration process as needed.

Elaboration

Individuals involved in establishing the set of organizational test process assets are trained in developing and maintaining processes.

Examples of training topics include the following:

- TMMi, CMMI and other (test) process reference models
- Planning, managing and monitoring processes
- Process modeling and definition
- Developing a tailorable standard process
- Developing work environment standards
- Ergonomics

Test management, and other individuals or groups involved, are trained in master test planning and the accompanying procedures and techniques.

Examples of training topics include the following:

- Planning principles
- Test strategy
- Product and project risk assessment process and techniques
- Defining a test approach
- Test plan templates and standards
- Organizational structures
- Test estimation and test scheduling
- Supporting test planning tools

GP 2.6 Manage configurations

Place selected work products of the Test Lifecycle and integration process under appropriate levels of configuration control.

Elaboration

Examples of training topics include the following:

- Planning principles
- Test strategy
- Product and project risk assessment process and techniques
- Defining a test approach
- Test plan templates and standards
- Organizational structures
- Test estimation and test scheduling
- Supporting test planning tools

GP 2.7 Identify and involve relevant stakeholders

Identify and involve relevant stakeholders of the Test Lifecycle and Integration process as planned.

Elaboration

Examples of activities for stakeholder involvement include the following:

- Reviewing the organization's set of standard test processes
- Reviewing the organization's integrated lifecycle models
- Resolving issues with tailoring guidelines
- Assessing the definitions of the common set of test process and product quality measurement data
- Reviewing the work environment standards
- Selecting the product and product components to be tested
- Identifying the risk level and risk types of the product and product components to be tested by being involved in a product risk assessment
- Providing input to test estimates
- Reviewing and resolving issues on test project risks
- Explicitly committing to test resources needed
- Reviewing and approval of master test plan

GP 2.8 Monitor and control the process

Monitor and control the Test Lifecycle and Integration process against the plan for performing the process and take appropriate actions.

Elaboration

Examples of measures used in monitoring and control the Test Lifecycle and Integration process include the following:

- Percentage of projects using the test process elements of the organization's set of standard test processes
- Number of change requests for each test process element of the organization's set of standard test processes
- Amount of staff members' compensation claims due to ergonomic problems
- Days required for development of a test process or test process change
- Number of revisions to the master test plan
- Effort spent and actual lead-time compared to the effort planned and planned lead-time in the master test plan
- Number of test items with risk level changes per test plan revision
- Cost, schedule and effort variance per plan revision

Execution of the master test plan is typically monitored and controlled by means of the practices of the process area Test Monitoring and Control.

GP 2.9 Objectively evaluate adherence

Objectively evaluate adherence of the Test Lifecycle and Integration process and selected work products against the process description, standards, and procedures, and address any areas of non-compliance.

Elaboration

Examples of review and/or audit topics for evaluation and adherence include the following:

- Activities for establishing organizational test process assets
- Organization's set of standard test processes
- Description of test lifecycle models
- Tailoring guidelines for the organization's set of standard test processes
- Organization's test process data
- Compliance with the test strategy
- Compliance with standards (procedures and templates)
- Quality of the master test plan
- Defined test approach
- Product risk assessment process
- Test estimation process
- Activities for reviewing and making test commitments

GP 2.10 Review status with higher level management

Review the activities, status and results of the Test Lifecycle and Integration process with higher level management and resolve issues.

GG 3 Institutionalize a Defined Process

GP 3.1 Establish a defined process

Establish and maintain a description of a defined Test Lifecycle and Integration process

GP 3.2 Collect improvement information

Collect process related experiences derived from planning and performing the Test Lifecycle and Integration process to support the future use and improvement of the organization's processes and process assets.

Elaboration

Examples of measures include the following:

- Submission of lessons learned to the organization's process asset library
- Submission of data to the organization's test process database
- Status of change requests submitted to modify the organization's standard process
- Percentage of master test plans established according to procedure and template
- Percentage of master test plans that have documented product risk assessment results and a test approach
- Percentage of master test plans formally reviewed and approved by management
- Master test planning effort
- Test estimation accuracy

Process Area 3.4 Non-functional Testing

Purpose

The purpose of the Non-functional Testing process area is to improve test process capability to include non-functional testing during test planning, test design and execution. This is done by defining a test approach based on the identified non-functional product risks, establishing non-functional test specifications and executing a structured test execution process focused on non-functional testing.

Introductory Notes

Quality of products is all about satisfying stakeholders' needs. These needs have to be translated to well-described functional ('what' the product does) and non-functional ('how' the product does it) requirements. Often the non-functional requirements are highly important for customer satisfaction. This process area addresses the development of a capability for non-functional testing. There is a set of principal non-functional attributes that are used to describe the quality of software products or systems. These quality attributes can be assessed using non-functional test techniques. Application of the various test techniques varies depending on the ability of the tester, the knowledge of the domain, and the attributes being addressed.

A test approach needs to be defined based on the outcome of a non-functional product risk assessment. Depending on the level and type of non-functional risks, it is decided which requirements of the product will be tested, to what degree and how. The non-functional product risks and test approach are defined in close cooperation between test specialists and the stakeholders; testers should not make these decisions in isolation.

Non-functional test techniques are applied, possibly supported by tools. Test techniques are used to derive and select non-functional test conditions and create test cases from non-functional requirements and design specifications. The test cases are subsequently translated into manual test procedures and/or automated test scripts. Specific test data required to execute the non-functional test is created. During the test execution stage, the non-functional tests will be executed, incidents found and incident reports written.

Scope

The process area Non-functional Testing involves performing a non-functional product risk assessment and defining a test approach based on the non-functional risks identified. It also addresses the test preparation phase to derive and select non-functional test conditions and test cases, the creation of specific test data and the execution of the non-functional tests. Test environment practices, which are often critical for non-functional testing, are not addressed within this process area. They are addressed as part of the TMMi level 2 process area Test Environment and should now also support non-functional testing.

Specific Goal and Practice Summary

SG 1 Perform a Non-functional Product Risk Assessment
- SP 1.1 Identify non-functional product risks
- SP 1.2 Analyze non-functional product risks

SG 2 Establish a Non-functional Test Approach
- SP 2.1 Identify features to be tested
- SP 2.2 Define the non-functional test approach
- SP 2.3 Define non-functional exit criteria

SG 3 Perform Non-functional Test Analysis and Design
- SP 3.1 Identify and prioritize non-functional test conditions
- SP 3.2 Identify and prioritize non-functional test cases
- SP 3.3 Identify necessary specific test data
- SP 3.4 Maintain horizontal traceability with non-functional requirements

SG 4 Perform Non-functional Test Implementation
- SP 4.1 Develop and prioritize non-functional test procedures
- SP 4.2 Create specific test data

SG 5 Perform Non-functional Test Execution
- SP 5.1 Execute non-functional test cases
- SP 5.2 Report non-functional test incidents
- SP 5.3 Write test log

Specific Practices by Goals

SG 1 Perform a Non-functional Product Risk Assessment

A product risk assessment is performed to identify the critical areas for non-functional testing.

SP 1.1 Identify non-functional product risks

Non-functional product risks are identified and documented.

Example work products

1. Identified non-functional product risks

Sub-practices

1. Identify and select stakeholders that need to contribute to the risk assessment

2. Identify non-functional product risks based on defined non-functional product risk categories using input from stakeholders and requirements documents

Examples of product risk identification techniques include the following:
- Risk workshops
- Brainstorming
- Expert interviews
- Checklists
- Lessons learned

3. Document the context-of-use and potential effects of the non-functional risk
4. Identify the relevant stakeholders for each non-functional risk

Note that in practice the identification of non-functional products risk may be combined with SP 1.2 Identify product risks of the Test Planning process area and/or with the SP 3.1 Perform a product risk assessment of the Test Lifecycle and Integration process area when establishing a master test plan.

SP 1.2 Analyze non-functional product risks

Non-functional product risks are evaluated, categorized and prioritized using predefined categories and parameters.

Example work products

1. Non-functional product risk list, with a category and priority assigned to each risk

Sub-practices

1. Analyze the identified non-functional products risks using the predefined parameters, e.g., likelihood and impact
2. Categorize and group non-functional product risks according to the defined risk categories

Examples of non-functional risks categories include the following [ISO 9126]:
- Usability
- Reliability
- Efficiency
- Maintainability
- Portability

3. Prioritize the non-functional product risks for mitigation

4. Establish traceability between non-functional product risks and requirements to ensure that the source of product risks is documented
5. Generate a non-functional requirements / product risks traceability matrix
6. Review and obtain agreement with stakeholders on the completeness, category and priority level of the non-functional product risks
7. Revise the non-functional product risks as appropriate

> *Examples of when product risks may need to be revised include the following:*
>
> - New or changing non-functional requirements
> - Change of the software development approach
> - Lessons learned on quality issues in the project

Note that product risk categories and parameters as defined in the Test Planning process area (SP1.1 Define product risk categories and parameters) are largely re-used and potentially also enhanced within this and the next specific practice.

SG 2 Establish a Non-functional Test Approach

A test approach for non-functional testing, based on identified non-functional product risks, is established and agreed upon.

SP 2.1 Identify non-functional features to be tested

The non-functional features to be tested, and not to be tested, are identified based on the non-functional product risks.

Example work products

1. List of non-functional features to be tested and not to be tested

Sub-practices

1. Breakdown the prioritized non-functional product risks into non-functional features to be tested and not to be tested
2. Document the risk level and source documentation (test basis) for each identified feature to be tested

SP 2.2 Define the non-functional test approach

The test approach is defined to mitigate the identified and prioritized non-functional product risks.

Example work products

1. Non-functional test approach (documented in a test plan)

The approach should be described in sufficient detail to support the identification of major test tasks and estimation of the time required to do each one.

Sub-practices

1. Select the non-functional test techniques to be used

Examples of non-functional test techniques to be selected include the following:

- Heuristic evaluation, survey and questionnaires for usability
- Operational profiles for reliability
- Load, stress and volume testing for efficiency

Note that also black box techniques, white box techniques and experienced-based techniques such as exploratory testing and checklists can be selected to test specific non-functional quality attributes.

2. Define the approach to reviewing test work products
3. Define the approach for non-functional re-testing
4. Define the approach for non-functional regression testing
5. Define the supporting test tools to be used
6. Identify significant constraints regarding the non-functional test approach, such as test resource availability, test environment features and deadlines
7. Align the non-functional test approach with the defined organization-wide or program-wide test strategy
8. Identify any areas of non-compliance with the test strategy and the rationale
9. Review the non-functional test approach with the stakeholders
10. Revise the non-functional test approach as appropriate

Examples of when the non-functional test approach may need to be revised include the following:

- New or changed priority level of non-functional product risks
- Lessons learned on applying the non-functional test approach in the project

SP 2.3 Define non-functional exit criteria

The exit criteria for non-functional testing are defined to plan when to stop-testing.

Example work products

1. Non-functional exit criteria

Sub-practices

1. Define a set of exit criteria related to the non-functional product quality attributes to be tested

> *Examples of exit criteria related to non-functional product quality attributes include the following:*
> - For reliability: Mean Time Between Failures (MTBF), Mean Time to Repair (MTTR)
> - For usability: user satisfaction, average time to perform functions
> - For efficiency: mean response time, memory utilization
> - For maintainability: average effort to change, availability of documentation

2. Review the non-functional exit criteria with the stakeholders

Note that the exit criteria of a test level should be aligned with the entry criteria of a subsequent test level.

Note that entry, suspension and resumption criteria are not explicitly defined within this process area by means of specific practices. The criteria that were defined as part of the process area Test Planning generally are applicable to non-functional testing. For example, entry criteria such as the availability of a test environment, a successful intake test and the availability of test release notes are applicable to all types of testing, both functional and non-functional.

SG 3 Perform Non-functional Test Analysis and Design

During test analysis and design the test approach for non-functional testing is translated into tangible test conditions and test cases.

SP 3.1 Identify and prioritize non-functional test conditions

Test conditions are identified and prioritized, based on an analysis of the non-functional features as specified in the test basis

Example work products

1. Test basis issue log
2. Non-functional test conditions
3. Non-functional test design specification

Sub-practices

1. Study and analyze the test basis (such as non-functional requirements, architecture, design and interface specifications)
2. Discuss issues regarding the test basis with the document owner
3. Derive the test conditions from the test basis according to the documented non-functional test approach
4. Prioritize the test conditions based on identified product risks
5. Document the test conditions in a test design specification based on the test design specification standard

Examples of elements of a test design specification include the following [after IEEE 829]:

- Test design specification identifier
- Features (and/or items) to be tested
- Approach refinements
- Test conditions
- Pass/fail criteria

6. Review the test design specifications with stakeholders
7. Revise the test design specifications and test conditions as appropriate, e.g., whenever the requirements change.

SP 3.2 Identify and prioritize non-functional test cases

Non-functional test cases are identified and prioritized to address the defined test conditions.

Example work products

1. Non-functional test cases
2. Non-functional test case specification

Sub-practices

1. Derive the test cases from the test conditions according to the documented non-functional test approach.
2. Prioritize the test cases based on identified non-functional product risks
3. Document the non-functional test cases in a test case specification based on the test case specification standard

Examples of elements of a test case specification include the following [IEEE 829]:

- Test case specification identifier
- Features (and/or items) to be tested
- Input specifications
- Output specifications
- Environmental needs
- Special procedural requirements
- Inter-case dependencies

4. Review the test case specifications with stakeholders
5. Revise the test case specifications as appropriate

SP 3.3 Identify necessary specific test data

Specific test data necessary to support the non-functional test conditions and test cases is identified

Example work products

1. Test data specification

Sub-practices

1. Identify and specify the necessary specific test data required to implement and execute the non-functional test cases
2. Document the necessary specific test data, possibly as part of the test case specification

SP 3.4 Maintain horizontal traceability with non-functional requirements

Maintain horizontal traceability from non-functional requirements to non-functional test conditions.

Example work products

1. Non-functional requirements / test conditions traceability matrix

Sub-practices

1. Maintain non-functional requirements traceability to ensure that the source of non-functional test conditions is documented
2. Generate a non-functional requirements / test conditions traceability matrix

3. Set up the traceability matrix such that monitoring of non-functional requirements coverage during test execution is facilitated

SG 4 Perform Non-functional Test Implementation

Non-functional test procedures are developed and prioritized, and specific test data required for non-functional testing is created.

SP 4.1 Develop and prioritize non-functional test procedures

Non-functional test procedures are developed and prioritized.

Example work products

1. Non-functional test procedure specification
2. Automated test script

Sub-practices

1. Develop non-functional test procedures by combining the non-functional test cases in a particular order and including any other information needed for test execution
2. Prioritize the non-functional test procedures based on identified product risks
3. Document the non-functional test procedures in a test procedure specification based on the test procedure specification standard

Examples of elements of a test procedure specification include the following [IEEE 829]:

- Test procedure specification identifier
- Purpose
- Special requirements (execution preconditions)
- Procedure steps (test actions and checks)

4. Review the non-functional test procedure specifications with stakeholders
5. Revise the non-functional test procedure specifications as appropriate
6. Optionally, the non-functional test procedures can be automated and translated into automated test scripts, e.g., for endurance testing or performance testing
7. Schedule the non-functional test procedures as part of the overall test execution schedule
   Refer to SP 2.4 Develop test execution schedule from the process area Test Design and Execution for scheduling the execution of test procedures and test scripts.

SP 4.2 Create specific test data

Specific test data is created to support the Non-functional testing as specified during the test analysis and design activity.

Example work products

1. Specific test data

Sub-practices

1. Create specific test data required to perform the non-functional tests as specified in the test procedures
2. Archive the set of specific test data to allow a restore of the initial situation in the future

Refer to SP 3.2 Perform test data management from the process area Test Environment for managing the created test data.

SG 5 Perform Non-functional Test Execution

Non-functional tests are executed according to previously specified test procedures. Incidents are reported and test logs are written.

SP 5.1 Execute non-functional test cases

The non-functional test cases are executed manually using documented test procedures and/or automatically using test scripts.

Example work products

1. Test results

Sub-practices

1. Execute the non-functional test cases using documented test procedures and/or test scripts
2. Record actual results
3. Compare actual results with expected results
4. Repeat non-functional test activities as a result of an action for an incident found by performing re-testing (confirmation testing)
5. Perform non-functional regression testing as appropriate.

Note that some non-functional testing will be conducted informally without using pre-defined detailed test procedures, e.g., a heuristic evaluation to test the usability.

Note that the non-functional test execution is normally preceded by the overall intake test. Refer to the practices SP 2.3 Specify intake test procedure and SP 3.1 Perform intake test from the process area Test Design and Execution for more details on the intake test on the test object and to the practice SP 2.4 Perform test environment intake test from the process area Test Environment for more details on the intake test on the test environment.

SP 5.2 Report test incidents

Differences between actual and expected results are reported as non-functional test incidents.

Example work products

1. Non-functional test incident reports

Sub-practices

1. Log non-functional test incidents when a discrepancy is observed.
2. Analyze the non-functional test incident for further information on the problem
3. Establish the cause of the non-functional test incident, e.g., system under test, test documentation, test data or test execution mistake
4. Assign an initial priority and severity level to the non-functional test incident
5. Formally report the test incident using an incident classification scheme

> *Examples of elements of a test incident report include the following [IEEE 829]:*
>
> - Test incident report identifier
> - Summary
> - Incident description (input, expected results, actual results, anomalies, date and time, test procedure step, environment, attempts to repeat, testers, observers)
> - Priority level
> - Severity level

6. Review the non-functional test incident report with stakeholders
7. Store non-functional test incidents in a central repository
   Refer to the goal SG 4 Manage test incidents to closure from the process area Test Design and Execution for more details on how test incidents are processed and managed to closure.

SP 5.3 Write test log

Test logs are written to provide a chronological record of relevant details about the execution of the non-functional tests.

Example work products

1. Test logs

Sub-practices

1. Collect test execution data
2. Document the test execution data by means of a test log, based on the test log standard

> *Examples of elements of a test log include the following [IEEE 829]:*
> - Test log identifier
> - Description (items being tested, environment in which the testing has been executed)
> - Activity and event entries (execution description, test results, anomalous events, incident report identifiers)

3. Review the test log with stakeholders

Generic Practices by Goals

GG 2 Institutionalize a Managed Process

GP 2.1 Establish an organizational policy

Establish and maintain an organizational policy for planning and performing the Non-functional Testing process.

Elaboration

The policy for non-functional testing typically specifies:

- Typical quality attributes that are important to the business and products
- A set of important and relevant quality attributes per test level
- The level of test automation and type of tools required
- The incident classification scheme to be used when non-functional test incidents are documented and reported
- The document procedure to be used to evaluate, classify and process reported non-functional test incidents

GP 2.2 Plan the process

Establish and maintain the plan for performing the Non-functional Testing process.

Elaboration

Typically, the plan for performing the Non-functional Testing process is included in the test plan, which is described in the Test

Planning process area. The activities for non-functional testing are explicitly scheduled as part of the test plan.

GP 2.3 Provide resources

Provide adequate resources for performing the Non-functional Testing process, developing the test work products, and providing the services of the process.

Elaboration

- Adequate time is provided to perform the non-functional test planning, design and execution activities
- Experienced individuals, who have expertise in non-functional testing activities and tools are available
- Experienced individuals, who have expertise in the application domain of the test object and those who have expertise in the development process are available to support the development of the non-functional test approach, e.g., participating in product risk analysis sessions and the non-functional test designs, as well as participating at reviews
- Tools to support the non-functional test design and execution process are available

Examples of tools include the following:

- Monitoring tool
- Performance tool
- Static analysis tool
- Dynamic analysis tool

GP 2.4 Assign responsibilities

Assign responsibility and authority for performing the Non-functional Testing process, developing the work products, and providing the services of Non-functional Testing process.

GP 2.5 Train people

Train the people performing or supporting the Non-functional Testing process as needed.

Elaboration

Test specialists, and other individuals or groups, involved in non-functional testing, are trained in non-functional testing and the accompanying procedures, techniques and tools.

Examples training topics include the following:

- The importance of non-functional testing
- Quality attributes (e.g., ISO 9126)
- Product risk analysis for non-functional testing
- Defining a test approach for non-functional testing
- Formal and informal test techniques for non-functional testing
- Exit criteria for non-functional attributes
- Supporting tools

GP 2.6 Manage configurations

Place selected work products of the Non-functional Testing process under appropriate levels of configuration control.

Elaboration

Examples of work products placed under configuration management include the following:

- Non-functional product risk assessment data
- Non-functional test design specifications
- Non-functional test case specifications
- Non-functional test procedure specifications (and/or test scripts)
- Test logs

GP 2.7 Identify and involve relevant stakeholders

Identify and involve relevant stakeholders of the Non-functional Testing process as planned.

Elaboration

Examples of activities for stakeholder involvement include:

- During the product risk assessment, identifying the non-functional risks of the product and product components to be tested
- Reviewing and approving the non-functional test designs and test cases
- Executing tests, e.g., usability testing by end users

GP 2.8 Monitor and control the process

Monitor and control the Non-functional Testing process against the plan for performing the process and take appropriate actions.

Elaboration

Examples of review and/or audit topics for evaluation and adherence include the following:

- Number of non-functional test specifications completed
- Number of non-functional tests executed
- Number of non-functional risks mitigated
- Number of outstanding non-functional incidents (per priority level)

GP 2.9 Objectively evaluate adherence

Objectively evaluate adherence of the Non-functional Testing process and selected work products against the process description, standards, and procedures, and address non-compliances.

Elaboration

Examples of review and/or audit evaluation adherence topics include the following:

- Compliance with the non-functional aspects of the test strategy
- The defined test approach for non-functional testing
- The non-functional product risk assessment process
- The effectiveness and efficiency of non-functional test design techniques
- The quality of the non-functional test cases

GP 2.10 Review status with higher level management

Review the activities, status and results of Non-functional Testing process with higher level management and resolve issues.

GG 3 Institutionalize a Defined Process

GP 3.1 Establish a defined process

Establish and maintain a description of a defined Non-functional Testing process.

GP 3.2 Collect improvement information

Collect process related experiences derived from planning and performing the Non-functional Testing process to support the future use and improvement of the organization's processes and process assets.

Elaboration

Examples of measures include the following:

- Effort ratio of non-functional testing versus functional testing
- Test effort spent per non-functional attribute
- Number of non-functional attributes tested per project
- Incident reports for non-functional attributes by priority and severity
- Coverage achieved for non-functional requirements

Process Area 3.5 Peer Reviews

Purpose

The purpose of the Peer Review process area is to verify that work products meet their specified requirements and to remove defects from selected work products early and efficiently. An important corollary effect is to develop a better understanding of the work products and of defects that might be prevented.

Introductory Notes

Reviews involve a methodical examination of work products by peers to identify defects and areas where changes are needed. Reviews are conducted with a small group of engineers, generally between 2-7 persons. The work product to be reviewed could be a requirements specification, design document, source code, test design, a user manual, or another type of document. In practice, there are many ways by which the group of reviewers is selected. Reviewers may be:

- Specialists in reviewing (quality assurance or audit)
- People from the same project
- People invited by the author because of their specific knowledge
- People, e.g., business representatives, who have a significant interest in the product

Several types of reviews are defined, each with its own purpose and objective. In addition to informal reviews, more formal review types such as walkthroughs, technical reviews and inspections are used [IEEE 1028]. In a walkthrough, the author guides a group of people through a document and his thought process, so everybody understands the document in the same way and they reach a consensus on the content or changes to be made. In a technical review the group discusses, after an individual preparation, the content and the (technical) approach to be used. An inspection, the most formal review type, is a technique where a document is checked for defects by each individual and by the group, using sources and standards and following prescribed rules.

Scope

The Peer Review process area covers the practices for performing peer reviews on work products, e.g., testers reviewing a requirements specification for testability. It also includes the practices for establishing the peer review approach within a project. Project reviews (also known as management reviews) are outside the scope of this process area. At TMMi maturity level 3 peer reviews are not yet fully integrated with the dynamic testing process, e.g., part of the test strategy, test plan and test approach.

Specific Goal and Practice Summary

SG 1 Establish a Peer Review Approach
- SP 1.1 Identify work products to be reviewed
- SP 1.2 Define peer review criteria

SG 2 Perform Peer Reviews
- SP 2.1 Conduct peer reviews
- SP 2.2 Testers review test basis documents
- SP 2.3 Analyze peer review data

Specific Practices by Goals

SG 1 Establish a Peer Review Approach

A review approach is established and agreed upon.

SP 1.1 Identify work product to be reviewed

The work products to be reviewed are identified, including the type of review and critical participants (stakeholders) to involve.

Example work products

1. List of work products to be reviewed
2. Review approach
3. Review log
4. Peer review schedule

Sub-practices

1. Select work products that will undergo a peer review based on the peer review policy and the identified product risks
2. Determine what type(s) of peer review will be conducted for the selected work products

> *Examples of types of peer reviews include the following (IEEE 1028):*
> - Inspection
> - Walkthrough
> - Technical Review
> - Informal review
>
> Note, it is possible that multiple types of reviews are selected for the same work product, e.g., for work products related to critical product risks.

3. Identify key participants who shall be involved in a peer review
4. Review the defined review approach with stakeholders
5. Develop a detailed peer review schedule, including the dates for peer review training and when material for peer reviews will be available
6. Obtain commitments to undertake the review approach and schedule from key stakeholders

SP 1.2 Define peer review criteria

Preparation for peer reviews on selected work products is accomplished by defining and maintaining entry and exit criteria for peer reviews.

Example work products

1. Peer review entry and exit criteria
2. Criteria for requiring another peer review

Sub-practices

1. Establish and maintain entry criteria for peer reviews

Examples of peer review entry criteria include the following:

- A short cursory check of a product sample by the review leader (or an expert) does not reveal a large number of major defects
- The document has been cleaned up by a spelling checker or other computer analysis, e.g., static code analysis
- References needed for the review are up to date and available
- All source (i.e. higher level) documents shall have exited their own review
- The document author is prepared to join the review and feels confident regarding the quality of the document

Note that entry criteria will differ depending on the type of review that will be performed.

2. Establish and maintain exit criteria for peer reviews

Examples of peer review exit criteria include the following:

- Number of major defects found per page
- Preparation time spent as agreed upon
- All pages checked according to plan
- All issues and action items addressed
- Estimated residual defect density

3. Establish and maintain criteria for requiring another peer review

4. Review the defined criteria with stakeholders

SG 2 Perform Peer Reviews

Peer reviews are performed on selected work products and peer review data is analyzed.

SP 2.1 Conduct peer reviews

Selected work products are peer reviewed and issues are identified.

Example work products

1. Peer review logging forms (defects found)
2. Peer review action items
3. Peer review data (e.g., documented on process forms)
4. Peer review report (e.g., documented on process form)

Sub-practices

1. Ensure that the work product satisfies the peer review entry criteria prior to distribution
2. Select participants to be involved in the review and define a specific review task for them to perform
3. Distribute the work product to be reviewed and its related information to participants early enough to enable participants to adequately prepare for peer review
4. Assign individuals to roles for the peer review as appropriate

> *Examples of roles include the following:*
> - Review Leader (Moderator)
> - Checker (Reviewer)
> - Scribe
> - Author

5. Perform the assigned roles in the peer review
6. Identify and document defects and other issues in the work product
7. Record the results of the peer review, e.g., on logging forms
8. Identify action items and communicate the issues to relevant stakeholders
9. Conduct an additional peer review if the defined criteria indicate the need
10. Ensure that the exit criteria for the peer review are satisfied
11. Record peer review data related to the preparation, conduct, and results of the peer review

Typical data are product type, product size, type of peer review, number of reviewers, preparation time per reviewer, length of the review meeting, number of (major) defects found, etc.

SP 2.2 Testers review test basis documents

The documents that are used as a basis for testing are reviewed by the testers.

Example work products

1. Testability defects
2. Testability review report

Sub-practices

1. Testers review the test basis documents for testability, e.g., whether the chosen test design techniques can be applied to the test basis
2. Defects found during the review of the test basis documents are logged and reported
3. Test basis documents are improved based on the defects reported by testing

SP 2.3 Analyze peer review data

The peer review data regarding preparation, conduct, and results of the reviews is analyzed.

Example work products

1. Peer review database
2. Peer review analysis communication report

Sub-practices

1. Store the peer review data for future reference and analysis
2. Protect the review data to ensure that it is not used inappropriately

Examples of inappropriate use of peer review data include using the data to evaluate the performance of people and using data for attribution.

3. Analyze the peer review data

Examples of peer review data that can be analyzed include the following:

- Phase defect was injected
- Preparation effort or rate versus expected effort or rate
- Actual review effort versus planned review effort
- Number of defects versus number expected
- Types and severity level of defects detected
- Causes of defects
- Defect resolution impact

4. Communicate peer review analysis results to stakeholders

Generic Practices by Goals

GG 2 Institutionalize a Managed Process

GP 2.1 Establish an organizational policy

Establish and maintain an organizational policy for planning and performing the Peer Review process.

Elaboration

The peer review policy typically specifies:

- Reviews will be applied to identify defects early in the development lifecycle
- The organization identifies a standard set of work products that will undergo review, including test deliverables
- Each project selects the work products that will undergo review and the associated review type(s)
- Peer review leaders and other participants will be trained for their role
- Testers shall participate in reviews on development documents to address testability issues

GP 2.2 Plan the process

Establish and maintain the plan for performing the Peer Review process.

Elaboration

At TMMi level 3, peer reviews are most often not a full part of the testing process; therefore, typically the plan for performing the peer review process is included in the project plan, which is described in the CMMI Project Planning process area. Resources, e.g., review leaders, are explicitly planned for in order to allow the performance of peer reviews.

At higher TMMi levels, peer reviews become an integral part of the testing process and the plan for performing the Peer Review process is included in the (master) test plan.

GP 2.3 Provide resources

Provide adequate resources for performing the Peer Reviews process, developing the test work products, and providing the services of the process.

Elaboration

- Meeting rooms are available for the review meeting
- Trained peer review leaders are available
- Supporting artifacts such as defect logging forms and review process forms to support data collection and reporting are available
- Checklists are established and maintained, e.g., on testability, to ensure that the work products are reviewed in a consistent way

Examples of items addressed by the checklists include the following:

- Compliance with standards
- Adherence to design guidelines
- Completeness
- Correctness
- Testability
- Maintainability
- Common defect types

- The checklists are modified as necessary to address the specific type of work product and peer review. The checklists themselves are reviewed by peers and potential users.
- Tools to support the peer review process are available, e.g., communication tools, data analysis tools and peer review process tools

GP 2.4 Assign responsibilities

Assign responsibility and authority for performing the Peer Review process, developing the work products, and providing the services of the Peer Review process.

Elaboration

Peer review leaders are designated to be responsible for coordinating the peer review process within projects.

GP 2.5 Train people

Train the people performing or supporting the Peer Review process as needed.

Elaboration

- Peer review leaders (moderators) receive training in how to lead peer reviews

> *Examples of training topics for peer review leaders include the following:*
> - Developing a peer review approach
> - Type of reviews
> - Peer review leader tasks and responsibilities
> - Leading and facilitating a meeting
> - Achieving buy-in for reviews
> - Peer review metrics

- Participants in peer reviews receive training for their roles in the peer review process

> *Examples of training topics for peer review participants include the following:*
> - Objectives and benefits of peer reviews
> - Types of reviews
> - Peer review roles and responsibilities
> - Peer review process overview
> - Peer review preparation
> - Document rules and checklists, e.g., regarding testability
> - Peer review meetings

GP 2.6 Manage configurations

Place selected work products of the Peer Review process under appropriate levels of configuration control.

Elaboration

> *Examples of work products placed under configuration management include the following:*
> - Peer review approach
> - Peer review logging and process forms
> - Peer review data(base)
> - Peer review training material

GP 2.7 Identify and involve relevant stakeholders

Identify and involve relevant stakeholders of the Peer Review process as planned.

Elaboration

Select relevant stakeholders to participate in peer reviews from customers, end users, developers, testers, suppliers, marketers, maintenance, service and any others who may be affected by, or may affect, the (work) products.

GP 2.8 Monitor and control the process

Monitor and control the Peer Review process against the plan for performing the process and take appropriate actions.

Elaboration

Examples of measures used in monitoring and controlling the peer review process include the following:

- Number of peer reviews planned and performed
- Number of work products reviewed compared to plan
- Number and type of defects found during peer reviews
- Schedule of peer review process activities (including training activities)
- Effort spent on peer reviews compared to plan

GP 2.9 Objectively evaluate adherence

Objectively evaluate adherence of the Peer Review process and selected work products against the process description, standards, and procedures, and address any areas of non-compliance.

Elaboration

Examples of review and/or audit topics for evaluation and adherence include the following:

- Verify whether peer reviews are performed
- Training for peer review leaders and other participants
- The process followed during peer reviews, including adherence to the defined criteria
- The actual performance on follow-up action items
- Peer review reporting regarding completeness and accuracy
- Peer review checklists used

GP 2.10 Review status with higher level management

Review the activities, status and results of the Peer Review process with higher level management and resolve issues.

GG 3 Institutionalize a Defined Process

GP 3.1 Establish a defined process

Establish and maintain a description of a defined Peer Review process

GP 3.2 Collect improvement information

Collect process related experiences derived from planning and performing the Peer Review process to support the future use and improvement of the organization's processes and process assets.

Elaboration

Examples of measures include the following:

- Peer review data such as average preparation time, average total time spent per peer review and average number of pages
- Number of defects found through peer reviews by phase in the development lifecycle
- Return on investment calculations

TMMi Level 4: Measured

Achieving the goals of TMMi levels 2 and 3 has the benefits of putting into place a technical, managerial, and staffing infrastructure capable of thorough testing and providing support for test process improvement. With this infrastructure in place, testing can become a measured process to encourage further growth and accomplishment. In TMMi level 4 organizations, testing is a thoroughly defined, well-founded and measurable process. Testing is perceived as evaluation; it consists of all lifecycle activities concerned with checking products and related work products.

An organization-wide test measurement program will be put into place that can be used to evaluate the quality of the testing process, to assess productivity, and to monitor improvements. Measures are incorporated into the organization's measurement repository to support fact-based decision making. A test measurement program also supports predictions relating to test performance and cost.

With respect to product quality, the presence of a measurement program allows an organization to implement a product quality evaluation process by defining quality needs, quality attributes and quality metrics. (Work) products are evaluated using quantitative criteria for quality attributes such as reliability, usability and maintainability. Product quality is understood in quantitative terms and is managed to the defined objectives throughout the lifecycle.

Reviews and inspections are considered to be part of the test process and are used to measure product quality early in the lifecycle and to formally control quality gates. Peer reviews as a defect detection technique is transformed into a product quality measurement technique in line with the process area Product Quality Evaluation.

TMMi level 4 also covers establishing a coordinated test approach between peer reviews (static testing) and dynamic testing and the use of peer reviews results and data to optimize the test approach with both aiming at making testing more effective and more efficient. Peer reviews are now fully integrated with the dynamic testing process, e.g. part of the test strategy, test plan and test approach.

The process areas at TMMi level 4 are:
4.1 Test Measurement
4.2 Product Quality Evaluation
4.3 Advanced Peer Reviews

Each of these is discussed in more detail in the sections hereafter.

Process Area 4.1 Test Measurement

Purpose

The purpose of Test Measurement is to identify, collect, analyze and apply measurements to support an organization in objectively evaluating the effectiveness and efficiency of the test process, the productivity of its testing staff, the resulting product quality and the results of test improvement. As such, the test organization will develop and sustain a test measurement capability that is used to support management information needs.

Introductory Notes

Achieving the goals of TMMi levels 2 and 3 has had the benefits of putting into place a technical, managerial, and staffing infrastructure capable of thorough testing and providing support for test process improvement. With this infrastructure in place, a formal test measurement program can be established to encourage further growth and accomplishment.

Test measurement is the continuous process of identifying, collecting, and analyzing data on both the test process and the products being developed in order to understand and provide information to improve the effectiveness and efficiency of the test processes and possibly also the development processes. Measurement and analysis methods and processes for data collection, storage, retrieval and communication are specified to support a successful implementation of a test measurement program. Note that a test measurement program has two focal areas: it supports test process and product quality evaluation and it supports process improvement.

In order to be successful, a test measurement program needs to be linked to the business objectives, test policy and test strategy [Van Solingen and Berghout]. The business objectives are the starting point for defining test measurement goals and metrics. From the business objectives, goals are derived for the organization's standard test process. When implemented successfully, the test measurement program will become an integral part of the test culture, and measurement will become a practice adopted and applied by all test groups and teams. Test measurement is the continuous process of identifying, collecting, and analyzing data in order to improve the test process and product quality. It should help the organization improve planning for future projects, train its employees more effectively, etc. Examples of test related measurements include test costs, number of test cases executed, defect data and product measures such as mean time between failures.

The Test Measurement process area involves the following:

- Specifying the objectives of test measurement such that they are aligned with identified information needs and business objectives
- Specifying measures, analysis and validation techniques as well as mechanisms for data collection, data storage, retrieval, communication and feedback
- Implementing the collection, storage, analysis, and reporting of the data
- Providing objective results that can be used in making informed decisions and in taking appropriate actions.

It is suggested at lower TMMi levels that an organization should begin to collect data related to the testing process, e.g., test performance indicators within Test Policy and Strategy. It is recommended that an organization at the lower TMMi levels begin to assemble defect-related measurements in the context of a simple defect repository. When moving towards TMMi level 4, an organization will realize the need for additional measures to achieve greater levels of test process maturity. In anticipation of these needs, the TMMi calls for a formal test measurement program as a goal to be achieved at TMMi level 4. For most organizations it may be practical to implement such a test measurement program as a supplement to a general measurement program.

At TMMi level 4 and above the test measurement activities are at the organizational level addressing organizational information needs. However, test measurement will also provide support to individual projects by providing data, e.g., to support objective planning and estimation. Because the data is shared widely across projects, it is often stored in an organization-wide test measurement repository.

Scope

The process area Test Measurement addresses the measurement activities at an organizational level. For organizations that have multiple test groups or teams, test measurement will be performed identically across all test groups as part of one overall test measurement program. Test Measurement covers practices such as defining measurement objectives, creating the test measurement plan, gathering data, analyzing data and reporting the results. It will also encompass organizational test measurement activities that were defined at lower TMMi levels, such as test performance indicators (a specific type of test measure) from Test Policy and Strategy and generic practice 3.2 Collect improvement information. This process area also will provide support to the measurement activities for the other TMMi level 4 process areas: Product Quality Evaluation and Advanced Reviews. The measurement activities at the project level, e.g., the process area Test Monitoring and Control, will remain at the project level but will interface with the organizational Test Measurement process area.

Specific Goal and Practice Summary

SG 1 Align Test Measurement and Analysis Activities
- SP 1.1 Establish test measurement objectives
- SP 1.2 Specify test measures
- SP 1.3 Specify data collection and storage procedures
- SP 1.4 Specify analysis procedures

SG 2 Provide Test Measurement Results
- SP 2.1 Collect test measurement data
- SP 2.2 Analyze test measurement data
- SP 2.3 Communicate results
- SP 2.4 Store data and results

Specific Practices by Goals

SG 1 Align Test Measurement and Analysis Activities

Test measurement objectives and activities are aligned with identified information needs and objectives.

SP 1.1 Establish test measurement objectives

Test measurement objectives that are derived from identified information needs and business objectives are established and maintained.

Example work products

1. Test measurement objectives
2. Information needs / test measurement objectives traceability matrix

Sub-practices

1. Identify and select stakeholders that need to contribute to the identification of the information needs
2. Identify and document information needs and test measurement objectives using input from stakeholders and other sources
3. Prioritize information needs and test measurement objectives
   It may be neither possible nor desirable to subject all initially identified information needs to test measurement and analysis. Priorities may also need to be set within the limits of the available resources.
4. Review and update test measurement objectives

The test measurement objectives are reviewed by management and other relevant stakeholders, and updated as necessary. Stakeholders are not only those that have the information needs, but should also include users of the test measurement and analysis results and possibly those who provide the test measurement data.

5. Maintain traceability of the test measurement objectives to the identified information needs

   There must always be a good answer to the question, 'Why are we measuring this?'

SP 1.2 Specify test measures

The test measures are specified that will address the test measurement objectives.

Test measures may be either 'base' or 'derived.' Data for base test measures are obtained by direct measurement. Data for derived test measures come from other data, typically by combining two or more base test measures.

Example work products

1. Specification of test measures

Sub-practices

1. Identify test measures based on documented test measurement objectives

> *Examples of commonly used test measures include the following:*
> - Estimates and actual measures of test effort and test cost
> - Estimates and actual measures of number of test cases
> - Number of defects by severity and/or priority
> - Total number of defects
> - Defect detection rate
> - Defect density
> - Peer review coverage
> - Structural coverage, e.g., code coverage
> - Requirements coverage
> - Reliability measures, e.g., Mean Time Between Failures (MTBF) and Mean Time To Repair (MTTR)
> - Burn down measurements, e.g., Test case execution rate per week

2. Document the test measures including their related test measurement objective
3. Specify operational definitions in exact and unambiguous terms for the identified test measures

4. Review and update the specification of test measures
   Proposed specifications of the test measures are reviewed for their appropriateness with potential end users and other relevant stakeholders and updated as necessary.

SP 1.3 Specify data collection and storage procedures

Collection methods are explicitly specified to ensure that the right data are collected properly. Storage and retrieval procedures are specified to ensure that data are available and accessible for future use.

Example work products

1. Data collection and storage procedures
2. Data collection tools

Sub-practices

1. Identify the measurement data that is currently not available for the identified test measures
2. Identify existing sources of the data
   Existing sources of data may already have been identified when specifying the test measures.
3. Specify how to collect and store the data for each required measure
   Explicit specifications are made of how, where, when and by whom the data will be collected. Procedures for collecting valid data are specified.

Examples of topics that need to be included in the collection and storage procedures include the following:

- Frequency of collection
- Points in the process where data will be collected
- Time lines and security rules for storing data
- Responsibilities for obtaining the data and data storage (including security)
- Links to supporting tools

4. Create data collection mechanisms and process guidance
   Data collection mechanisms may include manual or automated forms and templates. Clear, concise guidance on correct procedures is made available to those responsible for doing the work.
   Depending on the measurement objectives, related test measures and measurement data needed, a detailed defect classification scheme could be needed to address the test measurements process needs. Refer to SP 1.1 Define defect selection parameters and defect classification scheme of the

Defect Prevention process area at TMMi level 5 for more information on a defect classification scheme.

5. Support automatic collection of the data where appropriate and feasible
6. Review data collection and storage procedures
   Proposed procedures are reviewed for their appropriateness and feasibility with those who are responsible for providing, collecting, and storing the data.
7. Update test measures and test measurement objectives as necessary
   Priorities may need to be reset based on the amount of effort required to obtain the data. Considerations include whether new forms, tools, or training would be required to obtain the data.

SP 1.4 Specify analysis procedures

Data analysis procedures are specified in advance to ensure that appropriate analysis will be conducted and reliable test measurement data is reported to address the documented test measurement objectives (and thereby the information needs and objectives on which they are based).

Example work products

1. Data analysis procedures
2. Data analysis tools

Sub-practices

1. Specify the analysis that will be conducted and the reports that will be prepared
   The analysis should explicitly address the documented test measurement objectives. Presentation of the results should be clearly understandable by the stakeholders to whom the results are addressed. Priorities may have to be reset within available resources.
2. Select appropriate data analysis methods and tools

Examples of issues to be considered when selecting appropriate data analysis methods and tools include the following:

- Choice of visual display and other presentation techniques (e.g., pie charts, bar charts, histograms, line graphs, scatter plots, or tables)
- Choice of appropriate descriptive statistics (e.g., arithmetic mean or median)
- Decisions about statistical sampling criteria when it is impossible or unnecessary to examine every data element
- Decisions about how to handle analysis in case of missing data elements
- Selection of appropriate analysis tools
- How to examine distributions on the specified test measures
- How to examine interrelationships among the specified test measures

3. Specify administrative procedures for analyzing the data and communicating the results
4. Review and update the proposed content and format of the specified analysis procedures and communication reports
5. Update test measures and test measurement objectives as necessary
   Just as measurement needs to drive data analysis, clarification of analysis criteria can affect measurement. Specifications for some measures may be refined further based on the specifications established for data analysis procedures. Other measures may prove to be unnecessary, or a need for additional measures may be recognized.

SG 2 Provide Test Measurement Results

Test measurement results that address identified information needs and objectives are provided.

SP 2.1 Collect test measurement data

The test measurement data necessary for analysis are obtained and checked for completeness and integrity.

Example work products

1. Test measurement data sets
2. Results of data integrity tests

Sub-practices

1. Gather test measurement data from project records or from elsewhere in the organization

2. Generate the data for derived test measures and calculated their values
3. Perform data integrity checks as close to the source of the data as possible
   All measurements are subject to error in specifying or recording data. It is always better to identify such errors and to identify sources of missing data early in the measurement and analysis cycle. Checks can include scans for missing data, out-of-bounds data values, and unusual patterns and correlation across measures.

SP 2.2 Analyze test measurements data

The collected test measurement data are analyzed as planned and additional analysis is conducted as necessary.

Example work products

1. Analysis results
2. Draft test measurement reports

Sub-practices

1. Conduct initial analysis, interpret the results, and draw preliminary conclusions
2. Conduct additional measurement and analysis as necessary and prepare results for presentation
   The results of planned analysis may suggest (or require) additional, unanticipated analysis.
3. Review the initial results with relevant stakeholders
   It is appropriate to review initial interpretations of the results and the way in which they are presented before disseminating and communicating them more widely. Reviewing the initial results before their release may prevent needless misunderstandings and lead to improvements in the data analysis and communication.

SP 2.3 Communicate results

Results of test measurement activities are communicated to all relevant stakeholders.

Example work products

1. Test measurement reports and related analysis results

Sub-practices

1. Keep relevant stakeholders informed of test measurement results on a timely basis
2. Assist relevant stakeholders in understanding the results

Examples of actions to assist in understanding of results include the following:

- Discussing the results with the relevant stakeholders in feedback sessions
- Providing a transmittal memo that provides background and explanation
- Briefing users on the results
- Providing training on the appropriate use and understanding of test measurement results

3. Define corrective and improvement actions based on the analyzed test measurement results

SP 2.4 Store data and results

The test measurement data, measurement specification and analysis results are stored and managed.

Example work products

1. Stored test measurement data inventory, including measurement plans, specifications of measures, sets of data that have been collected and analysis reports and presentations

Sub-practices

1. Review the measurement data to ensure their completeness, integrity, accuracy, and currency
2. Store the test measurement data according to the data storage procedures
3. Restrict access to the data to the appropriate groups and personnel
4. Prevent the stored information from being used inappropriately, e.g. by controlling access to the test measurement data

Generic Practices by Goals

GG 2 Institutionalize a Managed Process

GP 2.1 Establish an organizational policy

Establish and maintain an organizational policy for planning and performing the Test Measurement process.

Elaboration

This policy establishes organizational expectations for aligning test measurement objectives and activities at the organizational level with identified information needs and objectives and for providing measurement results. The test measurement policy should answer questions such as the purpose of the process, the purpose of the measurements, who will use them, how much the organization is willing to invest in the test measurement process, what are the benefits, which levels of management support the process, and what is the priority level of the test measurement process.

GP 2.2 Plan the process

Establish and maintain the plan for the Test Measurement process.

Elaboration

The plan for performing the test measurement process can be included (or referenced by) the test process improvement plan, which is described in the Test Organization process area, or the organization's quality plan.

GP 2.3 Provide resources

Provide adequate resources for performing the Test Measurement process, developing the test work products, and providing the services of the process.

Elaboration

- Adequate time is provided to perform the test measurement activities
- Measurement personnel may be employed full time or part time. A test measurement group (within the test organization) may or may not exist to support test measurement activities across multiple projects.
- Tools to support the test measurement activities are available

GP 2.4 Assign responsibilities

Assign responsibility and authority for performing the Test Measurement process, developing the work products, and providing the services of the Test Measurement process.

GP 2.5 Train people

Train the people performing or supporting the Test Measurement process as needed.

Elaboration

Examples of training topics include the following:

- Quality and measurement concepts
- Statistical techniques
- Data collection, analysis, and reporting processes
- Development of goal-related measurements (e.g., Goal Question Metric)
- People issues – in general, people do not like to be measured

GP 2.6 Manage configurations

Place selected work products of the Test Measurement process under appropriate levels of configuration control.

Elaboration

Examples of work products placed under configuration management include the following:

- Specifications of base and derived test measures
- Data collection and storage procedures
- Base and derived test measurement data sets
- Analysis results and reports
- Data analysis tools

GP 2.7 Identify and involve relevant stakeholders

Identify and involve relevant stakeholders of the Test Measurement process as planned.

Elaboration

Examples of activities for stakeholder involvement include:

- Eliciting information needs and objectives
- Establishing procedures
- Assessing test measurement data
- Providing meaningful feedback to those responsible for providing the raw data on which the analysis and results depend

GP 2.8 Monitor and control the process

Monitor and control the Test Measurement process against the plan for performing the process and take appropriate actions as needed.

Elaboration

Examples of measures used to monitor and control the test measurement process include the following:

- Percentage of projects submitting data for establishing test measures
- Percentage of measurement objectives addressed
- Schedule for collection and review of measurement data
- Number of test measurement results feedback sessions held

GP 2.9 Objectively evaluate adherence

Objectively evaluate adherence of the Test Measurement process and selected work products against the process description, standards, and procedures, and address any non-compliances.

Elaboration

Examples of review and/or audit evaluation adherence topics include the following:

- Aligning test measurement and analysis activities
- Providing test measurement results
- Specifications for base and derived test measures
- Data collection and storage procedures
- Analysis results and reports

GP 2.10 Review status with higher level management

Review the activities, status and results of the Test Measurement process with higher level management and resolve issues.

GG 3 Institutionalize a Defined Process

GP 3.1 Establish a defined process

Establish and maintain a description of a defined Test Measurement process.

GP 3.2 Collect improvement information

Collect process related experiences derived from planning and performing the Test Measurement process to support the future use and improvement of the organization's processes and process assets.

Examples of measures include the following:

- Data currency status
- Results of data integrity tests
- Data analysis reports
- Cost of measurement training and tools
- Cost of maintaining the test measurement database

Process Area 4.2 Product Quality Evaluation

Purpose

The purpose of Product Quality Evaluation is to develop a quantitative understanding of the quality of the products and thereby support the achievement of specific projects' product quality goals.

Introductory Notes

Product Quality Evaluation involves defining the project's quantitative product quality goals and establishing plans to achieve those goals. It also involves defining quality metrics for evaluating (work) product quality. Subsequently the plansü products, activities and product quality status are monitored and adjusted when necessary. The overall objective is to contribute to satisfying the needs and desires of the customers and end users for quality products.

The practices of the Product Quality Evaluation build on the practices of process areas at TMMi maturity levels 2 and 3. The Test Design and Execution, Test Monitoring and Control and Non-functional Testing process areas establish and implement key test engineering and measurement practices at the project level. Test Measurement establishes a quantitative understanding of the ability of the project to achieve desired results using the organization's standard test process.

In this process area quantitative goals are established for the products based on the needs of the organization, customer, and end users. In order for these goals to be achieved, the organization establishes strategies and plans, and the projects specifically adjust their defined test process to accomplish the quality goals.

Scope

The Product Quality Evaluation process area covers the practices at the project level for developing a quantitative understanding of the product that is being developed and achieving defined and measurable product quality goals. Both functional and non-functional quality attributes are to be considered when defining the goals and practices for this process area. Product Quality Evaluation is strongly supported by the Test Measurement process area that provides the measurement infrastructure.

Specific Goal and Practice Summary

SG 1 Project Goals for Product Quality and their Priorities are Established
- SP 1.1 Identify product quality needs
- SP 1.2 Define the project's quantitative product quality goals

SP 1.3 Define the approach for measuring progress toward the project's product quality goals

SG 2 Actual Progress toward Achieving the Project's Product Quality Goals is Quantified and Managed

SP 2.1 Measure product quality quantitatively throughout the lifecycle

SP 2.2 Analyze product quality measurements and compare them to the product's quantitative goals

Specific Practices by Goals

SG 1 Measurable Project Goals for Product Quality and their Priorities are Established

A set of measurable and prioritized project goals for product quality is established and maintained.

SP 1.1 Identify product quality needs

Project product quality needs are identified and prioritized.

Example work products

1. Identified and prioritized product quality needs for the project

Sub-practices

1. Review the organization's objectives for product quality
The intent of this review is to ensure that the project stakeholders understand the broader business context in which the project will need to operate. The project's objectives for product quality are developed in the context of these overarching organizational objectives.
2. Identify and select stakeholders that need to contribute to the identification of the project's product quality needs
3. Elicit product quality needs using input from stakeholders and other sources

Examples of ways to elicit product quality needs include the following:

- Surveys
- Questionnaires [Pinkster], [Trienekens and Van Veenendaal]
- Focus groups
- Product evaluation by users
- Quality Function Deployment [Hauser and Clausing]
- Brainstorming

Examples of sources for product quality needs include the following:

- Requirements, e.g., non-functional requirements
- Organization's product quality objectives
- Customer's product quality objectives
- Business objectives
- Market surveys
- Quality targets as defined in the test policy
- Quality assurance process and results
- Service level agreements

4. Analyze and prioritize the identified set of product quality needs
5. Resolve conflicts among product quality needs (e.g. if one need cannot be achieved without compromising another need)
6. Establish traceability between the project's product quality needs and their sources
7. Review and obtain agreement with stakeholders on the completeness and priority level of the product quality needs
8. Revise the product quality needs as appropriate

Examples of when product quality needs may need to be revised include the following:

- New or changing requirements
- Evolved understanding of product quality needs by customers and end users
- Lessons learned on product quality issues within the project

SP 1.2 Define the project's quantitative product quality goals

The project's quantitative product quality goals are defined based on the project's product quality needs.

Example work products

1. Identified and prioritized project-specific quantitative product quality goals
2. Interim quantitative product quality goals (e.g., for each lifecycle phase)

Sub-practices

1. Identify the attributes of product quality that are required to address the project's product quality needs

Examples of product quality attributes include the following [ISO 9126]:

- Functionality
- Reliability
- Maintainability
- Usability
- Portability
- Efficiency

2. Prioritize the identified set of product quality attributes based on the priorities of the product quality needs
3. Define quantitative product goals for each of the selected product quality attributes
   To support this sub-practice selected product quality attributes are often broken down into product quality sub-attributes. For each of the quality goals measurable numeric values based on the required and desired values are identified [Gilb]. The quality goals will act as acceptance criteria for the project.
4. Assess the capability of the project's defined process to satisfy the product quality goals
5. Define interim quantitative product quality goals for each lifecycle phase and corresponding work products, as appropriate, to be able to monitor progress towards achieving the project's product quality goals
   The interim quality goals will act as exit criteria for the appropriate lifecycle phases.
6. Allocate project product quality goals to subcontractors, as appropriate
7. Specify operational definitions in exact and unambiguous terms for the identified (interim) product quality goals
8. Establish traceability between the project's quantitative product quality goals and the project's product quality needs
9. Revise the product quality goals as appropriate

SP 1.3 Define the approach for measuring progress toward the project's product quality goals

The approach is defined for measuring the level of accomplishment toward the defined set of product quality goals.

Refer to the Test Measurement process area for how to define measures.

Example work products

1. Measurement approach for product quality
2. Definitions of (test) measurement techniques to be used

Sub-practices

1. Select the (test) measurement techniques to be used to measure the progress toward achieving the (interim) product quality goals

Examples of (test) measurement techniques include the following:

- Peer reviews
- Prototype development
- Static (code) analysis
- Dynamic testing
- Defect numbers during development testing to predict defects found later in the lifecycle

2. Define the points in the lifecycle, e.g., the test levels, for application of each of the selected techniques to measure product quality
3. Specify data collection and storage procedures
   Refer to the Test Measurement process area for more information on data collection and storage procedures.
4. Select analysis techniques to be used to analyze the product quality measurement data
5. Define the supporting (test) measurement tools to be used
6. Identify any significant constraints regarding the approach being defined

Examples of constraints regarding the approach being defined include the following:

- Source data quality constraints
- Measurement data scheduling constraints due to overlapping points in the lifecycle
- Test measurement techniques and/or data analysis techniques requiring specific skills
- Budget and resource constraints
- Test environment constraints

7. Review the product quality measurement approach with stakeholders
8. Revise the product quality measurement approach as appropriate

SG 2 Actual Progress toward Achieving the Project's Product Quality Goals is Quantified and Managed

The project is monitored to determine whether the project's product quality goals will be satisfied, and to identify corrective action as appropriate.

SP 2.1 Measure product quality quantitatively throughout the lifecycle

The quality of the product and work products delivered by the project are quantitatively measured throughout the lifecycle based on the defined approach.

Example work products

1. Product quality measurement data sets
2. Results of product quality data integrity tests

Sub-practices

1. Perform product quality measurements on work products in accordance with the selected (test) measurement techniques and the defined approach at defined points in the lifecycle

> *Examples of work products include the following:*
> - Requirements documents
> - Design documents
> - Interface specifications
> - Prototypes
> - Code
> - Individual components

2. Perform product quality measurements on the product in accordance with the selected (test) measurement techniques and the defined approach
3. Collect product quality measurement data as necessary
4. Review the product quality measurement data to ensure quality

> *Examples of quality attributes of measurement data include the following:*
> - Completeness
> - Integrity
> - Accuracy
> - Currency

5. Revise the product quality measurement approach and product quality measures as appropriate

SP 2.2 Analyze product quality measurements and compare them to the product's quantitative goals

The (interim) product quality measurements are analyzed and compared to the project's (interim) product quality goals on an event-driven and periodic basis.

Example work products

1. Analysis results
2. Product quality measurement report
3. Documented product quality review results, e.g., minutes of the meetings
4. List of product quality issues needing corrective actions

Sub-practices

1. Conduct initial analysis on the (interim) product quality measurements

   Refer to the Test Measurement process area for more information on data analysis.

2. Compare the product quality measures against the project's product quality goals, and draw preliminary conclusions
   Metrics that indicate low product quality should be subject to further scrutiny
3. Conduct additional product quality measurements and analysis as necessary, and prepare results for communication
4. Communicate product quality measurement results and the level of achievement of (interim) product quality quantitative goals to relevant stakeholders on a timely basis.
5. Review the results of product quality measurements and the level of achievement of (interim) product quality quantitative goals with relevant stakeholders
6. Identify and document significant product quality issues and their impacts
7. Define corrective actions to be taken based on the analyzed product quality measurement results
8. Manage corrective actions to closure
   Refer to SG 3 Manage corrective actions to closure from the process area Test Monitoring and Control for more information on managing corrective actions to closure

9. Revise the product quality goals and measurement approach as appropriate

Generic Practices by Goals

GG 2 Institutionalize a Managed Process

GP 2.1 Establish an organizational policy

Establish and maintain an organizational policy for planning and performing the Product Quality Evaluation process.

Elaboration

The product quality evaluation policy typically specifies:

- The product quality evaluation activities support the organization's commitment to improve the quality of the products
- The project defines and collects the measurements used for product quality evaluation based on the project's defined (test) process
- The project defines quantitative quality goals for the products and monitors actual progress towards them
- Responsibilities for product quality evaluation are defined and assigned to the test group and other related groups, e.g., quality assurance and/or configuration management

GP 2.2 Plan the process

Establish and maintain the plan for performing the Product Quality Evaluation process.

Elaboration

Typically, the plan for performing the product quality evaluation process is included in the test plan, which is described in the TMMi Test Planning process area. The activities for product quality evaluation, e.g., the definition of product quality goals and the (test) measurement activities, are explicitly scheduled as part of the plan. Alternatively, the plan for performing the product quality evaluation process may be described as part of the project's quality plan.

GP 2.3 Provide resources

Provide adequate resources for performing the Product Quality Evaluation process, developing the test work products, and providing the services of the process.

Elaboration

- Adequate time is provided to perform the product quality evaluation activities
- Specialists in measurement and non-functional testing, e.g., for performance, safety or reliability, may be needed to define the quality goals and measures, and select the (test) measurement techniques. They may also be needed to analyze and interpret the collected data.
- Tools to support the product quality evaluation activities are available

GP 2.4 Assign responsibilities

Assign responsibility and authority for performing the process, developing the work products, and providing the services of the Product Quality Evaluation process.

When defining the responsibility for this process area, it must be made clear what the role and responsibility of quality assurance is in this context. The quality assurance group is, by nature, defining process and product quality goals and evaluating the project's performance in achieving these goals.

GP 2.5 Train People

Train the people performing or supporting the Product Quality Evaluation process as needed.

Elaboration

Examples of training topics include the following:

- Understanding the goals and benefits of quantitatively managing product quality
- Understanding product quality measurements
- Methods for defining, selecting and collecting measurement
- Quality attributes (e.g. ISO 9126)
- Methods and techniques to elicit product quality needs
- Techniques to measure product quality
- Supporting measurement tools

GP 2.6 Manage configurations

Place selected work products of the Product Quality Evaluation process under appropriate levels of configuration control.

Elaboration

Examples of work products placed under configuration management include the following:

- Product quality needs documents
- Definitions of product quality goals, operational measures and their collection points during the processes
- Collected measurements

GP 2.7 Indentify and involve relevant stakeholders

Identify and involve relevant stakeholders of the Product Quality Evaluation process as planned.

Elaboration

Examples of activities for stakeholder involvement include the following:

- Eliciting product quality needs
- Reviewing product quality needs, product quality goals and test measurement approaches
- Assessing product quality being achieved against the product quality goals
- Reviewing product quality achieved

GP 2.8 Monitor and control the process

Monitor and control the Product Quality Evaluation process in accordance with the plan for performing the process and take appropriate actions as needed.

Elaboration

Examples of measures used to monitor and control the Product Quality Evaluation process include the following:

- Percentage of product quality goals actually being achieved by the projects
- Percentage of product quality goals actually being measured in the projects
- Schedule of data collection, analysis and reporting activities related to the product quality goals

GP 2.9 Objectively evaluate adherence

Objectively evaluate adherence of the Product Quality Evaluation process and selected work products against the process description, standards, and procedures, and address any areas of non-compliance.

Elaboration

Examples of review and/or audit evaluation adherence topics include the following:

- Definition of the quantitative product quality goals
- Collected measures
- Information in the test plan regarding product quality evaluation activities to be performed
- The process for establishing and monitoring the product quality goals

GP 2.10 Review status with higher level management

Review the activities, status and results of Product Quality Evaluation process with higher level management and resolve issues.

GG 3 Institutionalize a Defined Process

GP 3.1 Establish a defined process

Establish and maintain a description of a defined Product Quality Evaluation process.

GP 3.2 Collect improvement information

Collect process related experiences derived from planning and performing the Product Quality Evaluation process to support the future use and improvement of the organization's processes and process assets.

Examples of measures include the following:

- Cost of poor quality
- Cost for achieving the product quality goals

Process Area 4.3 Advanced Reviews

Purpose

The purpose of Advanced Reviews, building on the practices of the TMMi level 3 process area Peer Reviews, is to measure product quality early in the lifecycle and to enhance the test strategy and test approach by aligning peer reviews (static testing) with dynamic testing.

Introductory Notes

The definition of testing clearly states that 'it is a process that encompasses of all lifecycle activities, both static and dynamic, concerned with planning, preparation and evaluation of software products and related work products'. This view of testing which originates from the evolutionary test model [Gelperin and Hetzel] holds the position that testing should cover both validation and verification and include both static and dynamic analysis. In line with this view of testing, reviews are an intrinsic part of testing, serving as a verification, validation and static analysis technique. At TMMi level 4 this view is supported by a coordinated approach to manage peer reviews (static testing) and dynamic testing. This expands upon the peer review process at TMMi level 3, where peer reviews are performed but are not coordinated with dynamic testing.

Peer reviews, as an isolated process, are an effective way to identify defects and product risks before the actual product is built. When peer reviews and dynamic testing are coordinated, the early review results and data are used to influence the test approach. Building on the testing principle of defect clustering [Graham], the types and quantity of defects found during reviews can help to select the most effective tests, and may also influence the test approach or even the test objectives. Typically, at project milestones, the test approach is re-evaluated and updated. Peer review data should be one of the drivers for this update.

At TMMi level 4, the organization sets quantitative goals for software products and related work products. Peer reviews play an essential role in achieving these goals. Whereas at TMMi level 3 peer reviews are mainly performed to find defects, the emphasis is now on measuring product (document) quality. Building on the experiences of performing peer reviews at TMMi level 3, the review practices are enhanced to include practices like sampling, applying exit criteria, and prescribing rules. To improve the reliability of the measurements, advanced defect finding techniques such as perspective-based reading [Veenendaal] are practiced. The measurement results are also used by (project) management to control product quality early in the lifecycle (see Product Quality

Evaluation for more information on measuring and managing product quality).

Scope

The Advanced Review process area builds on the practices of the TMMi level 3 Peer Reviews process area. It covers the practices for establishing a coordinated test approach between peer reviews and dynamic testing and the use of peer review results and data to optimize the test approach. At TMMi maturity level 4, peer reviews are fully integrated with the dynamic testing process, e.g., part of the test strategy, test plan and test approach. The Advance Review process area also covers the practices that facilitate the shift from peer reviews as a defect detection technique to a product quality measurement technique in line with the process area Product Quality Evaluation. These practices include document sampling, definition of rules, strict exit criteria and perspective-based reading.

Specific Goal and Practice Summary

SG 1 Coordinate the Peer Review Approach with the Dynamic Test Approach
- SP 1.1 Relate work products to items and features to be tested
- SP 1.2 Define a coordinated test approach

SG 2 Measure Product Quality Early in the Lifecycle by Means of Peer Reviews
- SP 2.1 Define peer review measurement guidelines
- SP 2.2 Define peer review criteria based on product quality goals
- SP 2.3 Measure work product quality using peer reviews

SG 3 Adjust the Test Approach Based on Review Results Early in the Lifecycle
- SP 3.1 Analyze peer review results
- SP 3.2 Revise the products risks as appropriate
- SP 3.3 Revise the test approach as appropriate

SG 1 Coordinate the Peer Review Approach with the Dynamic Test Approach

The approach for peer reviews (static testing) is aligned and coordinated with the approach for dynamic testing.

SP 1.1 Relate work products to items and features to be tested

For the item and features to be tested, as identified by the test approach, the related work products are identified.

Example work products

1. Bi-directional traceability matrix mapping the test items and features to the work products

Sub-practices

1. Review the project's product risk analysis report

The project's product risk analysis report, including the rationale, is reviewed to establish a detailed understanding of the identified product risks and the importance of the items and features to be tested.
Refer to SG 1 Perform a Product Risk Assessment from the process area Test Planning for more details on product risk analysis.

2. Review the product work breakdown as defined in the project plan
   The product work breakdown as defined in the project plan is reviewed to establish a detailed understanding of the identified project's work products and their relationship to the final product and thereby to the items and features to be tested.
3. Establish bi-directional traceability from the items and features to be tested to the work products
   The work products, as candidates for reviews, are linked by means of a bi-directional traceability matrix to the items and features to be tested as identified by the project's product risk analysis.

SP 1.2 Define a coordinated test approach

A test approach is defined that coordinates both static and dynamic testing.

Example work products

1. List of work products to be reviewed
2. Coordinated test approach documented in a (master) test plan
3. Documented commitments

Sub-practices

1. Identify the project's work products and test work products to be reviewed
   From the list of work products those that are associated with high or medium risk items and/or features are selected to be reviewed.
2. Document the associated risk level and type, derived from the related item and/or feature to be tested, for each of the identified work products to be reviewed.
3. Prioritize the identified work product reviews based on the associated product risks
4. Review the list of work products to be reviewed including priority level and work products not to be reviewed with stakeholders

5. Define the review type(s) per work product, including the rationale, that will be applied to review the identified work products in accordance with the associated product risk levels and types
   Refer to the Peer Review process area for an overview of the various review types and for other aspects of a peer review approach.
6. Revisit the dynamic test approach
   The dynamic test approach is revisited to determine whether the effort level can be reduced as a result of the product risk coverage attained by static testing.
7. Identify any significant constraints regarding the coordinated test approach

Examples of constraints regarding the coordinated test approach include the following:

- Review resource availability
- Knowledge and skills of potential reviewers
- Project deadlines

8. Estimate the effort and costs required to perform the coordinated test approach
9. Review the coordinated test approach with the stakeholders
10. Document the coordinated test approach as part of a (master) test plan
11. Obtain commitment to the coordinated test approach with management
12. Revise the coordinated test approach as appropriate

SG 2 Measure Product Quality Early in the Lifecycle by Means of Peer Reviews

Early in the lifecycle, product quality is measured against set criteria by means of peer reviews.

SP 2.1 Define peer review measurement guidelines

Guidelines to support the peer reviews as a measurement practice are defined and documented.

Example work products

1. Rules and review checklists
2. Sampling guidelines
3. Perspective-based reading procedures

Sub-practices

1. Define and document rules and review checklists
   The rules provide a set of generic requirements regarding the content and format of a document type. The rule set provides a basis for defining peer review criteria and objectively measuring document quality. Review checklists are a specialized set of questions designed to help reviewers find more defects, and, in particular, more significant defects by checking against the defined rule set. Checklist questions interpret specific rules and preferably are defined per review role. [Gilb and Graham]
2. Define and document sampling guidelines
   To measure the quality of a work product, it is neither necessary nor efficient to review every page of a document. Sampling is a proven method for being able to accurately measure product quality. With sampling, only a limited number of pages of the document is reviewed. Defects, objectively defined as a violation to a rule, are used to provide a quality measure such as the number of defects per page. If a valid sample is chosen, the quality measure of the sample can be used as a quality measure for the whole document.

> *Examples of issues to be addressed in sampling guidelines include the following:*
> - Sample size
> - Sample representativeness
> - Actions based on sampling review results such as distribution of defects found
> - Checking rate (number of pages reviewed per hour)

3. Define and document perspective based reading procedures
   The use of a defined, systematic process for individual defect detection (known as a reading technique) allows reviewers to focus better on the important aspects of the document being reviewed. More importantly, by making the review process explicit, reading techniques allow the reviews to be adapted over time, to better meet the needs of the organization. For example, if a particular type of defect is consistently missed by the reviews, then a procedure for how to identify that type of defect should be developed and applied by at least one of the reviewers in the future. Using reading techniques also leads to being less people

dependent and provides more reproducible review results and product quality measurements. [Veenendaal]

4. Review the peer review measurement guidelines (rules, review checklists, sampling guidelines and perspective-based reading procedures) with relevant stakeholders
5. Optimize the peer review measurement guidelines based on practical experiences

SP 2.2 Define peer review criteria based on product quality goals

Peer review criteria, especially quantitative exit criteria, are defined based on the project's (interim) product quality goals.

Example work products

1. Quantitative project-specific exit criteria

Sub-practices

1. Review the project's (interim) product quality goals
   The project's product quality needs and goals are reviewed to establish a detailed understanding of the identified project's product quality goals and their priority.
   Refer to SG 1 Measurable Project Goals for Product Quality and their Priorities are Established, from the process area Product Quality Evaluation for more details on product quality goals.
2. Define quantitative exit criteria for peer reviews based on the project's (interim) product quality goals
   Refer to SP 1.2 Define peer review criteria from the process area Peer Reviews for more details on exit criteria for peer reviews.
3. Review the quantitative exit criteria with the stakeholders
4. Tailor the organizational peer review measurement guidelines based on the project's product quality goals and defined peer review exit criteria
   Organizational peer review measurement guidelines should only be used in a specific project if the guidelines are relevant for the project. The goals and requirements of the project determine the applicability of the guidelines. For example, rules and checklists concerning maintainability and documentation can be irrelevant for some type of projects, such as throw-away products, data conversions or migrations.

SP 2.3 Measure work product quality using peer reviews

The quality of the work products is measured early in the lifecycle using peer reviews.

Example work products

1. Peer review logging forms (defects found)
2. Peer review action list
3. Peer review data
4. Peer review reports

Sub-practices

1. Perform peer reviews on selected work products using measurement guidelines
   Refer to SG 2 Perform Peer Reviews from the process area Peer Reviews for more details on performing peer reviews.
2. Analyze peer review data and results
3. Compare peer review results against defined exit criteria
4. Identify action items and communicate issues and results to the relevant stakeholders
5. Record peer review data

SG 3 Adjust the Test Approach Based on Review Results Early in the Lifecycle

Based on results of peer reviews early in the lifecycle, the test approach is adjusted as appropriate.

SP 3.1 Analyze peer review results

The collected peer review measurement data on work product quality are analyzed as planned.

Example work products

1. Peer review measurement analysis results
2. Peer review measurement reports on work product quality

Sub-practices

1. Conduct analysis on the peer review measurements regarding work product quality
2. Compare the outcome of the analysis of peer reviews against the defined exit criteria and product risks and draw preliminary conclusions
3. Conduct additional peer review measurements and analysis as necessary and prepare results for communication

4. Keep relevant stakeholders informed of peer review measurement results regarding work product quality on a timely basis
5. Assist relevant stakeholders in understanding the results

SP 3.2 Revise the product risks as appropriate

Based on the peer review measurement data on work product quality, product risks are re-evaluated and re-prioritized using predefined categories and parameters.

Example work products

1. Updated product risk list, with a category and priority assigned to each risk (including documented rationale)

Sub-practices

1. Identify new product risks to which a changed risk level or risk type should be attributed
   Using the peer review measurement data on work product quality and based on information such as defect numbers and types of defects, some areas of the product may demonstrate a higher or lower level of product risk. This relates especially to the likelihood of being defect-prone. New product risks also can be identified using the peer review data on work product quality.
   Using the latest information on product quality to re-focus and tune testing supports a more effective and efficient test process.
2. Analyze the identified product risks using the predefined parameters, e.g., likelihood and impact

   Note that both newly identified product risks and previously identified product risks are subject to the analysis.

3. (Re-)categorize and (re-)group the product risks according to the defined risk categories
4. (Re-)prioritize the product risks for mitigation
5. Document the rationale for the updates of the project's product risk list
6. Review and obtain agreement with stakeholders regarding the completeness, category and priority level of the revised product risks
7. Revisit the set of product risks based on peer review measurement data at project milestones and on an event-driven basis

SP 3.3 Revise the test approach as appropriate

Based on identified product risks, the coordinated test approach is revised as appropriate and agreed upon.

Example work products

1. Updated dynamic test approach

Sub-practices

1. Revisit the list of items to be tested (including risk level) and not to be tested based on the revised set of product risks
2. Revisit the list of features to be tested (including risk level) and not to be tested based on the revised set of product risks
3. Review the revised list of items and feature to be tested and not to be tested with stakeholders
4. Revisit the coordinated test approach as appropriate
   The coordinated test approach, which includes both the dynamic test approach (functional and non-functional) and the peer review approach is revisited and updated as appropriate based on the revised list of items and features to be tested, and not to be tested.
   Refer to SG 2 Establish a Test Approach from the process area Test Planning, and to SG 2 Establish a Non-functional Test Approach from the process area Non-functional Testing for more details on defining a test approach. Refer to SG 1 Establish a Peer Review Approach from the process area Peer Reviews for more details on defining a peer review approach.
5. Document the revised coordinated test approach as part of a (master) test plan
6. Review and obtain commitment from the stakeholders to the revised coordinated test approach with management

Generic Practices by Goals

GG 2 Institutionalize a Managed Process

GP 2.1 Establish an organizational policy

Establish and maintain an organizational policy for planning and performing the Advanced Reviews process.

Elaboration

The advanced review policy typically specifies:
- Reviews will be applied to measure product quality early in the development lifecycle

- Reviews are part of the test process and should be part of the test approach, project test plan and test reports
- Peer reviews are led by trained peer review leaders or moderators
- Review measurement data is collected and used to tune the dynamic test approach, improve the review process, and predict product quality

GP 2.2 Plan the process

Establish and maintain the plan for performing the Advanced Reviews process.

Elaboration

At TMMi level 4, peer reviews are an integral part of the testing process. The plan for performing the Advanced Reviews process is included in the (master) test plan.

GP 2.3 Provide resources

Provide adequate resources for performing the Advanced Reviews process, developing the test work products, and providing the services of the process.

Elaboration

- Adequate time is provided to perform the advanced review activities
- Trained peer review leaders are available
- Meeting rooms are available for review meetings
- Supporting artifacts such as defect logging forms and review process forms to support data collection, analysis and reporting are available
- Rules and checklists, reading procedures and sampling guidelines are established and maintained
- Tools to support the advanced review process are available, e.g., defect logging tools, communication tools, measurement tools and peer review process tools

GP 2.4 Assign responsibilities

Assign responsibility and authority for performing the process, developing the work products and providing the services of the Advanced Reviews process.

Elaboration

Since at TMMi level 4 peer reviews are part of the test process, test managers are designated to be responsible for coordinating the advanced review process within projects.

Peer review leaders will support the test manager and are designated to be responsible for coordinating the individual peer reviews to measure work product quality.

GP 2.5 Train people

Train the people performing or supporting the Advanced Reviews process as needed.

Elaboration

Examples of training topics for advanced reviews include the following:

- Product risk assessment
- Defining a coordinated test approach
- Types of reviews
- Defining peer review quantitative exit criteria
- Document rules and checklists
- Sampling practices
- Perspective-based reading
- Data collection, analysis, and reporting processes

GP 2.6 Manage configurations

Place selected work products of the Advanced Reviews process under appropriate levels of configuration control.

Elaboration

Examples of work products placed under configuration management include the following:

- Coordinated test approach
- Coordinated test approach review report
- Test plan
- Peer review data(base)
- Peer review measurement data
- Peer review measurement analysis results and reports
- Advanced reviews training material
- Product risk assessment data

GP 2.7 Identify and involve relevant stakeholders

Identify and involve relevant stakeholders of the Advanced Reviews process as planned.

Elaboration

Select relevant stakeholders from customers, end users, developers, testers, suppliers, marketers, maintenance, service, management and others who may be affected by, or may affect, the (work) products to participate in advanced reviews.

Examples of activities for stakeholder involvement include the following:

- Selecting work products to be reviewed
- Explicitly committing the resources needed
- Reviewing and approving the coordinated test approach
- Performing peer reviews
- Assessing peer review measurement data

GP 2.8 Monitor and control the process

Monitor and control the Advanced Reviews process against the plan for performing the process and take appropriate actions as needed.

Elaboration

Examples of measures to monitor and control the Advanced Reviews process include the following:

- Actual effort spent compared to effort planned for peer reviews and dynamic testing
- Number of peer reviews planned and performed
- Number of work products measured on product quality compared to plan
- Number of revisions to the test plan
- Number of new or changed product risks per revision
- Number of test items affected by risk level changes per revision

GP 2.9 Objectively evaluate adherence

Objectively evaluate adherence of the Advanced Reviews process and selected work products against the process description, standards, and procedures, and address any areas of non-compliance.

Elaboration

Examples of review and/or audit evaluation adherence topics include the following:

- The presence of a coordinated test approach in the test plan
- The compliance of the peer reviews performed to the measurement guidelines
- The effectiveness and efficiency of the peer review measurement guidelines
- The usage of peer review results to revisit the product risk list
- The effectiveness of the updates of the test plans based on the peer review results

GP 2.10 Review status with higher level management

Review the activities, status and results of the Advanced Reviews process with higher level management and resolve issues.

Elaboration

Examples of activities, status and results of the Advanced Reviews process that can be reviewed with higher management:

- Number of projects with a coordinated test approach
- Number of peer reviews planned and performed
- Results of the performed reviews
- Measurement data of performed reviews, e.g., software defect removal effectiveness and yield

GG 3 Institutionalize a Defined Process

GP 3.1 Establish a defined process

Establish and maintain a description of a defined Advanced Reviews process.

GP 3.2 Collect improvement information

Collect process related experiences derived from planning and performing the Advanced Reviews process to support the future use and improvement of the organization's processes and process assets.

Elaboration

Examples of measures include the following:

- Peer review coverage
- Defect density (per page) on documents measured by means of peer reviews
- Percentage of test plans that encompass a peer review approach
- Percentage of peer reviews performed using perspective-based reading techniques
- Number of product risks revisited based on peer review results
- Number of test plans and test approaches updated based on peer review results

TMMi Level 5: Optimization

The achievement of all previous test improvement goals at levels 1 through 4 of TMMi has created an organizational infrastructure for testing that supports a completely defined and measured process. At TMMi maturity level 5, an organization is capable of continually improving its processes based on a quantitative understanding of statistically controlled processes. Improving test process performance is carried out through incremental and innovative process and technological improvements. The testing methods and techniques are optimized and there is a continuous focus on fine-tuning and process improvement. An optimized test process, as defined by the TMMi, is one that is:

- Managed, defined, measured, efficient and effective
- Statistically controlled and predictable
- Focused on defect prevention
- Supported by automation as much as is deemed an effective use of resources
- Able to support technology transfer from the industry to the organization
- Able to support re-use of test assets
- Focused on process change to achieve continuous improvement.

To support the continuous improvement of the test process infrastructure, and to identify, plan and implement test improvements, a permanent test process improvement group is formally established and is staffed by members who have received specialized training to increase the level of their skills and knowledge required for the success of the group. In many organizations this group is called a Test Process Group. Support for a Test Process Group formally begins at TMMi level 3 when the test organization is introduced. At TMMi level 4 and 5 the responsibilities grow as more high level practices are introduced, e.g., identifying reusable test (process) assets and developing and maintaining the test (process) asset library.

The Defect Prevention process area is established to identify and analyze common causes of defects across the development lifecycle and define actions to prevent similar defects from occurring in the future. Outliers to test process performance, as identified as part of process quality control, are analyzed to address their causes as part of Defect Prevention.

The test process is now statistically managed by means of the Quality Control process area. Statistical sampling, measurements of confidence levels, trustworthiness, and reliability drive the test process. The test process is characterized by sampling-based quality measurements.

At TMMi level 5, the Test Process Optimization process area introduces mechanisms to fine-tune and continuously improve testing. There is an established procedure to identify process enhancements as well as to select and evaluate new testing technologies. Tools support the test process as much as is effective during test design, test execution, regression testing, test case management, defect collection and analysis, etc. Process and testware re-use across the organization is also common practice and is supported by a test (process) asset library.

The three TMMi level 5 process areas, Defect Prevention, Quality Control and Test Process Optimization all provide support for continuous process improvement. In fact, the three process areas are highly interrelated. For example, Defect Prevention supports Quality Control, e.g., by analyzing outliers to process performance and by implementing practices for defect causal analysis and prevention of defect re-occurrence. Quality Control contributes to Test Process Optimization, and Test Process Optimization supports both Defect Prevention and Quality Control, for example by implementing the test improvement proposals. All of these process areas are, in turn, supported by the practices that were acquired when the lower level process areas were implemented. At TMMi level 5, testing is a process with the objective of preventing defects.

The process areas at TMMi level 5 are:
5.1 Defect Prevention
5.2 Quality Control
5.3 Test Process Optimization

Each of these is discussed in more detail in the sections hereafter.

Process Area 5.1 Defect Prevention

Purpose

The purpose of Defect Prevention is to identify and analyze common causes of defects across the development lifecycle and define actions to prevent similar defects from occurring in the future.

Introductory Notes

In line with the evolutionary test model [Gelperin and Hetzel], testing at TMMi level 5 completes its journey from being detection-focused to being a prevention-focused process. In line with this view of testing, testing is focused on the prevention of defects that otherwise might have been introduced rather than just their detection during testing activities. Defect Prevention involves analyzing defects that were encountered in the past, identifying causes and taking specific actions to prevent the occurrence of those types of defects in the future. The selection of defects to be analyzed should be based on various factors including risk. Focus needs to be given to those areas where prevention of defects has the most added value (usually in terms of reduced cost or risk) and/or where the defects are most critical. Attention should be given to both existing types of defects as well as new types of defects such as defects that are new to the organization but are known to occur in the industry. Defect Prevention activities are also a mechanism for spreading lessons learned across the organization, e.g., across projects.

Defect Prevention improves quality and productivity by preventing the introduction of defects into a product. Industry data shows that reliance on detecting defects after they have been introduced is usually not cost effective [Boehm]. It is usually more cost effective to prevent defects from being introduced by integrating Defect Prevention practices into each phase of the project. At TMMi level 5, an organization will know which is more cost effective, prevention or detection of a certain type of defect. Many process improvement models emphasize the use of causal analysis as a means of continually improving the maturity of the process. Examples of methods for causal analysis are specific causal analysis meetings, using tools such as fault tree analysis and cause/effect diagrams, project retrospectives, causal analysis during formal reviews, and usage of standard defect classifications.

Defect Prevention is a mechanism to evaluate the complete development process and identify the most effective improvements regarding product quality. As part of the Defect Prevention practices, trends are analyzed to track the types of defects that have been encountered and where they were introduced, and to identify defects that are most likely to reoccur. A (test) measurement process is already in place having been introduced at level 4. The available measures can be used, though some new measures may be needed to analyze the effects of the process changes. Based on an understanding of the organization's defined standard development and test process and how it is implemented, the root causes of the defects and the implications of the defects for future activities are determined. Specific actions are defined and taken to prevent reoccurrence of the identified defects. Defect Prevention is an essential part of a mature test process. Defects found during development, testing or even during production must be systematically analyzed, prioritized and action must be undertaken to prevent them from occurring in the future. The test organization coordinates the Defect Prevention activities. This should be done in close cooperation with other disciplines, e.g., requirements engineering, system engineering and/or software development, as improvement actions will often affect other disciplines.

Scope

The process area Defect Prevention addresses the practices for identifying and analyzing common causes of defects, and defining specific actions to remove the common causes of those types of defects in the future both within the project and elsewhere in the organization. All defects, whether found during development, testing or in the field, are within the scope of the process area. Process defects that have resulted in outliers and not meeting expected process performance also are within the scope. Since Defect Prevention needs measurement data and measurement processes as an input, Defect Prevention builds on the TMMi level 4 measurement practices and available measurement data regarding development, testing and product quality.

Specific Goals

SG 1 Determine Common Causes of Defects

- SP 1.1 Define defect selection parameters and defect classification scheme
- SP 1.2 Select defects for analysis
- SP 1.3 Analyze causes of selected defects

SG 2 Prioritize and Define Actions to Systematically Eliminate Root Causes of Defects

- SP 2.1 Propose solutions to eliminate common causes
- SP 2.2 Define action proposals and submit improvement proposals

Specific Practices by Goals

SG 1 Determine Common Causes of Defects

Root and common causes of selected defects are systematically determined.

SP 1.1 Define defect selection parameters and defect classification scheme

Selection parameters for the defects to be analyzed and a detailed defect classification scheme are defined.

Example work products

1. Defect selection parameters
2. Defect classification scheme

Sub-practices

1. Determine defect selection parameters
   The selection of defect should be based on various factors including risks. Focus needs to be given to those areas where prevention of defects has the most added value and/or where the defects are most critical.

Examples of defect selection parameters include the following:

- The potential damage a defect of this type can have
- The frequency of a defects occurrence
- The effort it takes to repair the defect
- An estimation of the effort it takes to prevent the defect from recurring
- The rework costs of the defect
- The extent to which the defect has a negative impact on process performance

2. Review the defined defect selection parameters with relevant stakeholders
3. Define a detailed defect classification scheme
   A common defect classification allows statistics to be obtained regarding improvement areas to be analyzed across the organization. The defects to be analyzed will be recorded from all lifecycle phases, including maintenance and operation. Standards such as [IEEE 1044] allow a common classification of anomalies leading to an understanding of the project stages when faults are introduced, the project activities occurring when faults are detected, the cost of rectifying the faults, the cost of failures, and the stage where the defect was raised versus where it should have been found (also known as defect leakage) [ISTQB ITP].

IEEE 1044 distinguishes the following four phases in the incident/defect lifecycle:

- Recognition - When the incident is found
- Investigation - Each incident is investigated to identify all known related issues and proposed solutions
- Action - A plan of action is formulated on the basis of the investigation (resolve, retest)
- Disposition - Once all actions required are complete the incident shall be closed

In each phase a number of attributes have been defined by the standard that can be used for classification. IEEE 1044 provides comprehensive lists of classifications and related data items, such as the following:

- During recognition the following classifications (including related data items) are provided: project activity, phase, suspected cause, repeatability, system, product status, etc.
- During investigation the following classifications (including related data items) are provided: actual cause, defect source, defect type, etc.

Note that the defect classification scheme introduced shall now be applied during defect logging activities such as SP 3.3 Report test incidents (process area Test Design and Execution) and SP 5.2 Report non-functional test incidents (process area Non-functional Testing).Note that a Defect Classification Scheme can be defined in PA 2.4 Test Design and Execution that can be re-used in this sub-practice.

4. Review the defined defect classification scheme with relevant stakeholders.

SP 1.2 Select defects for analysis

Defects are selected from the defect repository for detailed analysis.

Example work products

1. Defects selected for further analysis (including rationale)

Sub-practices

1. Identify and select stakeholders who need to contribute to the defect selection process
   The participants can be selected from business, development, maintenance, service management, application support, testing and relevant third parties. The participants can also be a standard team under the

umbrella of the Test Process Group, enhanced with ad hoc participants for specific defects.

2. Execute kick off

   The kick off has the following purposes:
   - Explaining the process that will be followed during the defect selection meeting
   - Making concrete arrangements about the preparation and the time and place of the meeting
   - Explaining the selection parameters and classification scheme

   If all participants are experienced in the defect selection process, the kick off may not be needed.

3. Prepare for the defect selection

Examples of activities to be carried out during the preparation for defect selection include the following:
- Establish a comprehensive list of all defects. Defects reports can originate from static testing, dynamic testing, actual usage in operation and from process performance outliers.
- Make an initial selection from the defect repository. During this activity, the defects that have a small likelihood of being selected, for instance minor defects, are removed from the list. Defects that adhere to the defect selection parameters are identified.
- Perform an initial analysis on the defects, e.g., to identify defect types that have high occurrence, using techniques such as Pareto Analysis and Histograms.

4. The stakeholders decide which defects (or defect types) will be analyzed in detail. The defect selection parameters and other information prepared are used to make this decision. Attention should be given to both existing types of defects as well as new types of defects.

SP 1.3 Analyze causes of selected defects

Perform causal analysis of selected defects to determine their root causes and identify common causes.

Example work products

1. Root causes of selected defects
2. Common causes of defects

Sub-practices

1. Analyze selected defects to determine their root cause

The root causes is to be found in the specific activity within the development or testing phase where the defect was injected. The root cause of the defects is determined using supporting methods. Depending on the number of defects, it may make sense to first group the defects, e.g., by type, before identifying their root causes.

Examples of supporting methods to determine root causes include the following [ISTQB ITP]:

- Cause/effect diagrams
- Ishikawa fishbone diagrams
- Fault tree analysis
- Process analysis
- Use of standard defect classifications [IEEE 1044]
- Checklists
- FMEA (Failure Mode Effects Analysis)
- Hardware Software Interaction Analysis

2. Determine common causes of the selected defects
The selected defects are grouped based on their root causes.

Examples of categories of common root causes include the following:

- Process
- People (skills and knowledge)
- (Project) organization
- Communication
- Architecture
- Technology, e.g., tools, test environment

SG 2 Prioritize and Define Actions to Systematically Eliminate Common Causes of Defects

Actions are defined and prioritized to systematically address root and common causes of defects.

SP 2.1 Propose solutions to eliminate common causes

Solutions are proposed to eliminate root causes.

Example work products

1. Possible solutions
2. Clustered common / root causes of defects

Sub-practices

1. Cluster common causes that can possibly be addressed through one or more related solutions
   For example, common causes can be clustered by development phase, technology, development lifecycle, or discipline.
2. Determine the type(s) of solutions that are most likely to address the common cause

Examples of types of solutions include the following:

- Process
- Work product standards
- Requirement rules
- Architecture
- Training
- Recruiting
- Coaching
- Organizational structure
- Communication and collaboration activities
- Employee recognition
- Review activities
- Test strategy and/or test approach
- Methods and techniques
- Checklist(s)
- Coding standards
- Tools

3. Define solutions
   Define the solutions to the common cause based on the identified type(s) of solutions.
   Possibly appropriate methods, tools and techniques are selected as part of the solutions. Methods, tools and techniques can help the organization define coherent solutions that prevent the defects from occurring again. Methods, tools and techniques can deliver solutions that are not yet used in or known by the organization.
   It is also possible that best practices from within the organization are part of the solutions. Best practices performed in a specific project or specific part of the organization can support the organization in defining coherent solutions that prevent defects from reoccurring
4. Validate proposed solutions
   Validate the proposed solution to determine if the solutions prevent the selected defects from occurring again.

The following are examples of techniques applied to validate proposed solutions:

- Prototype
- Walkthrough
- Technical review
- (Manual) simulation

5. Prioritize proposed solutions
   Criteria for prioritization of proposed solutions include the following:
   - Contribution to the business
   - The extent to which it contributes to remove common causes
   - Impact and cost of the implementation of the solution to the organization
   - Implications of not addressing the defects
   - Expected impact on quality.

SP 2.2 Define action proposals and submit improvement proposals

Action proposals that fulfill the proposed solutions are defined and submitted as improvement proposals.

Example work products

1. Developed action proposals
2. Recorded data
3. Submitted improvement proposals

Sub-practices

1. Develop action proposals

The following are examples of information provided in an action proposal [CMMI]:

- Person responsible for implementing it
- Description of the areas affected by it
- Person(s) who will be informed of its status
- Next date that the status will be reviewed
- Rationale for key decisions
- Description of implementation activities
- Estimated cost of not fixing the problem, for instance the costs for identifying and correcting the defect when it occurs again

2. Review action proposals with relevant stakeholders
   The action proposals can be reviewed to assess the expected reduction of business risk and/or technical risk, feasibility and impact on the organization.

3. Record data
   Data are recorded so that other projects and other parts of the organization can implement the defined solution.

The following are examples of information data to be recorded:
- Data on defects and other problems that were analyzed
- Rationale for decisions
- Prioritized proposed solutions
- Defined actions
- Defined solutions
- Data from pilots or tests
- Post project evaluation
- Solution refinements
- Cost of the analysis and resolution activities
- Measures of changes to the performance

4. Submit action proposal as improvement proposal
   Action proposals and recorded data are handed over to the process improvement team for implementation. Improvement proposals concerning the test process are handed over to the Test Process Group; improvement proposals concerning other areas are handed over to the improvement group or (senior) manager responsible for that area.
5. Monitor improvement proposals
   The progress of the implementation of the improvement proposals should be monitored. If the progress is not in line with the expectations, the relevant stakeholders should be informed.

Generic Practices by Goals

GG 2 Institutionalize a Managed Process

GP 2.1 Establish an organizational policy

Establish and maintain an organizational policy for planning and performing the Defect Prevention process.

Elaboration

The Defect Prevention policy typically specifies the following:
- The organizational objectives for defect prevention
- Key measures to monitor actual progress towards the defined objectives

- The organizational expectations for identifying and systematically addressing root causes of defects and other problems
- The long term commitments for funding, staffing, and providing other resources for Defect Prevention
- Defect Prevention activities are to be implemented across the organization to improve processes and products
- Defect Prevention activities are to be coordinated by a Test Process Group or process improvement team.

GP 2.2 Plan the process

Establish and maintain the plan for performing the Defect Prevention process.

Elaboration

The activities for Defect Prevention, e.g., the activities for identifying and addressing root and common causes, are explicitly planned and scheduled at an organizational cross-project level.

GP 2.3 Provide Resources

Provide adequate resources for performing the Defect Prevention process, developing the test work products, and providing the services of the Defect Prevention process.

Elaboration

Adequate time and supporting tools are needed to perform the Defect Prevention activities.

Examples of tools that support defect prevention activities include:

- Database systems to capture and mine historical data
- Statistical analysis packages
- Tools, methods and analysis techniques (e.g., Ishikawa fishbone diagrams, Pareto analysis, histograms, cause/effect graphing, process modeling tools)

GP 2.4 Assign responsibilities

Assign responsibility and authority for performing the Defect Prevention process, developing the work products, and providing the services of the Defect Prevention process.

Elaboration

Responsibilities for Defect Prevention are defined and typically assigned to a defect prevention analysis team, possibly under the umbrella of a Test Process Group. A defect prevention analysis team typically consists of representatives from the following areas:

- Management
- Development
- Quality assurance
- Process improvement
- Testing.

GP 2.5 Train people

Train the people performing or supporting the Defect Prevention process as needed.

Elaboration

Examples of training topics include the following:

- Defect prevention techniques such as cause/effect diagrams, Ishikawa fishbone diagrams, Pareto analysis, fault tree analysis and process analysis
- Defect selection parameters
- Defect classification schemes
- Conducting root cause analysis

GP 2.6 Manage configurations

Place selected work products of the Defect Prevention process under appropriate levels of configuration control.

Elaboration

Examples of work products placed under configuration management include the following:

- Defect selection parameters
- Selected defects
- Identified root causes and common causes
- Causal analysis records
- Proposed solutions
- Action proposals

GP 2.7 Identify and involve relevant stakeholders

Identify and involve relevant stakeholders of the Defect Prevention process as planned.

Elaboration

Examples of activities for stakeholder involvement include the following:

- Defining defect selection parameters
- Defining defect classification schemes
- Selecting defects for analysis
- Conducting causal analysis
- Validating proposed solutions
- Defining action proposals

GP 2.8 Monitor and control the process

Monitor and control the Defect Prevention process against the plan for performing the process and take appropriate actions.

Elaboration

Examples of measures used to monitor and control the Defect Prevention process include the following:

- The costs of defect prevention activities
- Number of defects analyzed
- Number of root causes identified
- Number of action proposals outstanding and for how long
- The number of action proposals submitted

GP 2.9 Objectively evaluate adherence

Objective evaluate adherence of the Defect Prevention process and selected work products against the process description, standards, and procedures, and address non-compliances.

Elaboration

Examples of review and/or audit evaluation adherence topics include the following:

- Selecting defects using selection parameters
- Analyzing defects using selection parameters
- Determining causes of defects
- Analyzing causes of defects
- Determining solutions
- Submitting action proposals
- Implementing action proposals

GP 2.10 Review status with higher level management

Review the activities, status and results of the Defect Prevention process with higher level management and resolve issues.

> *Examples of issues to be reviewed with higher level management include the following:*
> - Status of Defect Prevention activities
> - Determined common and root causes
> - Results of Defect Prevention activities, e.g., submitted improvement proposals
> - Effort and other resources spent compared to plan

GG 3 Institutionalize a Defined Process

GP 3.1 Establish a defined process

Establish and maintain a description of a defined Defect Prevention process.

Elaboration

The activities for Defect Prevention, e.g., the activities for identifying and addressing root causes, are defined in an organizational set of standard processes. The organization should have standard processes that cover the process area, as well as have guidelines for tailoring these standard processes to meet the needs of a specific part of the organization.

GP 3.2 Collect improvement information

Collect process-related experiences derived from planning and performing the Defect Prevention process to support the future use and improvement of the organization's processes and process assets.

> *Examples of measures include the following:*
> - Cost of weaknesses, and the results of implementing action proposals
> - Number and type of defects found per development stage
> - The number and characteristics of defects injected in each development stage

Process Area 5.2 Quality Control

Purpose

The purpose of Quality Control is to statistically manage and control the test process. At this level, test process performance is fully predictable and stabilized with acceptable limits. Testing at a project level is performed using statistical methods based on representative samples in order to predict product quality and make testing more efficient.

Introductory Notes

Quality Control consists of the procedures and practices employed to ensure that a work product or deliverable conforms to standards or requirements. In a broad view, the Quality Control procedures and practices can also be applied to the processes creating the product, thereby creating a feedback loop in line with the prevention-oriented and optimizing approach of TMMi level 5. At TMMi level 5, organizations use Quality Control to drive the testing process.

Process Quality Control is supported by statistical techniques and methodologies. The basis for process quality control is the view of the testing process as a series of steps, each of which is a process in itself with a set of inputs and outputs. Ideally the output of each step is determined by rules, procedures and/or standards that prescribe how it is to be executed. Practically speaking the outcome of a step may be different than expected. The differences are caused by variations. Variations may be due to human error, influences outside of the process, unpredictable events such as hardware/software malfunctions and so forth. If there are many unforeseen variations impacting the process step, then the process will be unstable, unpredictable, and out of control. When a process is unpredictable then it cannot be relied upon to give quality results.

An organization that controls its processes quantitatively will be able to do the following:

- Determine the stability of process
- Identify the process performance within the defined natural boundaries
- Identify unpredictable processes
- Identify the improvement opportunities in existing processes
- Identify the best performing processes.

Process quality control involves establishing objectives for the performance of the standard test process, which is defined in the Test Lifecycle and Integration process area. These objectives should be based on the defined test policy. As already stated in the Test Lifecycle and Integration process area, multiple standard test processes may be present to address the needs of different application domains, test levels, lifecycle models, methodologies, and tools in use in the organization. Based on the measurements taken on test process performance from the projects, analysis takes place and adjustments are made to maintain test process performance within acceptable limits. When the test process performance is stabilized within acceptable limits, the defined test process, the associated measurements and the acceptable limits for measurements are established as a baseline and used to control test process performance statistically. The test process capability, i.e., the test process performance a new project can expect to attain, of the organization's standard test process is now fully understood and known. As a result, the deviations from these expectations can be acted upon in a project early and consistently to ensure that the project perform within the acceptable limits. The test process capability can be used to establish unambiguous quantitative test process performance objectives for the project.

Product quality control builds on operational profiles [Musa] and usage models of the product in its intended environment to make statistically valid inferences resulting in a representative sample of test cases. This approach, especially useful at the system test level, uses statistical testing methods to predict product quality based on this representative sample. In other words, when testing a subset of all possible usages as represented by the usage or operational profile, the test results can serve as the basis for conclusions about the product's overall performance. At TMMi level 5, an organization is able to quantify confidence levels and trustworthiness because the infrastructure has been provided to reflect the most frequently requested operations or paths through an operational profile using historical data. Using test data from statistical testing, models such as reliability growth models are built to predict the confidence level and trustworthiness of the system. Confidence level, usually expressed as a percentage, provides information as to the likelihood that the product is defect free. Trustworthiness is defined as the probability that there are no defects in the product that will cause the system to fail. Both the level of confidence and trustworthiness are typically used as exit criteria when applying statistical testing. At TMMi level 5 these factors are used in combination and are usually the main drivers to determine when to stop-testing.

Note that addressing product quality control and statistical testing requires a great deal of expertise with statistical techniques including modeling, usage modeling, statistics, testing, and measurements. Specialists must be selected and trained to become leaders in this area of testing.

Scope

The process area Quality Control addresses the practices for establishing a statistically controlled test process (process quality control) and testing based on statistical methods and techniques (product quality control). Process quality control strongly builds on the deployed measurement practices from the Test Measurement process area from TMMi level 4. Product quality control builds on the deployed practices from the Product Quality Evaluation process area from TMMi level 4. Both types of quality control make use of available measurement data regarding the test process and product quality from the TMMi level 4 process areas.

Specific Goal and Practice Summary

SG 1 Establish a Statistically Controlled Test Process
- SP 1.1 Establish test process performance objectives
- SP 1.2 Establish test process performance measures
- SP 1.3 Establish test process performance baselines
- SP 1.4 Apply statistical methods to understand variations
- SP 1.5 Monitor performance on the selected test processes

SG 2 Testing is Performed using Statistical Methods
- SP 2.1 Develop operational profiles
- SP 2.2 Generate and execute statistically selected test cases
- SP 2.3 Apply statistical test data to make stop-test decisions

Specific Practices by Goals

SG 1 Establish a Statistically Controlled Test Process

A statistically controlled test process is established whereby baselines that characterize the expected test process performance of the organization's standard test processes are established and maintained.

SP 1.1 Establish test process performance objectives

Establish and maintain quantitative objectives for test process performance.

Note this specific practice correlates to and builds upon the SP 1.1 Establish test measurement objectives of the Test Measurement process area at TMMi level 4.

Example work products

1. List of test processes identified for test process performance analysis
2. Quantitative objectives for the organization's test performance

Sub-practices

1. Study the business needs and objectives regarding product quality and test process performance
2. Study the test policy with respect to the defined test goals and test performance indicators
   Refer to the Test Policy and Strategy process area for more information on business needs and objectives, test goals and test performance indicators.
   Explicitly select test processes from the organization's set of standard test processes that are to be included in the set of statistically controlled test processes.
   Typically it will not be possible, useful, or economically justifiable to apply statistical management techniques to all test processes of the organization's standard set of test processes. Selection of the test processes is based on the needs and objectives of both the organization and projects.
3. Define the organization's quantitative objectives for test process performance in cooperation with relevant stakeholders
   Objectives may be established directly for test process measurements (e.g., test effort and defect removal effectiveness) or indirectly for product quality measurements (e.g., reliability) that are the result of the test process.
4. Define the priorities of the organization's quantitative objectives for test process performance in cooperation with relevant stakeholders, e.g., customers and end users
5. Resolve conflicts among the test process performance objectives (e.g., if one objective cannot be achieved without compromising another objective)
6. Revise the organization's quantitative objectives for test process performance as necessary

Examples of when the organization's quantitative objectives for test process performance may need to be revised include the following:

- Based on findings and recommendations from regular test process assessments. (Refer to the Test Organization process area at TMMi level 3 for more information on test process assessments. Note that at TMMi level 5 test process assessments, both formal and informal, are typically performed more frequently.)
- When the organization's business objectives change
- When the organization's (test) processes change
- When actual test process performance differs significantly from the objectives

SP 1.2 Establish test process performance measures

Establish and maintain definitions of measures that are to be included in the organization's test process performance analyses.

Refer to the Test Measurement process area at TMMi level 4 for more information about selecting and establishing measures, especially SP1.2 Specify test measures.

Example work products

1. Definitions for selected measures for test process performance

Sub-practices

1. Select measures that provide appropriate insight into the organization's test process performance
   Interim measures for each lifecycle phase may need to be selected, as appropriate, to monitor progress early toward achieving the objectives.
2. Identify measures that are appropriate for statistical management, e.g., those that are controllable
3. Review the set of test process performance measures for statistical management
4. Incorporate the selected measures into the organization's set of common test measures
5. Revise the set of test process performance measures as appropriate

SP 1.3 Establish test process performance baselines

Establish and maintain the organization's test process performance baselines.

The organization's test process performance baselines are a measurement of test performance for the organization's set of standard test processes at various levels of detail, as appropriate. There may be several test process performance baselines to characterize test performance for subgroups of the organization, e.g., application domains, complexity, project size and lifecycle models.

Example work products

1. Baseline data on test process performance

Sub-practices

1. Collect and analyze measurements from projects
   Refer to the Test Measurement and Analysis process area for more information on collecting and analyzing data.

2. Establish and maintain the organization's test process performance baselines from the collected measurements and analyses
   Test process performance baselines (possibly including minimum and maximum tolerances) are derived by analyzing the collected measures to establish a distribution and range of results that characterize the expected performance for selected test processes when used on an individual project in the organization.
3. Review the validity and get agreement with relevant stakeholders about the test process performance baselines
4. Make the test process performance baselines available across the organization
   The test process performance baselines are used by the projects to estimate the upper and lower boundaries for test process performance. (Refer to SP 1.4 Apply statistical methods and understand variations for more information on upper and lower boundaries of test process performance.)
5. Revise the set of test process performance baselines as appropriate

Examples of when the organization's test process performance baselines may need to be revised including the following:

- When the organization's business objectives change
- When the organization's (test) processes change
- When actual test process performance differs significantly from the baselines

SP 1.4 Apply statistical methods to understand variations

Establish and maintain an understanding of the performance variations of the selected test processes using the selected measures.

Understanding variation is achieved, in part, by collecting and analyzing measures so that (common) causes of variation can be identified and addressed to achieve predictable performance.

Example work products

1. Collected measures
2. Upper and lower boundaries of test process performance for each measured attribute of each selected test process
3. Test process performance compared to the upper and lower boundaries of test process performance for each measured attribute of each selected test process

Sub-practices

1. Establish trial upper and lower boundaries (control limits) for test process performance using suitable historical data
   Boundaries of an attribute are the range within which variation normally occurs. All processes will show some variation in measures each time they are executed. Generally control limits (upper and lower boundaries) are set to 2 or 3 sigma. Control limits may also be set to 1 sigma, which is the most restricted interval. The control limits help the Test Process Group to separate the signals from the noise. The variation of data points inside the control limits is due to noise in the process (common cause or normal variations).
2. Collect data, as defined by the selected measures, on the test processes as they execute
   Data is collected and validated from projects across the organization according to the selected procedures. The data is stored in the test measurement database.
3. Calculate the boundaries of test process performance for each measured attribute

   Examples of where boundariesare calculated include the following:
   - Control charts
   - Histograms
   - Run charts
   - Confidence intervals
   - Prediction intervals

4. Identify causes of variation
   The criteria for detecting causes of variation are based on statistical theory, e.g., 3-sigma control limits, experience, and economic justification. An important activity during the identification of causes of variation is to determine if a process variation is caused by special circumstances (an assignable or specific cause) which may be linked to a specific time or location, or by the variation inherent in the nature of the process itself (common or natural cause). In general it is recommended to first solve assignable causes, since these may partly decrease common causes.
5. Analyze the cause of test process variation to determine the reason the anomaly occurred

Examples of techniques for analyzing the reasons for causes of variation include the following:

- Cause and effect (fishbone) diagrams
- Designed experiments
- Control charts (applied to input or underlying test sub-processes)
- Subgrouping

Note that some anomalies may simply be extremes of underlying distribution rather than problems.

Refer to the Defect Prevention process area for more information about analyzing the cause of an anomaly.

6. Determine what corrective action should be taken when causes of variations are identified
   Refer to the Test Process Optimization process area for more information about taking corrective action.
7. Recalculate the upper and lower boundaries for each measured attribute of the selected test processes as necessary.
8. Record statistical management data in the organization's measurement repository
   Refer to the Test Measurement process area for more information about managing and storing data, measurement definitions, and results

SP 1.5 Monitor performance on the selected test processes

Monitor the performance of the selected test processes to determine their capability to satisfy their process performance objectives and to identify corrective actions as needed.

The intent of this specific practice is to determine statistically the process behavior expected from the process and appraise the probability that the process will meet its process performance objectives.

Example work products

1. The process capability for each test process
2. Boundaries of test process performance for each selected test process compared to its established objectives
3. For each test process, documentation of actions needed to address deficiencies in its process capability

Sub-practices

1. Compare the test process performance objectives to the boundaries of the measured attributes
   This comparison provides an appraisal of the test process capability for each measured attribute of a test process.
2. Periodically review the performance of each selected test process, its capability to be statistically managed and appraise progress towards achieving the test process performance objectives
3. Identify and document test process capability deficiencies
4. Determine and document actions needed to address test process capability deficiencies

SG 2 Testing is Performed using Statistical Methods

Tests are designed and executed using statistical methods based on operational or usage profiles.

SP 2.1 Develop operational profiles

Operational profiles (or usage models) are developed early in the development lifecycle to serve as a basis from which a statistically correct sample of test cases can be derived.

Example work products

1. Operational profile of the system to be tested

Sub-practices

1. Develop the customer profile
   A customer is the person, group or organization that is acquiring the product being developed. A customer group is the set of customers that will be using the product in the same way. The customer profile is the complete set of customer groups and their associated frequency distribution across the profile.
2. Develop the user profile
   The user profile is the complete set of user groups (the set of actual users that will engage the system in the same way) and their associated frequency distribution across the profile.
3. Develop the system mode profile
   The system mode profile is the set of system modes (a set of functions or operations grouped in order to analyze execution behavior) and their associated occurrence probabilities.
4. Develop the functional profile

The functional profile provides (per system mode) a quantitative view of the relative use of each of the different system functions.

5. Develop the operational profile
   An operation represents a task being accomplished by a system. A series of steps needs to be performed for developing the final operational profile using information from the profiles already developed, including the following [Musa]:
   - Dividing the execution into runs
   - Identifying the input space (a comprehensive list of input variables)
   - Partitioning the input space into operations
   - Determining the occurrence probability for operations
6. Review the operational profile with stakeholders
7. Revise the operational profile as appropriate

SP 2.2 Generate and execute statistically selected test cases

Test cases are generated based on statistically selected samples of the usage of the product, and subsequently executed.

Example work products

1. Test cases
2. Test results
3. Record of representativeness monitoring

Sub-practices

1. Select samples of the usage of the product based on the developed usage model or operational profile
2. Generate test cases based on the selected usage samples that are characteristic of the operational use of the product
   The generated test cases will reflect probabilities in the usage model or operational profile and represent a sample of the input space according to the usage patterns
3. Review the test cases with stakeholders
4. Execute the test cases and record actual results
5. Monitor that the test coverage is representative of the actual usage
   Testing will use tools and measurements to determine if testing is representative of actual use. Only when testing is satisfied that the tests are sufficient to simulate expected operation in the field, they can use the test results along with other data to help make stop-testing decisions.
6. Revise the test cases as appropriate when test coverage of actual usage is not adequate

7. Analyze and draw statistical conclusions from test results
   At this sub-practice the statistical sample is used to develop conclusions about the entire population of customers and uses. This will typically be done using reliability models. Typical issues to be addressed include:
   - How quickly is product quality improving?
   - Can testing be completed within the constraints associated with the project and test resources?

SP 2.3 Apply statistical test data to make stop-test decisions

Estimations are made regarding the reliability of the product and confidence level regarding product quality. These estimations are the basis for making stop-test decisions.

Example work products

1. Definition of severity levels of failures
2. Reliability and confidence goals
3. Reliability and confidence measures
4. Documented review results, e.g., minutes of the review meeting

Sub-practices

1. Establish levels of severity of failures
   It is important to identify different classes or levels of failure and consider how they should be treated when measuring the reliability of the product. Typically, reliability requirements are established for each failure level.
2. Define quantitative reliability goals to be used as exit criteria and to make stop-test decisions

Examples of types of reliability goals include the following:
- Reliability, expressed in terms such as Mean Time Between Failure (MTBF), Mean Time To Repair (MTTR) and Mean Time To Failure (MTTF)
- Availability
- Recoverability
- Trustworthiness
- Confidence level (in case confidence levels are used as a reliability goal, the technique of fault seeding will typically be applied as part of the statistical testing process).

3. Review the reliability goals with stakeholders
4. Select a suitable reliability growth model

Examples of types of reliability growth models include the following [Musa and Ackerman]:

- Static model, which is best applied to unchanging software with an unchanged operational profile
- Basic model, which is useful for modeling failure occurrences for software being tested and continuously debugged
- Logarithmic poisson model, which is best applied when it is assumed that some defects are more likely to cause failures, and that on average the improvement in failure intensity with each correction decreases exponentially as the corrections are made.

5. Collect statistical data on failures and program execution time
6. Calculate and estimate reliability measures using the reliability growth model by fitting the model to the collected data
7. Review the status regarding the reliability goals with stakeholders
8. Document the results of the reviews, action items and stop-test decisions

Generic Practices by Goals

GG 2 Institutionalize a Managed Process

GP 2.1 Establish an organizational policy

Establish and maintain an organizational policy for planning and performing the Quality Control process.

Elaboration

The policy states organizational objectives and expectations for establishing test process performance baselines for the organization's set of standard test processes and statistically managing selected test processes.

The Quality Control policy typically specifies:

- The project's measurements of test process performance are analyzed to establish and maintain a test process capability baseline for the organization's standard test process
- The test process capability baseline for the organization's standard test process is used by the projects in establishing their test process performance goals.
- Testing is performed statistically based on operational profiles with the objective to measure the reliability of the product.

GP 2.2 Plan the process

Establish and maintain the plan for performing the Quality Control process.

Elaboration

Typically, the plan for performing the process quality control activities is included in or referenced by the organization's test process improvement plan, which is described in the Test Organization process area, or may be documented in a separate plan that described only the Quality Control process.

The activities to perform statistical testing are typically included in the test plan. The test plan will address activities such as developing/modifying the operational profile, running the tests, and collecting, cataloging, and analyzing the reliability data.

GP 2.3 Provide resources

Provide adequate resources for performing the Quality Control process, developing the test work products, and providing the services of the process.

Elaboration

- Adequate time is provided to develop an operational profile and perform the statistical testing activities
- Special expertise in statistics and statistical process control may be needed to establish the process performance baselines for the organization's standard set of test processes and to define the techniques for statistical management on the selected test processes
- Special expertise in statistics may also be needed for analyzing and interpreting the measures resulting for statistical management
- An organization-wide test measurement program exists
- Tools to support the Quality Control process are available.

Examples of tools include the following:

- Database management tools
- Process modeling tools
- Statistical analysis packages
- Incident management tools
- Coverage tools
- Statistical process and quality control packages
- Reliability measurement tools

GP 2.4 Assign responsibilities

Assign responsibility and authority for performing the Quality Control process, developing the work products, and providing the services of the Quality Control process.

Elaboration

Many groups must work together to achieve the goals of test process quality control. A Test Process Group is suggested as the umbrella organization for putting the process control team together. Team participants may be selected from various functional units, e.g., development, test and quality assurance. Both management and staff should participate.

GP 2.5 Train people

Train the people performing or supporting the Quality Control process as needed.

Elaboration

Examples of training topics include the following:

- Process modeling and analysis
- Process measurement data selection, definition, collection and validation
- Statistical process control
- Statistical methods and techniques (e.g., control charts, scatter diagrams and Pareto analysis)
- Statistical testing
- Usage models and operational profiles
- Reliability management (e.g., reliability models, measurements and reliability growth models)

GP 2.6 Manage configurations

Place selected work products of the Quality Control process under appropriate levels of configuration control.

Elaboration

Examples of work products placed under configuration management include the following:

- Organization's test process performance objectives
- Definitions of selected measures of test process performance, including their collection points in the processes and how the integrity of the measures will be determined
- Baseline data on the organization's test process performance
- Collected measures from projects
- Operational profiles
- Set of generated test cases

GP 2.7 Identify and involve relevant stakeholders

Identify and involve relevant stakeholders of the Quality Control process as planned.

Elaboration

Examples of stakeholder involvement include the following:

- Establishing the organization's test process performance objectives and their priorities
- Reviewing and resolving issues among the organization's test process performance objectives
- Appraising performance of the selected test processes
- Identifying what corrective action should be taken
- Defining the operational profiles
- Reviewing test results
- Making stop-test decisions

GP 2.8 Monitor and control the process

Monitor and control the Quality Control process against the plan for performing the process and take appropriate actions.

Elaboration

Examples of measures used in monitoring and controlling the Quality Control process include the following:

- Trends in the organization's test process performance with respect to changes in work products and task attributes (e.g., test effort, lead time and product quality)
- Profile of test processes under statistical management (e.g., number planned to be under statistical management, number currently being statistically managed, and number that are statistically stable)
- Number of causes of variation identified and resolved
- The degree to which actual testing experiences has become a good representative of expected usage
- Reliability trends

GP 2.9 Objectively evaluate adherence

Objectively evaluate adherence of the Quality Control process and selected work products against its process description, standards, and procedures, and address any areas of non-compliance.

Elaboration

Examples of review and/or audit topics for evaluation and adherence include the following:

- Establishing test process performance baselines
- Organization's test process performance objectives
- Definitions of the selected measures of test process performance
- Statistically managing selected test processes
- Collected measures
- The effectiveness and efficiency of statistical testing

GP 2.10 Review status with higher level management

Review the activities, status and results of Quality Control process with higher level management and resolve issues.

GG 3 Institutionalize a Defined Process

GP 3.1 Establish a defined process

Establish and maintain a description of a defined Quality Control process

GP 3.2 Collect improvement information

Collect process-related experiences derived from planning and performing the Quality Control process to support the future use and improvement of the organization's processes and process assets.

Elaboration

Examples of measures include the following:

- Upper and lower boundaries for defect density
- Review effort as a percentage of total development effort
- Test effort as a percentage of total development effort
- Coverage achieved
- Effectiveness of statistical testing, e.g., using Defect Detection Percentage (DDP)

Process Area 5.3 Test Process Optimization

Purpose

The purpose of Test Process Optimization is to continuously improve the existing testing processes used in the organization and to identify new testing technologies (e.g., test tools or test methods) that may be appropriate and to transition them into the organization in an orderly manner. Test Process Optimization also supports the re-use of test assets across the organization. The improvements support the organization's product quality and test process performance objectives as derived from the organization's business objectives.

Introductory Notes

At the highest level of the TMMi, the test process is subject to continuous improvement across projects and across the entire organization. The test process is quantified and can be fine-tuned in order for capability growth to become an ongoing process. An organizational infrastructure exists to support this continuous growth. This infrastructure, which consists of policies, standards, training facilities, tools and organizational structures, has been put in place through goal achievement processes that constitute the TMMi hierarchy. Test Process Optimization is in essence about developing a system to continuously improve testing. Optimizing the test process involves the following:

- Establishing test process assessment and improvement procedures with responsibilities assigned from a leadership perspective
- Identifying testing practices that are weak and those that are strong and suggesting areas for process asset extraction and re-use
- Deploying incremental and innovative improvements that measurably improve the organization's test processes and technologies
- Selecting and providing best practices to the organization
- Continuously evaluating new test-related tools and technologies for adaptation
- Supporting technology and knowledge transfer
- Re-use of high quality test assets.

Continuously improving the testing process involves proactively and systematically identifying, evaluating and implementing improvements to the organization's standard test process and the projects' defined processes on a continuous basis. Test process improvement activities are often also needed as a result of a changing environment, e.g., the business context, the test environment itself or a new development lifecycle. All of this is done with higher-level management sponsorship. Training and incentive programs are established to enable and encourage everyone in the organization to participate in test process improvement activities. Test improvement opportunities are identified and evaluated for potential return on investment to the organization using business goals and objectives as a point of reference. Pilots are performed to assess, measure and validate the test process changes before they are incorporated into organization's standard process.

To support Test Process Optimization the organization typically has established a group, e.g., a Test Process Group, that works with projects to introduce and evaluate the effectiveness of new testing technologies (e.g., test tools, test methods, and test environments) and to manage changes to existing testing technologies. Particular emphasis is placed on technology changes that are likely to improve the capability of the organization's standard test process (as established in the Test Lifecycle and Integration process). By maintaining an awareness of test-related technology innovations and systematically evaluating and experimenting with them, the organization selects appropriate testing technologies to improve the quality of its products and the productivity of its testing activities. Pilots are performed to assess new and unproven testing technologies before they are incorporated into standard practice.

Organizations now fully realize that both test processes and testware are corporate assets and that those of high quality should be documented and stored in a process repository in a format that is modifiable for re-use in future projects. Such a repository, possibly already established in a less mature format at TMMi level 3, is often called a test process asset library. At TMMi level 3 some informal re-use of testware across projects may already take place; however, re-use of test assets become a major goal at TMMi level 5. Note that test process re-use in this context means the use of one test process description to create another test process description.

Scope

The process area Test Process Optimization addresses the practices for continuously identifying test process improvements, evaluating and selecting new testing technologies and deploying them in the organization's standard test process, including planning, establishing, monitoring, evaluating and measuring the test improvement actions. It also covers the re-use of high quality test assets across the organization. This process area complements and extends the processes and practices defined by the Test Organization and Test Lifecycle and Integration process areas at TMMi level 3.

Specific Goal and Practice Summary

SG 1 Select Test Process Improvements

SP 1.1 Collect and analyze test process improvement proposals

SP 1.2 Pilot test process improvement proposals
SP 1.3 Select test process improvement proposals for deployment

SG 2 New Testing Technologies are Evaluated to Determine their Impact on the Testing Process
SP 2.1 Identify and analyze new testing technologies
SP 2.2 Pilot new testing technologies
SP 2.3 Select new testing technologies for deployment

SG 3 Deploy Test Improvements
SP 3.1 Plan the deployment
SP 3.2 Manage the deployment
SP 3.3 Measure improvement effects

SG 4 Establish Re-use of High Qquality Test Process Assets
SP 4.1 Identify re-usable test assets
SP 4.2 Select test assets to be added to the re-use library
SP 4.3 Deploy re-usable test assets
SP 4.4 Apply re-usable test assets in projects

Specific Practices by Goals

SG 1 Select Test Process Improvements

Test process improvements are selected which contribute to meeting product quality and test process performance objectives.

SP 1.1 Collect and analyze test process improvement proposals

Continuously collect and analyze proposals for improvements to the organization's standard test process.

The specific practice, Collect and analyze test process improvements, analyzes proposals that are internally collected. Refer to SP 2.1 Identify and analyze new testing technologies for a specific practice that actively searches externally for innovative and new testing technologies.

Example work products

1. Analyzed test process improvement proposals
2. List of test process improvement proposals to be piloted

Sub-practices

1. Collect test process improvement proposals
   A test process improvement proposal documents proposed improvements to a specific test process.

Examples of sources for test process improvement proposals include the following:

- Findings and recommendations from regular test process assessments (Refer to the Test Organization process area at TMMi level 3 for more information on test process assessments. Note that at TMMi level 5 test process assessments, both formal and informal, are typically performed more frequently.
- Analysis of data about customer/end user problems as well as customer/end user satisfaction
- Analysis of data about product quality and test process performance compared to the objectives
- Analysis of data to determine common defect causes, e.g., from Defect Prevention
- Operational product data
- Measured effectiveness and efficiency of test process activities
- Lessons learned documents (e.g., test evaluation reports)
- Spontaneous ideas from managers and staff
- Project retrospective meetings
- Test tool evaluations (Test tools are regularly evaluated regarding achieving their defined objectives.)

Refer to the Test Organization process area for more information about test process improvement proposals.

2. Analyze the costs and benefits of test process improvement proposals as appropriate

   Test process improvement proposals that do not have an expected positive return on investment are rejected.

Examples of criteria for evaluating costs and benefits include the following:

- Contribution towards meeting the organization's product quality and test process performance objectives
- Effect on mitigating identified test project and product risks
- Ability to respond quickly to changing circumstances
- Effect on related (test) processes and associated assets
- Cost of defining and collecting data that supports the measurement and analysis of the test process proposal
- Expected life span of the results of implementing the proposal

3. Analyze the project risks of test process improvement proposals

Examples of risk factors that affect the deployment of process improvements include the following:

- Complexity of the improvement
- Skills of potential users
- Multiple changes at the same time
- Unclear picture of expectations
- Lack of short-term benefits and visible successes
- Impact of the proposal not, or not completely, being implemented

4. Estimate the costs, effort and schedule required for deploying each process improvement proposal
5. Identify the process improvement proposal to be piloted prior to organization-wide deployment
   Alternatives to piloting are considered as appropriate e.g., controlled experiments, simulations, case studies.
6. Document the results of the evaluation of each process improvement proposal

SP 1.2 Pilot test process improvement proposals

Pilot test process improvements to select which ones to implement.

Pilots are performed to assess new and unproven major changes before they are organization-wide deployed, as appropriate.

Example work products

1. Pilot evaluation reports

Sub-practices

1. Plan the test process improvement pilots
2. Define pilot objectives and results evaluation criteria
3. Review the pilot plans and get stakeholder agreement
4. Coach and support the people performing the pilots
5. Perform each pilot in an environment that is sufficiently representative of the environment in which the test process improvement eventually will be deployed
6. Track the pilots against their plans
7. Review and document the results of each pilot
   Reviewing and documenting the results of the pilot usually involves the following:
   - Deciding whether to terminate the pilot, re-plan and continue the pilot, or proceed with deploying the test process improvement
   - Updating the disposition of the test process improvement proposal associated with the pilot

- Identifying and updating new test process improvement proposals as appropriate
- Identifying and documenting lessons learned and problems encountered during the pilot.

SP 1.3 Select test process improvements for deployment

Select test process improvement proposals for deployment across the organization.

A selection is made of test process improvement proposals for deployment across the organization based on quantifiable criteria derived from the organization's test process performance objectives.

Example work products

1. Test process improvement proposals selected for deployment
2. Selection process results documentation (including rationale for decisions made)

Sub-practices

1. Prioritize the candidate test process improvements for deployment
   Priority is based on an evaluation of the estimated return on investment with regard to the test process performance objectives.
   Refer to the Quality Control process area for more information about the test process performance objectives.

> *Examples of criteria to be used during the prioritization include the following:*
>
> - Contribution to meeting test performance objectives
> - Alignment with maturity model (e.g., trying to formally achieve a maturity level)
> - Visibility of improvement proposal
> - Cost of improvement proposal
> - Ease of implementation of improvement proposal
> - Expected acceptance of improvement proposal (some may cause severe resistance initially)
> - Risk mitigation as a result of implementing the improvement proposal

2. Select the test process improvement(s) to be deployed
   The selection of test process improvements is based on their priorities and the available resources.

3. Determine the approach for each test process improvement that will be deployed

Examples of topics to be addressed as part of the deployment approach include the following:

- Organizational test process assets affected
- All or a subset of the organization's projects
- All or a subset of the organization's applications

4. Document the results of the selection process

SG 2 New Testing Technologies are Evaluated to Determine their Impact on the Testing Process

New testing technologies such as tools, methods, techniques or technical innovations are identified, selected and evaluated to determine their effect on the organization's standard test process.

SP 2.1 Identify and analyze new testing technologies

Continuously identify and analyze innovative and new testing technologies, e.g., new test tools or methods, which could increase the quality and performance of the organization's standard test process.

The specific practice, SP 1.1 Collect and analyze test process improvements, analyzes proposals that are collected internally. The purpose of the specific practice SP 2.1 is to actively search externally for innovative and new testing technologies.

Example work products

1. New testing technology candidates
2. Analyzed new testing technologies
3. Test improvement proposals
4. List of testing technologies to be piloted

Sub-practices

1. Continuously investigate innovative and new testing technologies

Examples of investigative activities include the following:

- Systematically maintaining awareness of leading technical work and trends, e.g., by visiting conferences, attending webinars and studying literature
- Periodically searching for commercially available innovative and new testing technologies
- Studying new testing standards for their applicability in the organization
- Systematically reviewing test processes, tools and methods used externally and comparing them to those used within the organization
- Benchmarking test process performance against industry performance data
- Reviewing examples of test process improvements that were successfully adopted elsewhere
- Participating in special interest groups in testing
- Collaborating with other improvement initiatives in the organization to find opportunities that could be beneficial to testing as well

2. Analyze potential innovative and new testing technologies, e.g., new test tools or methods, to understand their effects on test process elements and to predict their influence on the process

   As part of the analysis consider constraints, prioritization of possible features, hardware/software issues, suppliers' track records, suppliers' presentations, and integration with existing technologies and processes.

3. Analyze the costs and benefits of potential new testing technologies

   Test process improvement proposals that do not have an expected positive return on investment are rejected. A major criterion is the expected contribution of the new testing technology toward meeting the organization's product quality and test process performance objectives.

   Both short term and long term recurring (maintenance) costs should be taken into account and also the compliance of the new testing technology with the test policy.

   As part of this sub-practice, alternative solutions, e.g., a test process change, whichprovide the same benefits but at lower costs, also are considered.

4. Create an improvement proposal for those new testing technologies that could result in improving the organization's way of working

As part of the improvement proposal estimate the cost, effort and schedule required for deploying the new testing technology.

5. Identify the new testing technologies to be piloted before organization-wide deployment
   Alternatives to piloting are considered, e.g., controlled experiments, simulations, case studies.
6. Document the results of the evaluation of each new testing technology

SP 2.2 Pilot new testing technologies

Pilot new testing technologies to select which ones to implement.

Pilots are performed to assess new, unproven testing technologies, especially those that have a major impact before they are organization-wide deployed.

Example work products

1. Pilot evaluation reports

Sub-practices

1. Plan the testing technology pilots
2. Define pilot results evaluation criteria

Sub-practices

1. Plan the pilots of the new testing technologies
2. Define pilot objectives and results evaluation criteria
3. Review the pilot plans and get stakeholder agreement
4. Coach and support the people performing the pilots
   Coaching and support can be performed by internal test consultants, possibly with support of an external supplier.
5. Perform each pilot in a environment that is sufficiently representative of the environment in which the new testing technology will be deployed
   Allow for additional resources for the pilot project, as necessary.
6. Track the pilots against their plans
7. Review and document the results of the pilots
   Refer to SP 1.2 Pilot test process improvement proposals for more details on this sub-practice.

SP 2.3 Select new testing technologies for deployment

Select new testing technologies for deployment across the organization.

A selection is made of new testing technologies for deployment across the organization based on quantifiable criteria derived from the organization's test process performance objectives.

Example work products

1. New testing technologies selected for deployment
2. Selection process results documentation

Sub-practices

1. Prioritize the candidate new testing technologies for deployment
   Priority is based on an evaluation of the estimated return on investment with regard to the test process performance objectives.
   Refer to the Quality Control process area for more information about the test process performance objectives.

Examples of criteria to be used during the prioritization include the following:

- Contribution to meeting test performance objectives
- Alignment with maturity model (e.g., trying to formally achieve a maturity level)
- Visibility of testing technologies
- Cost of testing technologies
- Ease of implementation of testing technologies
- Expected acceptance of testing technologies (some may cause severe resistance initially)
- Risk mitigation as a result of implementing the testing technologies

2. Select the testing technologies to be deployed
   The selection of the new testing technologies is based on their priorities and the available resources.
3. Determine the approach for each new testing technology that will be deployed

Examples of topics to be addressed as part of the deployment approach include the following:

- Organizational test process assets affected
- All or a subset of the organization's projects
- All or a subset of the organization's applications
- Incremental or single deployment; note that in general an incremental approach is preferred
- Comprehensiveness of consulting and support to projects and organizational groups

4. Document the results of the selection process

SG 3 Deploy Test Improvements

Test process improvements and appropriate new testing technologies are deployed across the organization to improve the testing process.

Their benefits are measured and information about new innovations is disseminated across the organization.

SP 3.1 Plan the deployment

Establish and maintain the plans for deploying the selected test process and testing technology improvements.

This specific practice addresses the planning of the deployment of individual test process and testing technology improvements. The generic practice GP 2.2 Plan for Process addresses a comprehensive planning that covers all practices in this process area.

Example work products

1. Deployment plan(s)

Sub-practices

1. Determine the changes necessary to deploy each test process and testing technology improvement

> *Examples of changes needed to deploy a test process and testing technology improvement include the following:*
>
> - Test process descriptions, standards and procedures
> - Test environments
> - Education, training and skill development
> - Existing management commitments
> - Existing testing activities in projects

2. Identify approaches to address potential problems to deploying each test process and testing technology improvement
   When defining the plan, changes and stability for the organization and project must be carefully balanced. The lifecycle model being used (e.g., sequential, iterative, agile) will influence the frequency cycle for changes in process that will be acceptable to projects.
3. Determine change management activities that are required to successfully deploy the test improvements

Examples of change management activities include the following:

- Presentation to stakeholders
- Kick-off with all parties involved
- Discussion sessions
- Publications, e.g., for information purposes and on successes achieved
- Recognition awards

4. Establish measures and objectives for determining the value of each test process and testing technology improvement with respect to the organization's test performance objectives

Examples of measures for determining the value of a test process and testing technology improvement include the following:

- Return on investment
- Payback period
- Measured improvement to product quality
- Measured improvement in the project's test process performance
- Number and type of project and product risks mitigated

Refer to the Test Measurement process area for more information on establishing measures and the measurement and analysis process.

5. Document the plan for deploying each test process and testing technology improvement
6. Review and get agreement with relevant stakeholders on the plan for deploying each test process and testing technology improvement
7. Revise the plan for deploying each test process and testing technology improvement as necessary

SP 3.2 Manage the deployment

Manage the deployment of the selected test process and testing technology improvements.

Example work products

1. (Updated) training materials
2. Documented results of deployment activities
3. Revised test process and testing technology improvement measures, objectives, priorities and deployment plans

Sub-practices

1. Monitor the deployment of the test process and testing technology improvements using the deployment plan
2. Coordinate the deployment of test process and testing technology improvements across the organization and within projects
   As part of the coordination activities the deployment team is assembled, which typically includes a management sponsor.
3. Incorporate the test process and testing technology improvements into organizational test process assets, as appropriate
   Refer to the Test Lifecycle and Integration process area at TMMi level 3 for more information about organization test process assets.
4. Provide consulting, as appropriate, to support deployment of the test process and testing technology improvements
5. Provide (updated) training material and perform the training as planned
   Refer to the Test Training Program process area at TMMi level 3 for more information about training and training materials.
6. Perform marketing inside and outside testing regarding deployment successes achieved to keep staffing motivated and involved and to decrease resistance
7. Confirm that the deployment of all test process and testing technology improvements is completed
8. Determine whether the ability of the defined test process to meet test process performance objectives is adversely affected by the test process and testing technology improvement, and take corrective action as necessary.
9. Document and review the results of test process and testing technology improvements deployment.
   Documenting and reviewing the results of the test process and testing technology improvement deployment usually involves the following:
   - Identifying and documenting lessons learned and problems encountered during the deployment
   - Identifying and documenting new test process and testing technology improvement proposals
   - Revising test process and testing technology improvement measures, objectives, priorities and deployment plans.

SP 3.3 Measure improvement effects

Measure the effect of deployed test process and testing technology improvements.

Refer to the Test Measurement process area for more information on establishing measures, the measurement and analysis process, and reporting results.

Example work products

1. Documented measures of the effects of the deployed test process and testing technology improvements

Sub-practices

1. Measure the actual cost, effort and schedule for deploying each test process and testing technology improvement
2. Measure the value of each test process and testing technology improvement
3. Measure the progress toward achieving the organization's test process performance objectives
4. Analyze the progress toward achieving the organization's test process performance objectives and take corrective action as needed
   Refer to the Quality Control process area for more information about test process performance analysis.
5. Store measures in the organization's test measurement repository

SG 4 Establish Re-use of High Quality Test Assets

Both test process components and testware are recognized as assets and re-used across the organization when creating another test asset.

SP 4.1 Identify re-usable test assets

Test assets (test process components or testware) of high quality that can possibly be re-used throughout the organization are identified.

Example work products

1. List of identified test assets for re-use

Sub-practices

1. Identify test assets for re-use evaluation

Examples of activities where test assets for re-use can be identified include the following:

- Project retrospectives / lessons learned sessions
- Test evaluation report
- Test process assessments, whereby areas of strength often indicate test process components and/or testware of high quality that are candidates for re-use
- Test improvement efforts

2. Document the background and context for each of the identified test assets for re-use
3. Submit re-use proposals to the Test Process Group

SP 4.2 Select test assets to be added to the re-use library

From the list of identified test assets for re-use, the test assets are selected that will be added to the re-use library.

A selection is made of test assets for re-use across the organization based on quantifiable criteria derived from the organization's test re-use policy.

Example work products

1. Test assets selected for re-use

Sub-practices

1. Prioritize the candidate test assets for re-use
   Priority is based on an evaluation of the added value with regard to the test process performance objectives and the organization's test re-use policy.
2. Analyze the candidate test assets for re-use
   The candidate test assets for re-use are analyzed for their compliance to the re-use criteria.

Examples of re-use criteria for test assets include the following:

- The test asset should be defined and documented according to the organizational standards
- The test asset should be easy to understand and implement
- The test asset, especially test process components, should have associated measurements available
- The test asset should have been carefully reviewed and successfully applied to ensure that it has been adequately tested
- Test process-related risk should be evaluated and documented
- The test asset, especially test process components, should have a well-defined interface to other related processes
- The test asset should be flexible and modifiable so it can be applied to different projects

3. Select the re-usable test assets to be deployed
   The selection of re-usable test assets is based on their priorities, the available resources and their compliance to the re-use criteria.
4. Document the results of the selection process and inform the stakeholders of the decision(s) made

SP 4.3 Deploy re-usable test assets

Manage and perform the deployment of the selected re-usable test assets, being either test process components or testware.

Example work products

1. Updated test process library
2. Re-usable test asset
3. Documented results of deployment activities

Sub-practices

1. Incorporate the selected re-usable test assets into the organizational test process assets library, as appropriate
   Work will typically need to be performed to make the test asset suitable for inclusion in the test process asset library (refer to the list of re-use criteria in the previous specific practice). To support re-use, each test asset meeting the re-use criteria should be represented by a template. The template should contain information that allows the test asset to be tailored for specific projects.

Examples of components for a re-use template include the following [Hollenbach and Frakes]:

- Test asset name
- General information
- Customer description
- Interface description
- Procedure description
- Context description
- Measurement description

Refer to the Test Organization process area for more information about the test process asset library.

2. Review and test the defined re-usable test asset to ensure it is fit for re-use
3. Disseminate the re-usable test assets across the organization and within projects

Examples of dissemination mechanisms include the following:

- Presenting in project and/or departmental meeting
- Submitting an informational email or general periodic newsletter
- Making it part of a introduction training program on the test process asset library
- Communicating and providing access to it on a central web portal

4. Provide consulting, as appropriate, to support deployment of the new or updated re-usable test assets
5. Provide (updated) training material and perform the training as necessary
6. Perform marketing inside and outside testing on successes achieved on the re-use process to keep staffing motivated and involved
7. Document and review the results of test asset re-use deployment

SP 4.4 Apply re-usable test assets in projects

Defined re-usable test assets stored in the test process asset library are applied and used in projects.

Example work products

1. Records of tailoring and using re-usable test assets in projects
2. Measurements on usage of re-usable test assets
3. Refined re-usable test assets

Sub-practices

1. Tailor the re-usable test asset to the project
   Tailoring consists of selecting and retrieving a suitable test asset (as a template from the test process asset library) and applying it to a new project. Changes may be needed to meet the requirements and environment of the new project.
2. Train the project staff
   The generic training package on the test asset is tailored to meet the specific project needs. The training package is used to instruct project staff.
3. Use the test asset on a project
   The (tailored) test asset is implemented (used) for the project. It is monitored and controlled using appropriate mechanisms. Measurements are taken during test process execution regarding the test asset.
4. Refine the re-usable test asset
   Using the measurements taken during process execution, it is determined whether the re-use of the test asset is efficient and effective. If there are issues, these are analyzed. Appropriate changes are made to the test asset definition.

Generic Practices by Goals

GG 2 Institutionalize a Managed Process

GP 2.1 Establish an organizational policy

Establish and maintain an organizational policy for planning and performing the Test Process Optimization process.

Elaboration

The Test Process Optimization policy typically specifies:

- Improving the testing process is performed on a continuous basis
- Defect prevention and Quality Control are performed to optimize the testing process
- Quantitative goals are defined for the test improvements, test process performance and the re-use of test assets
- Progress is measured based on the defined quantitative goals
- Objectives for testing technology transfer
- The test process improvements are coordinated by a test process group
- The role of formal and informal assessment in test process improvement

- All of the organization's test staff and managers are expected to participate in improving the test processes
- Test assets are identified for re-use, as appropriate
- Test assets are re-used in test process engineering and projects

GP 2.2 Plan the process

Establish and maintain the plan for performing the Test Process Optimization process.

Elaboration

The plan called for in this generic practice addresses the comprehensive organizational planning for all of the specific practices in this process area required to achieve the specific goals. The plan will cover collecting and analyzing improvement proposals all the way through measurement of improvement effects and performing the re-use process on test assets. The plan undergoes peer review and is reviewed by the affected managers.

The deployment plans are part of the specific practices within this process area and not the plan referred to by this generic practice.

GP 2.3 Provide resources

Provide adequate resources for performing the Test Process Optimization process, developing the test work products, and providing the services of the process.

Elaboration

- An annual budget is available for test process improvement activities, including assessments, deployment and the investigation and analysis activities for new testing technologies.
- Administrative and human resources functions are established and allocated to establish, operate and conduct the communications, motivation, and recognition activities needed to maintain a high level of employee involvement and satisfaction.
- Appropriate facilities and tools are made available to perform the Test Process Optimization activities, e.g., prototyping tools, simulation packages, process modeling tools, statistical packages and test process asset library.
- Individuals with in-depth expertise in test process improvement, re-use strategies and process optimization are available.

- An annual budget is available for the re-use activities on test assets.

GP 2.4 Assign responsibilities

Assign responsibility and authority for performing the Test Process Optimization process, developing the work products, and providing the services of the Test Process Optimization process.

Elaboration

A test process group is typically designated to be responsible for managing the test process with full support of management. Management now fully understands the value of process change and improvement and is therefore willing to invest in a high quality test process group. Testers and test teams are responsible for providing continuous feedback on the test processes and technologies they are using. Test process improvement and optimization is every tester's responsibility.

Examples of test process group responsibilities to be assigned include the following:

- Defining organizational goals and measurement plans for test process performance and reviewing these with senior management for their endorsement
- Defining test processes
- Controlling the quality of test processes
- Managing test process changes, e.g., defining and maintaining the procedures for handling test process improvement proposals and reviews, reviewing test process improvement proposals and coordinating the actions for these proposals
- Managing the defect prevention process
- Testing technology transfer
- Evaluating test processes
- Participating in the effort to define the organization's training needs for test process improvement and test asset re-use and supporting the development and presentation of training course material
- Identifying re-usable test assets
- Maintaining the test process asset library
- Conducting test process
- Participating in and communicating improvement initiatives from other groups within the organization

GP 2.5 Train people

Train the people performing or supporting the Test Process Optimization process as needed.

Elaboration

Examples of training topics include the following:

- Test process improvement
- Planning, designing and conducting pilots
- Test process assessments
- Cost/benefit analysis
- Tool selection and implementation process
- Process analysis and modeling
- Deployment strategies
- Technology transfer
- Change management
- Team building
- Re-use strategies and processes

GP 2.6 Manage configurations

Place selected work products of the Test Process Optimization process under appropriate levels of configuration control.

Elaboration

Examples of work products placed under configuration management include the following:

- Test process improvement proposals and their analysis
- Documented lessons learned from pilots
- Test improvement plans
- Deployment plans
- Training material
- Test process and testing technology improvement measures
- Updated set of the organization's standard test processes
- Re-usable test process components
- Re-usable testware

GP 2.7 Identify and involve relevant stakeholders

Identify and involve relevant stakeholders of the Test Process Optimization process as planned.

Elaboration

Examples of stakeholder involvement include the following:

- Engaging senior management for addressing commitment to a test process group, setting long-term goals, and providing the resources for test process improvement, testing technology transfer and test asset re-use
- Reviewing test process and testing technology improvement proposals with senior management, specific user roles and those with technical interest perspectives
- Providing feedback on the status and results of the deployment activities, including testing technology transfer, to senior management as well as operational stakeholders
- Disseminating information on new testing technologies

GP 2.8 Monitor and control the process

Monitor and control the Test Process Optimization process against the plan for performing the process and take appropriate actions as needed.

Elaboration

Examples of measures used to monitor and control the Test Process Optimization include the following:

- Number of test process improvements selected and deployed
- Number of technology innovations identified and deployed
- Effort and other resources spent, e.g., on establishing deployment plans
- Change in product quality
- Change in test process performance

GP 2.9 Objectively evaluate adherence

Objectively evaluate adherence of the Test Process Optimization process and selected work products against the process description, standards, and procedures, and address any areas of non-compliance.

Elaboration

Examples of review and/or audit topics for evaluation and adherence include the following:

- The process for determining test improvement opportunities
- Planning and coordinating test improvements
- The process for selecting, procuring and deploying new testing technologies
- Test improvement plans
- Test process assessments
- Deployment plans
- Testing technology transfer process
- Measurements on the effects of test improvements
- Measurements on the re-use of test assets

GP 2.10 Review status with higher level management

Review the activities, status and results of the Test Process Optimization process with higher level management and resolve issues.

Elaboration

Examples of issues to be reviewed with higher level management include the following:

- Status of improvements being developed by action teams
- Results of pilots and deployments
- Measurements on test process performance
- Effort and other resources spent compared to plan
- Status regarding the achievement of major milestones, e.g., readiness for a formal assessment
- Necessary strategy changes
- Testing technology transfer program
- Test assets re-use program

GG 3 Institutionalize a Defined Process

GP 3.1 Establish a defined process

Establish and maintain a description of a defined Test Process Optimization process

GP 3.2 Collect improvement information

Collect process-related experiences derived from planning and performing the Test Process Optimization process to support the future use and improvement of the organization's processes and process assets.

Elaboration

Examples of measures include the following:

- The overall testing technology change activity, including number, type and size of changes
- The effect of implementing the testing technology change compared to the goals
- Effort/costs of test process adjustments (test process changes)
- Cost of test process improvement and optimization
- Cost to maintain the test process asset library
- Number of test assets being re-used
- Cost/effort associated with re-use of a test asset
- Cost/effort of maintaining a Test Process Group

Part 3

Annexes, Glossary and References

Annex A: TMMi Assessments and Certification

A.1 Assessments Overview

Many organizations find value in evaluating and/or benchmarking their progress in test process improvement for both internal purposes and for external customers and suppliers. Test process assessments focus on identifying improvement opportunities and understanding the organization's position relative to the selected model or standard. The TMMi model provides an excellent standard reference to be used during such assessments. Assessment teams evaluate organizational units against the requirements of the TMMi model and this evaluation guides the identification and prioritization of findings. These findings, along with the guidance of TMMi practices, can (and should) be used to plan improvements for the organization. The assessment framework (e.g., how to undertake assessments using the model) is not prescribed within the TMMi model. However, in order to use the model effectively, it should be used within an overall assessment framework which, in turn, should be part of the overall improvement process (see Annex B).

A.2 The Assessment Framework

The TMMi model is a definition of staged levels of capability of an organization's test and test-related quality processes as part of the overall system and software engineering processes. It is developed from a number of published sources as well as inputs from a wide range of practitioners across the globe and contains best practices, both current and emerging. It is intended to be generic enough to apply to all delivery models but specific enough to identify all expected testing practices. However, it is 'only' a reference framework and if assessments against the framework are of poor quality, then the results will be less effective. Further it does not provide a predefined solution; the optimal solution depends on the context of the organization and the interpretation of what is fit for purpose while also satisfying the requirements of the model. This is a key element in interpreting the model during the assessments.

When conducting assessments against the TMMi model, there is a need to develop/purchase and implement an assessment framework (robust method, skilled resources, tools, etc.) that can effectively and efficiently use the model to evaluate organizational process capabilities. A good assessment framework will deliver high quality outputs in a consistent, repeatable and comparable way. The outputs also must be easily understood and usable. This also includes the prime tenet of being able to assess an organization's capability through accurate interpretation of the model requirements based on the context of the organization (size, industry sector, development methodology, etc.) and being able to interpret the capability based on fitness for purpose.

An assessment can be formal (leading to certification) or informal (indicative information only). The section 'Assessment Types' below provides more detailed information on the various types of assessments. An assessment process consists of three elements to be used as appropriate depending on the assessment type:

1. A reference model (e.g., the TMMi) that every assessment will use to evaluate an organization's processes, procedures, activities and deliverables including the organizational levels of institutionalization, management, adherence and quality assurance.
2. An assessment method that contains the process flow, detailed procedures, tools, etc., that will ensure consistency and auditability during the assessment.
3. Trained and skilled assessor and lead assessor resources that are qualified to manage and all aspects of an assessment in accordance with the defined assessment method.

The first element is provided via the TMMi standard reference model. The following sections provide guidance on acquiring an accredited assessment method and developing accredited assessor resources as outlined by the TMMi Foundation. For more information on assessment methods and assessor resource accreditation by the TMMi Foundation, please visit their website.

A.3 A TAMAR Compliant Assessment Method

The TMMi Assessment Method Accreditation Requirements (TAMAR) for TMMi assessments are described by the TMMi Foundation in a separate document [TAMAR]. These requirements are based upon the ISO 15504 standard (TAMAR contains a complete table defining the correlation with this standard). The achievement of a specific maturity level must mean the same thing for different assessed organizations. Rules for ensuring this consistency of assessment are contained in the TAMAR. TAMAR also contains guidelines for different classes of assessments.

The requirements contained in TAMAR ensure that the assessment method is:

- *Performable* - The assessment can be performed in a manner that satisfies the objectives of the assessment and complies with the requirements of the TMMi Foundation
- *Repeatable* - The assessment provides consistent benchmarks e.g., if the appraisal was re-run by a different assessment team on the same data, the same results, strengths and weaknesses would be identified.

A.3.1 Assessment Types

The TAMAR defines the requirements for two types of assessments: informal and formal.

Informal Assessments

Informal assessments are indicative and have fewer requirements for compliance. This means they are often more flexible and cheaper to perform because the corroboration of evidence is not required, which significantly reduces the time it takes to perform the assessment. The additional flexibility of an informal assessment enables the organization to focus an assessment on a particular business unit. Informal assessments will provide only an indicative view of the organization's maturity and cannot lead to a formal maturity rating or certification. An informal assessment is often used to identify the major improvements that need to be made and it can also be used determine the progress of a TMMi implementation. An informal assessment is often adequate as an initial survey, although a formal assessment can also be used for this.

Formal Assessments

Formal assessments must conform to all the TAMAR requirements and must be led by a qualified Lead Assessor.

There are two mandated data sources: interviews and artifacts (documentary evidence). All interview data must be supported by corroborating artifacts. Artifacts are evidence which could include documents, templates, screen shots or similar. A formal assessment, if undertaken against an accredited assessment method, can lead to a formal maturity rating or certification.

A.3.2 What does the TAMAR cover?

The requirements of the TAMAR state that there are a number of activities within the following phases of an assessment and that the requirements must be demonstrated as being satisfied within the method definition..

Planning and Preparation

During the Planning and Preparation phase, all the activities that are required to be carried out prior to the assessment activity are performed. This includes the following:

- Agreeing on the objectives of the assessment
- Agreeing on the plan of activities and the deliverables
- Arranging interviews
- Preparing the assessment team and tools.

Data Collection

During the Data Collection phase, the assessment team conducts interviews and gathers information to support the interviews by means of artifacts, questionnaires or surveys. All data is collected, logged and stored according to the requirements for confidentiality and security.

Data Analysis and Reporting

During the Data Analysis and Reporting phase the gathered information is analyzed and the results are reported. The analysis covers the following:

- Identifying process strengths
- Identifying process weaknesses
- Conducting the ratings activities and determining the TMMi maturity rating
- Creating a process improvement plan if it is one of the objectives
- Returning the results of the assessment, against the plans and objectives, to the stakeholders.

Assessment Closure

The Closure phase occurs when the assessment is complete. The main activities are:

- Archiving all assessment data according to required confidentiality and security requirements
- Completing the Data Submission Report (see below).

A.3.3 Data Submission Report (DSR)

There is a requirement for the results of all assessments (formal and informal) to be documented and submitted to the TMMi Foundation. This is done by completing and submitting the DSR for every assessment conducted using an accredited assessment method. The Foundation has a governance role to play in ensuring that any TMMi assessments undertaken using accredited methods are following due diligence in doing the assessments. The TMMi Foundation reserves the right to audit any assessment either during or after completion to ensure adherence to the method. A key element of this is the DSR. DSR requirements can be found at the web site of the TMMi Foundation. The DSR provides specific requirements for the submission of the assessment results and the assessor activity data to the Foundation.

Assessment Data
The TMMi Foundation will use the assessment data to analyze market trends and industry level maturity. Sanitized data is sent to the Foundation who will then;

- Establish initial consistency and completeness of assessments
- Enable the Foundation to perform market research (on sanitized data)
- Enable the Foundation to verify formal assessment ratings and issue certificates as appropriate.

Assessor Data
Assessor reporting criteria is set out in the DSR Requirements. Each assessor is responsible for maintaining his or her individual logs which must be sent to the TMMi Foundation. This is necessary to demonstrate to the Foundation that assessors not only have acquired the required skills, experience and training to be accredited by the Foundation, but also maintain these skills.

A.3.4 Access to a TAMAR Accredited Method

The TMMi standard reference model is in the public domain and, as such, anyone can use the standard TMMi reference model as a basis for process improvement, evaluation and change. Although test consultants can undertake assessments and assessed organizations can publish the 'results', this is subject to interpretation since there is little governance concerning the assessment process and method used. Therefore, there is no guarantee that the model has been applied consistently through a pre-verified, robust assessment process and that the results are sound. The TMMi Foundation provides a framework to verify assessment methods. Once a method is accredited, then there is an independent validation that the assessment method is following a valid process according to published standards, is fully performable and repeatable and is auditable. Further, if an organization is assessed using an accredited assessment method, this provides the added levels of credibility and auditability, not to mention an 'independent badge of authenticity'!

There are two ways to gain access to an accredited method and become an accredited assessment provider. This can be done either by using the assessment method of the TMMi Foundation or developing one's own assessment method. A list of accredited methods and accredited assessment providers can be found at the web site of the TMMi Foundation. An independent Accreditation Panel within the TMMi Foundation manages accreditation of methods. An accreditation for a method is valid for three years after which the method is subject to re-accreditation.

TMMi Foundation Assessment Method
The Foundation has developed and made available its own assessment method. This has been independently verified as compliant with the requirements of TAMAR and is maintained by the TMMi Foundation. Organizations can use this method under license and can receive the following benefits:

- There is minimal investment to gain access to an accredited method.
- There is no research, development or maintenance costs or effort incurred by the assessment provider. This is all managed by the TMMi Foundation.
- The approved Assessor and Lead Assessor training is available through the TMMi Foundation.

Commercial Organization Owned Assessment Methods
Assessment providers can develop their assessment method packages and submit these to the TMMi Foundation to be accredited as compliant with the requirements defined in TAMAR. While the obvious benefit is that the assessment method is defined and controlled within the assessment provider and remains their proprietary property, the potential disadvantages are the effort and costs to develop, accredit and maintain the method package. These can be significant disadvantages. An additional benefit is that the assessment method will be tailored to the specific needs of the organization and possibly combined with other assessment practices within the organization (e.g., CMMI, ISO 9000, etc.).

A.4 Accredited Assessors and Lead Assessors

The previous section outlined the requirements of an assessment method and provided guidance on how to develop/license an accredited method to conduct TMMi assessments. The third requirement is to ensure that the assessment resources are suitably trained and skilled to conduct assessments in a consistent way and with a high degree of proficiency.

A.4.1 Assessor Accreditation Criteria

The TMMi Foundation manages a framework for evaluating and accrediting Assessors and Lead Assessors. If an assessment provider intends to conduct formal assessments leading to certification, then the assessment must be led by an accredited lead assessor and the assessment team must include at least one accredited assessor. It is important to note that Assessors and Lead Assessors will be accredited against an already accredited assessment method (TMMi Foundation or commercially owned). The requirements for accreditation of both roles and application forms can be found at the web site of the TMMi Foundation. The requirements are summarized as:

Assessor Accreditation Criteria		
Area of expertise	Lead assessor	Assessor
Testing	A minimum of five years of experience in different kinds of testing and in different types of organizations. Must be ISTQB Advanced certified.	A minimum of five years of experience in different kinds of testing and in different types of organizations. Must be ISTQB Foundation certified.
Test Process Improvement	A minimum of two years of test process improvement experience, in which two years of experience in software process improvement equals one year of experience in test process improvement.	A minimum of one year of test process improvement experience, in which two years of experience in software process improvement equals one year of experience in test process improvement.
TMMi	Holds TMMi Professional certificate or has proven experience using TMMi.	Holds TMMi Professional certificate or has proven experience using TMMi.
Assessments	Attended assessment training and has at least 20 days of assessment experience	Attended assessment training and has at least 10 days of assessment experience

Table A1: Assessor Accreditation Criteria

All applications are reviewed by an independent Accreditation Panel in the TMMi Foundation. If the requirements are satisifed the assessor will be accredited as demonstrating the experience, knowledge and training sufficient to conduct TMMi assessments using a prescribed, accredited method. The Accreditation Panel will take into consideration equivalent experience and/or qualifications. Assessor resource accreditation is valid for one year and renewable subject to demonstrating that the skills and experience are still current (e.g., contributing sufficient assessment hours/activities, etc.). All accredited assessor and lead assessor resources are listed on the website of the TMMi Foundation.

A.4.2 Training

The TMMi Foundation does not provide training on the structure, contents or interpretation of the TMMi model. However, they have published learning objectives under the title 'TMMi Professional – TMMi model training' which must be covered by any training received. Further, they publish training providers of TMMi model courses and will run independent examinations and provide certification for attendees that have passed the exam.

The TMMi Foundation does provide approved training courses for assessors and lead assessors using the Foundation-owned assessment method. If the assessment provider is using a proprietary, accredited method, they need to demonstrate adequate training has been provided to the satisfaction of the accreditation panel of the TMMi Foundation.

Annex B: The Improvement Process[1]

B.1 Introduction

Primarily, TMMi is a list of best practices or a description of a mature test process. TMMi does not offer a standard approach to a change program in an organization. To support the implementation of models such as CMMI, the Software Engineering Institute (SEI) has developed a model for change processes: IDEAL [IDEAL]. This model has been proven to be very useful when implementing TMMi. IDEAL offers an extensive and practical reference standard for change processes and also shows what needs to be done when implementing TMMi improvements in an organization. The model contains a five phase improvement cycle as shown below:

Acronym	Phase	Goal
I	Initiating	Establishing the initial improvement infrastructure for a successful improvement process.
D	Diagnosing	Determining the organization's current state as opposed to what it wants to achieve.
E	Establishing	Planning and specifying how the chosen situation will be established.
A	Acting	Executing the plan.
L	Learning	Learning by experience and improving the abilities to implement changes.

Table B.1: IDEAL five phase improvement cycle

Organizations are free to choose the improvement approach for the implementation of TMMi. In addition to IDEAL, there are several other models for the implementation of process improvement. In general these models are based on Edward Deming's plan-do-check-act cycle. The Deming cycle starts with making a plan that determines the improvement goals and how they will be achieved (plan). Then the improvements are implemented (do) and it is determined whether the planned advantages

1 The text in this annex is re-used with permission from chapter 5 of 'The Little TMMi' [Veenendaal and Cannegieter]

have been achieved (check). Based on the results of this assessment further actions are taken as needed (act).

This annex provides an overview of the phases and activities of the IDEAL improvement process.

B.2 The Change Program

The phases of an improvement program in accordance with IDEAL are shown in Figure B.1.

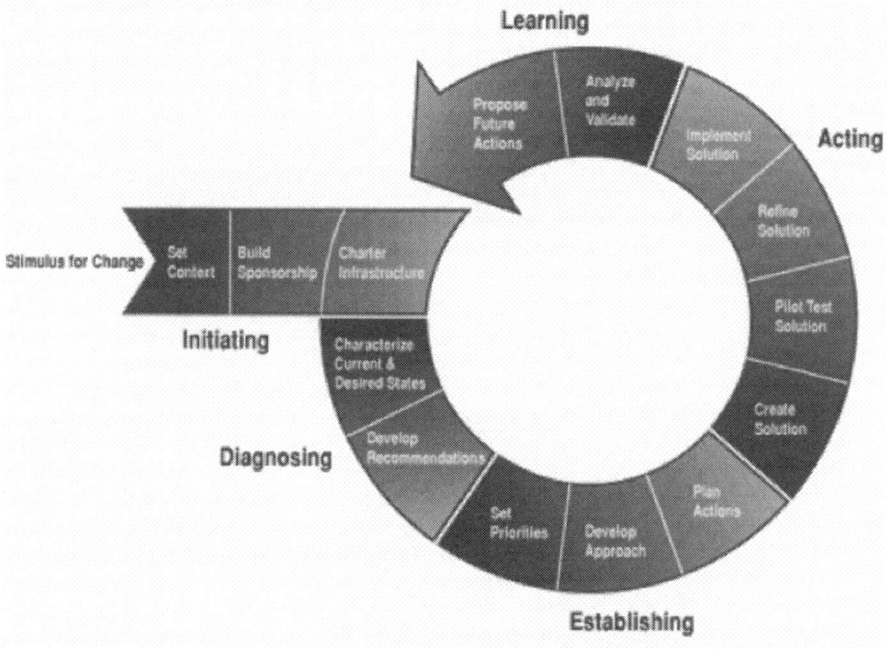

Figure B1: Phases of an improvement program in accordance with IDEAL [IDEAL]

The phases and activities are described briefly below.

B.2.1 I – Initiating: The Initiating Phase

In the Initiating phase the infrastructure for a successful change program is established. The goals and expected results with respect to the change and what needs to be contributed by the different parties concerned are defined. The goals of a TMMi implementation need to be in line with the quality goals and the organizational goals. In this phase the goals cannot always be formulated in a SMART (Specific, Measureable, Achievable,

Realistic and Time-based) way, which is why the goals are specified in more detail in the Establishing phase. In this phase, management commitment requires explicit attention; management commitment is needed from test management, ICT management and business management. The Initiating phase has the following activities:

- Identify Stimulus for Change
- Set Context
- Build Sponsorship
- Charter Infrastructure.

Identify Stimulus for Change

Before the actual change project is started, the organization needs to realize that change is necessary. This can be stimulated, for example, by dissatisfaction with the results of current testing, unexpected incidents, changing circumstances, a senior management initiative, a benchmark result, a TMMi assessment, customer demand, market trends or information taken from an internal measurement repository. The proposed change needs to contribute to the success of the organization and needs to complement the existing quality and organizational goals. The extent to which the change is in accordance with the organizational goals largely determines the success of the change.

Set Context

The management needs to determine how the change effort fits the quality and business strategy. Which specific organizational goals will be realized or supported by the TMMi implementation? How are current projects influenced by the improvement? Which proceeds need to be yielded, for example in terms of fewer issues and incidents or the shortening of the lead time for test execution? During the project, the context and effects will become more concrete, but it is important to be as clear as possible early in the project.

Build Sponsorship

Gaining support from the responsible managers, or building sponsorship, is extremely important in improvement projects. This concerns test management, IT management and business management sponsorship, because all these stakeholders will be influenced by the change. Sponsorship is important during the entire project, but because of the insecurity caused by changes, especially active support at the beginning of the project is important. Supporting the improvement program is an important part of sponsorship, but sponsorship also includes providing active participation or promoting the project when there is resistance.

Charter Infrastructure

As a final activity in the Initiating phase, the way in which a change project is executed is determined An infrastructure is put in place for this. The infrastructure must be described explicitly, including responsibilities and qualifications.

Usually the infrastructure consists of a project board guiding several improvement teams. On the project board are the sponsor, possibly the other sponsors of other improvement projects, the manager of the improvement program and possibly an external consultant. In addition there is often also an (external) TMMi expert. The project board is ultimately responsible for the improvement program and agrees on plans, milestones and final results. The project board has the ultimate power to decide and is the highest escalation level.

B.2.2 D – Diagnosing: The Diagnosing Phase

In the Diagnosing phase it is determined where the organization stands as opposed to what it wants to achieve. In order to do this, assessments are conducted in which measurements are compared to a reference standard, for example TMMi level 2. The current state of the organization is determined and its desired future state is clearly formulated. In the Diagnosing phase are the following activities:

- Characterize Current and Desired States
- Develop Recommendations.

Characterize Current and Desired States

TMMi can be used to define the desired state. An assessment, either formal or informal, is conducted to determine the current state (Chapter 4). The assessment may use the purposes and practices as a checklist to determine the maturity levels of the test processes. The desired state must align with the stimulus for change as determined in the Initiating phase and it must be within the realm of possibility for the organization.

Develop Recommendations

The recommendations suggest a way of proceeding in subsequent activities. Which TMMi process area is implemented first? Which part of a process area is to be addressed and in what way? The recommendations are formulated under the guidance of (internal or external) TMMi experts in the specific process area.

B.2.3 E – Establishing: The Establishing Phase

During this phase a detailed TMMi implementation plan is developed to implement the recommendations. The general goals as laid down in the Initiating phase are further specified as SMART goals. The recommendations are prioritized taking into account factors such as available resources, visibility, likely resistance, contribution to organizational goals, and so on. In the Establishing phase are the following activities:

- Set Priorities
- Develop Approach
- Plan Actions.

Set Priorities

The first activity of this phase is to set priorities for the change effort. For example, it is futile to implement all five process areas of level 2 at once. When priorities are set, it is determined which process area(s) and which parts of them are implemented first. Several factors, such as available resources, visibility of the results, likely resistance, contribution to organizational goals, etc., should be taken into account.

Develop Approach

Using the recommendations and priorities, a strategy is developed for achieving the desired situation, the desired TMMi level, and the resources needed to achieve them. Technical factors considered include new methods, techniques or resources. Attention must be paid to training, developing process descriptions and possible tool selection. Non-technical factors considered include knowledge and experience, implementation approach, resistance, support, sense of urgency, and the organization's culture, among other things.

Plan Actions

With the approach defined, detailed actions can be determined. Together with information taken from prior activities, these are combined into a plan including, among other things, actions, schedule, milestones, decision points, resources, responsibilities, measurement, tracking mechanisms, risks and implementation strategy.

B.2.4 A – Acting: The Acting Phase

This phase is about concrete activities; this is where the action is! The plan of approach must be executed. The recommendations must be specified in detail and must be implemented. Obviously this phase consumes most of the effort, because while developing the solution takes up about 30% of effort, implementing the solution takes up about 70% [Cannegieter]. In the Acting phase are the following activities:

- Create Solution
- Pilot/Test Solution
- Refine Solution
- Implement Solution.

Create Solution

The Acting phase begins with developing solutions to address the broadly outlined problems. These solutions should satisfy the purposes and practices of TMMi and contribute to achieving the desired situation. The solutions can include processes, templates, tools, knowledge, skills (training), information and support. The solutions, which can be quite complex, are often developed by improvement teams which include a TMMi expert. An approach using improvement teams that has been proven to be successful is the improvement team relay [Zandhuis]. In an improvement team relay, a number of successive improvement teams develop and implement (parts of) the solution in a short time. Some advantages of the improvement team relay include reducing the lead time that would be required if only one overall improvement team was used, achieving results quickly and allowing for more exact guidance. Every improvement team needs to have a clear goal and be given a clear assignment by management. As many employees as possible need to be involved in actually working out the solutions; an external consultant can provide guidance and content input.

Pilot/Test Solution

Following Tom Gilb's advice, 'If you don't know what you are doing, don't do it on a large scale,' the created solution first needs to be tested in one or more test projects. Sometimes only practical experience can show the exact effect of a solution. In pilots such as this, usually one or more test projects are appointed in which the improvements are implemented and evaluated before additional projects adopt the improvements.

Refine Solution

With the use of the results of the test or pilot, the solution can be optimized. Several iterations of the test-optimizing process may be necessary to reach a satisfactory solution that will work for all projects. A solution should be workable; waiting for a 'perfect' solution may unnecessarily delay the implementation.

Implement Solution

Once the solutions are deemed workable, they can be implemented throughout the (test) organization. This is usually the activity that provokes the most resistance. Several implementation approaches can be used, such as:

- Big bang - all the organizational changes are implemented at the same time
- One project at a time - in every project the change is implemented at a set moment in time
- Just in time - the change is implemented when the process is executed.

No single implementation approach is always better than another; the approach should be chosen based on the nature of the improvement and organizational circumstances. For a major change, implementation may require substantial time, resources, effort and attention from management.

B.2.5 L – Learning: The Learning Phase

The Learning phase completes the improvement cycle. One of the goals of the IDEAL model is to continuously improve the ability to implement change. In the Learning phase, the entire IDEAL experience is reviewed to determine what was accomplished, whether the intended goals were achieved, and how the organization can implement change more effectively and efficiently. In the Learning phase are the following activities:

- Analyze and Validate
- Propose Future Actions.

Analyze and Validate

This activity answers several questions, such as:

- How did the improvement program go?
- What has been accomplished; have the initial goals been achieved?
- What worked well?
- What could be done more efficiently or effectively?

Using these questions for guidance, lessons learned are collected, analyzed, summarized and documented.

Propose Future Actions

Based upon the previous activity, recommendations are formulated which are intended to improve future improvement programs, whether or not based upon TMMi. These recommendations are provided to higher management for consideration.

Glossary

acceptance criteria The exit criteria that a component or system must satisfy in order to be accepted by a user, customer, or other authorized entity. [IEEE 610]

acceptance testing Formal testing with respect to user needs, requirements, and business processes conducted to determine whether or not a system satisfies the acceptance criteria and to enable the user, customers or other authorized entity to determine whether or not to accept the system. [After IEEE 610]

action proposal The documented action to be taken to prevent the future occurrence of common causes or to incorporate best practices into test process assets.

actual result The behavior produced/observed when a component or system is tested.

alpha testing Simulated or actual operational testing by potential users/customers or an independent test team at the developers' site, but outside the development organization. Alpha testing is often employed for off-the-shelf software as a form of internal acceptance testing.

Audit An independent evaluation of software products or processes to ascertain compliance to standards, guidelines, specifications, and/or procedures based on objective criteria, including documents that specify:
(1) the form or content of the products to be produced
(2) the process by which the products shall be produced
(3) how compliance to standards or guidelines shall be measured. [IEEE 1028]

availability The degree to which a system or component is operational and accessible when required to use. [IEEE 610]

best practice A superior method or innovative practice that contributes to the improved performance of an organization under given context, usually recognized as 'best' by other peer organizations.

beta testing Operational testing by potential and/or existing users/customers at an external site not otherwise involved with the developers, to determine whether or not a component or system satisfies the user/customer needs and fits within the business processes. Beta testing is often employed as a form of external acceptance testing for off-the-shelf software in order to acquire feedback from the market.

black-box testing Testing, either functional or non-functional, without reference to the internal structure of the component or system.

black-box test design Technique/procedure to derive and/or select test cases based on an analysis of the specification, either functional or non-functional, of a component or system without reference to its internal structure.

boundary value analysis A black box test design technique in which test cases are designed based on boundary values.

branch coverage The percentage of branches that have been exercised by a test suite. 100% branch coverage implies both 100% decision coverage and 100% statement coverage.

branch testing A white box test design technique in which test cases are designed to execute branches.

Capability Maturity Model (CMM) A five level staged framework that describes the key elements of an effective software process. The Capability Maturity Model covers best-practices for planning, engineering and managing software development and maintenance. [CMM]

Capability Maturity Model Integration (CMMI) A framework that describes the key elements of an effective product development and maintenance process. The Capability Maturity Model Integration covers best-practices for planning, engineering and managing product development and maintenance. CMMI is the designated successor of the CMM. [CMMI]

capture/playback tool A type of test execution tool where inputs are recorded during manual testing in order to generate automated test scripts that can be executed later (i.e. replayed). These tools are often used to support automated regression testing.

cause-effect graphing A black box test design technique in which test cases are designed from cause-effect graphs. [BS 7925/2]

classification tree method A black box test design technique in which test cases, described by means of a classification tree, are designed to execute combinations of representatives of input and/or output domains. [Grochtmann]

checklist Checklists are 'stored wisdom' aimed at helping to interpret the rules and explain their application. Checklists are used to increase effectiveness at finding major defects in a specification during a review. A checklist usually takes the form of a list of questions. All checklist questions are derived directly and explicitly from cross-referenced specification rules. [Gilb and Graham]

code coverage An analysis method that determines which parts of the software have been executed (covered) by the test suite and which parts have not been executed, e.g., statement coverage, decision coverage or condition coverage.

common causes The underlying source of a number of defects of a similar type, so that if the root cause is addressed the occurrence of these types of defects is decreased or removed.

component A minimal software item that can be tested in isolation.

component integration testing Testing performed to expose defects in the interfaces and interaction between integrated components.

component testing The testing of individual software components. [After IEEE 610]

condition coverage The percentage of condition outcomes that have been exercised by a test suite. 100% condition coverage requires each single condition in every decision statement to be tested as True and False.

condition testing A white box test design technique in which test cases are designed to execute condition outcomes.

confidence level The likelihood that the software is defect-free. [Burnstein]

configuration The composition of a component or system as defined by the number, nature, and interconnections of its constituent parts.

configuration auditing The function to check on the contents of libraries of configuration items, e.g., for standards compliance. [IEEE 610]

configuration control An element of configuration management, consisting of the evaluation, co-ordination, approval or disapproval, and implementation of changes to configuration items after formal establishment of their configuration identification. [IEEE 610]

configuration control board (CCB) A group of people responsible for evaluating and approving or disapproving proposed changes to configuration items, and for ensuring implementation of approved changes. [IEEE 610]

configuration identification An element of configuration management, consisting of selecting the configuration items for a system and recording their functional and physical characteristics in technical documentation. [IEEE 610]

configuration item An aggregation of hardware, software or both, that is designated for configuration management and treated as a single entity in the configuration management process. [IEEE 610]

configuration management A discipline applying technical and administrative direction and surveillance to: identify and document the functional and physical characteristics of a configuration item, control changes to those characteristics, record and report change processing and implementation status, and verify compliance with specified requirements. [IEEE 610]

configuration management tool A tool that provides support for the identification and control of configuration items, their status over changes and versions, and the release of baselines consisting of configuration items.

continuous representation A capability maturity model structure wherein capability levels provide a recommended order for approaching process improvement within specified process areas. [CMMI]

coverage tool A tool that provides objective measures of what structural elements, e.g., statements, branches have been exercised by a test suite.

debugging tool A tool used by programmers to reproduce failures, investigate the state of programs and find the corresponding defect. Debuggers enable programmers to execute programs step by step, to halt a program at any program statement and to set and examine program variables.

decision coverage The percentage of decision outcomes that have been exercised by a test suite. 100% decision coverage implies both 100% branch coverage and 100% statement coverage.

decision table testing A black box test design technique in which test cases are designed to execute the combinations of inputs and/or stimuli (causes) shown in a decision table. [Veenendaal]

decision testing A white box test design technique in which test cases are designed to execute decision outcomes.

defect A flaw in a component or system that can cause the component or system to fail to perform its required function, e.g., an incorrect statement or data definition. A defect, if encountered during execution, may cause a failure of the component or system.

defect based test design technique A procedure to derive and/or select test cases targeted at one or more defect categories, with tests being developed from what is known about the specific defect category. See also defect taxonomy.

defect classification scheme A set of categories, including phase, defect type, cause, severity, priority, to describe a defect in a consistent manner.

defect density The number of defects identified in a component or system divided by the size of the component or system (expressed in standard measurement terms, e.g., lines-of-code, number of classes or function points).

Defect Detection Percentage (DDP) The number of defects found by a test phase, divided by the number found by that test phase and any other means afterwards.

defect management The process of recognizing, investigating, taking action and disposing of defects. It involves recording defects, classifying them and identifying the impact. [After IEEE 1044]

defect management tool A tool that facilitates the recording and status tracking of defects and changes. They often have workflow-oriented facilities to track and control the

	allocation, correction and re-testing of defects and provide reporting facilities. See also incident management tool.
defect masking	An occurrence in which one defect prevents the detection of another. [After IEEE 610]
defect prevention	The activities involved in identifying defects or potential defects, analyzing these defects to find their root causes and preventing them from being introduced into future products. [After Burnstein]
defect report	A document reporting on any flaw in a component or system that can cause the component or system to fail to perform its required function. [After IEEE 829]
defect taxonomy	A system of (hierarchical) categories designed to be a useful aid for reproducibly classifying defects.
defined process	A managed process that is tailored from the organization's set of standard processes according to the organization's tailoring guidelines; has maintained process description; and contributes work products, measures, and other process improvement information to the organizational process assets. [CMMI]
deliverable	Any (work) product that must be delivered to someone other than the (work) product's author.
driver	A software component or test tool that replaces a component that takes care of the control and/or the calling of a component or system. [After TMap]
dynamic analysis tool	A tool that provides run-time information on the state of the software code. These tools are most commonly used to identify unassigned pointers, check pointer arithmetic and to monitor the allocation, use and de-allocation of memory and to flag memory leaks.
dynamic testing	Testing that involves the execution of the software of a component or system.
efficiency	The capability of the software product to provide appropriate performance relative to the amount of resources used under stated conditions. [ISO 9126]
elementary comparison testing	A black box test design technique in which test cases are designed to execute combinations of inputs using the concept of condition determination coverage. [TMap]

emulator A device, computer program, or system that accepts the same inputs and produces the same outputs as a given system. [IEEE 610] See also simulator.

entry criteria The set of generic and specific conditions for permitting a process to go forward with a defined task, e.g., test phase. The purpose of entry criteria is to prevent a task from starting which would entail more (wasted) effort compared to the effort needed to remove the failed entry criteria. [Gilb and Graham]

equivalence partitioning A black box test design technique in which test cases are designed to execute representatives from equivalence partitions. In principle test cases are designed to cover each partition at least once.

error A human action that produces an incorrect result. [After IEEE 610]

error guessing A test design technique where the experience of the tester is used to anticipate what defects might be present in the component or system under test as a result of errors made, and to design tests specifically to expose them.

exhaustive testing A test approach in which the test suite comprises all combinations of input values and preconditions.

exit criteria The set of generic and specific conditions, agreed upon with the stakeholders, for permitting a process to be officially completed. The purpose of exit criteria is to prevent a task from being considered completed when there are still outstanding parts of the task which have not been finished. Exit criteria are used to report against and to plan when to stop-testing. [After Gilb and Graham]

expected result The behavior predicted by the specification, or another source, of the component or system under specified conditions.

experienced-based test design technique Procedure to derive and/or select test cases based on the tester's experience, knowledge and intuition.

exploratory testing An informal test design technique where the tester actively controls the design of the tests as those tests are performed and uses information gained while testing to design new and better tests. [After Bach]

failure	Deviation of the component or system from its expected delivery, service or result. [After Fenton]
feature	An attribute of a component or system specified or implied by requirements documentation (for example reliability, usability or design constraints). [After IEEE 1008]
formal review	A review characterized by documented procedures and requirements, e.g., inspection.
Function Point Analysis (FPA)	Method aiming to measure the size of the functionality of an information system. The measurement is independent of the technology. This measurement may be used as a basis for the measurement of productivity, the estimation of the needed resources, and project control.
functional testing	Testing based on an analysis of the specification of the functionality of a component or system. See also black box testing.
functionality	The capability of the software product to provide functions which meet stated and implied needs when the software is used under specified conditions. [ISO 9126]
generic goal	A required model component that describes the characteristics that must be present to institutionalize the processes that implement a process area. [CMMI]
generic practice	An expected model component that is considered important in achieving the associated generic goal. The generic practices associated with a generic goal describe the activities that are expected to result in achievement of the generic goal and contribute to the institutionalization of the processes associated with a process area. [CMMI]
Goal Question Metric (GQM)	An approach to software measurement using a three-level model: conceptual level (goal), operational level (question) and quantitative level (metric).
heuristic evaluation	A static usability test technique to determine the compliance of a user interface with recognized usability principles (the so-called "heuristics").
higher level management	The person or persons who provide the policy and overall guidance for the process, but do not to provide direct day-to-day monitoring and controlling of

the process. Such persons belong to a level of management in the organization above the intermediate level responsible for the process and can be (but are not necessarily) senior managers. [CMMI]

horizontal traceability The tracing of requirements for a test level through the layers of test documentation (e.g., test plan, test design specification, test case specification and test procedure specification or test script).

impact analysis The assessment of change to the layers of development documentation, test documentation and components, in order to implement a given change to specified requirements.

Improvement proposal A change request that addresses a proposed process or technology improvement typically also includes a problem statement, a plan for implementing the improvement, and quantitative success criteria for evaluating actual results of the deployment within the change process managed by the Test Process Group.

incident Any event occurring that requires investigation. [After IEEE 1008]

incident logging Recording the details of any incident that occurred, e.g., during testing.

incident management The process of recognizing, investigating, taking action and disposing of incidents. It involves logging incidents, classifying them and identifying the impact. [After IEEE 1044]

incident management tool A tool that facilitates the recording and status tracking of incidents. They often have workflow-oriented facilities to track and control the allocation, correction and re-testing of incidents and provide reporting facilities. See also defect management tool.

incident report A document reporting on any event that occurred, e.g., during the testing, which requires investigation. [After IEEE 829]

independence of testing Separation of responsibilities, which encourages the accomplishment of objective testing. [After DO-178b]

indicator A measure that can be used to estimate or predict another measure. [ISO 14598]

informal review A review not based on a formal (documented) procedure.

input A variable (whether stored within a component or outside) that is read by a component.

inspection A type of peer review that relies on visual examination of documents to detect defects, e.g., violations of development standards and non-conformance to higher level documentation. The most formal review technique and therefore always based on a documented procedure. [After IEEE 610, IEEE 1028] See also peer review.

institutionalization The ingrained way of doing business that an organization follows routinely as part of its corporate culture.

intake test A special instance of a smoke test to decide if the component or system is ready for detailed and further testing. An intake test is typically carried out at the start of the test execution phase. See also smoke test.

integration The process of combining components or systems into larger assemblies.

integration testing Testing performed to expose defects in the interfaces and in the interactions between integrated components or systems. See also component integration testing, system integration testing.

level test plan A test plan that typically addresses one test level. See also test plan.

maintainability The ease which a software product can be modified to correct defects, modified to meet new requirements, modified to make future maintenance easier, or adapted to a changed environment. [ISO 9126]

managed process A performed process that is planned and executed in accordance with policy; employs skilled people having adequate resources to produce controlled outputs; involves relevant stakeholders; is monitored, controlled and reviewed; and is evaluated for adherence to its process description. [CMMI]

management review A systematic evaluation of software acquisition, supply, development, operation, or maintenance process, performed by or on behalf of management that monitors progress, determines the status of plans and schedules, confirms requirements and their system allocation, or evaluates the effectiveness of management approaches to achieve fitness for purpose. [After IEEE 610, IEEE 1028]

master test plan A test plan that typically addresses multiple test levels. See also test plan.

maturity level Degree of process improvement across a predefined set of process areas in which all goals in the set are attained. [CMMI]

Mean Time Between Failures (MTBF) The arithmetic mean (average) time between failures of a system. The MTBF is typically part of a reliability growth model that assumes the failed system is immediately repaired, as a part of a defect fixing process.

Mean Time To Repair (MTTR) The arithmetic mean (average) time a system will take to recover from any failure. This typically includes testing to insure that the defect has been resolved.

measure The number or category assigned to an attribute of an entity by making a measurement. [ISO 14598]

measurement The process of assigning a number or category to an entity to describe an attribute of that entity. [ISO 14598]

measurement scale A scale that constrains the type of data analysis that can be performed on it. [ISO 14598]

metric A measurement scale and the method used for measurement. [ISO 14598]

milestone A point in time in a project at which defined (intermediate) deliverables and results should be ready.

moderator The leader and main person responsible for an inspection or other review process.

monitor A software tool or hardware device that runs concurrently with the component or system under test and supervises, records and/or analyzes the behavior of the component or system. [After IEEE 610]

non-functional testing Testing the attributes of a component or system that do not relate to functionality, e.g., reliability, efficiency, usability, maintainability and portability.

non-functional test design techniques Procedure to derive and/or select test cases for non-functional testing based on an analysis of the specification of a component or system without reference to its internal structure. See also black box test design technique.

operational profile The representation of a distinct set of tasks performed by the component or system, possibly based on user behavior when interacting with the component or system, and their probabilities of occurrence. A task is logical rather that physical and can be executed over several machines or be executed in non-contiguous time segments.

operational profile testing Statistical testing using a model of system operations (short duration tasks) and their probability of typical use. [Musa]

optimizing process A quantitatively managed process that is improved based on an understanding of the common causes of variation inherent in the process. The focus of an optimizing process is on continually improving the range of process performance through both incremental and innovative improvements.

output A variable (whether stored within a component or outside) that is written by a component.

Pareto analysis A statistical technique in decision making that is used for selection of a limited number of factors that produce significant overall effect. In terms of quality improvement, a large majority of problems (80%) are produced by a few key causes (20%).

pass/fail criteria Decision rules used to determine whether a test item (function) or feature has passed or failed a test. [IEEE 829]

peer review A review of a software work product by colleagues of the producer of the product for the purpose of identifying defects and improvements. Examples are inspection, technical review and walkthrough.

performance indicator A high level metric of effectiveness and/or efficiency used to guide and control progressive development, e.g., lead-time slip for software development. [CMMI]

phase test plan A test plan that typically addresses one test phase. See also test plan.

portability The ease with which the software product can be transferred from one hardware or software environment to another. [ISO 9126]

post condition Environmental and state conditions that must be fulfilled after the execution of a test or test procedure.

precondition Environmental and state conditions that must be fulfilled before the component or system can be executed with a particular test or test procedure.

pretest See intake test.

priority The level of (business) importance assigned to an item, e.g., defect.

process A set of interrelated activities, which transform inputs into outputs. [ISO 12207]

process area A cluster of related practices in an area that, when implemented collectively, satisfy a set of goals considered important for making improvements in that area. [CMMI]

process assessment A disciplined evaluation of an organization's software processes against a reference model. [after ISO 15504]

process capability The range of expected results that can be achieved by following a process.

process improvement A program of activities designed to improve the performance and maturity of the organization's processes, and the result of such a program. [CMMI]

process performance A measure of actual results achieved by following a process. [CMMI]

process performance baseline A documented characterization of the actual results achieved by following a process, which is used as a benchmark for comparing actual process performance against expected process performance. [CMMI]

process performance objectives Objectives and requirements for product quality, services quality and process performance.

product risk A risk directly related to the test object. See also risk.

project A project is a unique set of coordinated and controlled activities with start and finish dates undertaken to achieve an objective conforming to specific requirements, including the constraints of time, cost and resources. [ISO 9000]

project risk A risk related to management and control of the (test) project, e.g., lack of staffing, strict deadlines, changing requirements, etc. See also risk.

project test plan See master test plan.

quality assurance Part of quality management focused on providing confidence that quality requirements will be fulfilled. [ISO 9000]

quality attribute A feature or characteristic that affects an item's quality. [IEEE 610]

quantitatively managed process A defined process that is controlled using statistical and other quantitative techniques. The product quality, service quality, and process-performance attributes are measured and controlled throughout the project. [CMMI]

regression testing Testing of a previously tested program following modification to ensure that defects have not been introduced or uncovered in unchanged areas of the software, as a result of the changes made. It is performed when the software or its environment is changed.

release note A document identifying test items, their configuration, current status and other delivery information delivered by development to testing, and possibly other stakeholders, at the start of a test execution phase. [After IEEE 829]

reliability The capability of the software product to perform its required functions under stated conditions for a specified period of time, or for a specified number of operations. [ISO 9126]

reliability growth model A model that shows the growth in reliability over time during continuous testing of a component or system as a result of the removal of defects that result in reliability failures.

requirement A condition or capability needed by a user to solve a problem or achieve an objective that must be met or possessed by a system or system component to satisfy a contract, standard, specification, or other formally imposed document. [After IEEE 610]

requirements-based testing An approach to testing in which test cases are designed based on test objectives and test conditions derived from requirements, e.g., tests that exercise specific functions or probe non-functional attributes such as reliability or usability.

requirements management tool A tool that supports the recording of requirements, requirements attributes (e.g., priority, knowledge responsible) and annotation, and facilitates traceability through layers of requirements and requirements change management. Some requirements management tools also provide facilities for static analysis, such as consistency checking and violations to pre-defined requirements rules.

requirements phase The period of time in the software lifecycle during which the requirements for a software product are defined and documented. [IEEE 610]

result The consequence/outcome of the execution of a test. It includes outputs to screens, changes to data, reports, and communication messages sent out. See also actual result, expected result.

resumption criteria The testing activities that must be repeated when testing is re-started after a suspension. [After IEEE 829]

re-testing Testing that runs test cases that failed the last time they were run, in order to verify the success of corrective actions.

review An evaluation of a product or project status to ascertain discrepancies from planned results and to recommend improvements. Examples include management review, informal review, technical review, inspection, and walkthrough. [After IEEE 1028]

reviewer The person involved in the review that identifies and describes anomalies in the product or project under review. Reviewers can be chosen to represent different viewpoints and roles in the review process.

review tool A tool that provides support to the review process. Typical features include review planning and tracking support, communication support, collaborative reviews and a repository for collecting and reporting of metrics.

risk A factor that could result in future negative consequences; usually expressed as impact and likelihood.

risk analysis The process of assessing identified risks to estimate their impact and probability of occurrence (likelihood).

risk-based testing An approach to testing to reduce the level of product risks and inform stakeholders on their status, starting in the initial stages of a project. It involves the identification of product risks and their use in guiding the test process.

risk control The process through which decisions are reached and protective measures are implemented for reducing risks to, or maintaining risks within, specified levels.

risk identification The process of identifying risks using techniques such as brainstorming, checklists and failure history.

risk level The importance of a risk as defined by its characteristics, impact and likelihood. The level of risk can be used to determine the intensity of testing to be performed. A risk level can be expressed either qualitatively (e.g., high, medium, low) or quantitatively.

risk management Systematic application of procedures and practices to the tasks of identifying, analyzing, prioritizing, and controlling risk.

risk mitigation See risk control.

risk type A specific category of risk related to the type of testing that can mitigate (control) that category. For example the risk of user-interactions being misunderstood can be mitigated by usability testing.

root cause A source of a defect such that if it is removed, the occurrence of the defect type is decreased or removed. [CMMI]

root cause analysis An analysis technique aimed at identifying the root causes of defects. By directing corrective measures at root causes, it is hoped that the likelihood of defect recurrence will be minimized.

rule A rule is any statement of a standard on how to write or carry out some part of a systems engineering or business process. [Gilb and Graham]

sampling A statistical practice concerned with the selection of an unbiased or random subset of individual observations within a population of individuals intended to yield some knowledge about the population of concern as a whole.

scribe The person who records each defect mentioned and any suggestions for process improvement during a review meeting, on a logging form. The scribe has to ensure that the logging form is readable and understandable.

severity The degree of impact that a defect has on the development or operation of a component or system. [After IEEE 610]

simulator A device, computer program or system used during testing, which behaves or operates like a given system when provided with a set of controlled inputs. [After IEEE 610, DO178b] See also emulator.

smoke test A subset of all defined/planned test cases that cover the main functionality of a component or system, ascertaining that the most crucial functions of a program work, but not bothering with finer details. A daily build and smoke test is among industry best practices. See also intake test.

software lifecycle The period of time that begins when a software product is conceived and ends when the software is no longer available for use. The software lifecycle typically includes a concept phase, requirements phase, design phase, implementation phase, test phase, installation and checkout phase, operation and maintenance phase, and sometimes, retirement phase. Note these phases may overlap or be performed iteratively.

specific goal A required model component that describes the unique characteristics that must be present to satisfy the process area. [CMMI]

specific practice An expected model component that is considered important in achieving the associated specific goal. The specific practices describe the activities expected to result in achievement of the specific goals of a process area. [CMMI]

specification A document that specifies, ideally in a complete, precise and verifiable manner, the requirements,

	design, behavior, or other characteristics of a component or system, and, often, the procedures for determining whether these provisions have been satisfied. [After IEEE 610]
specified input	An input for which the specification predicts a result.
staged representation	A model structure wherein attaining the goals of a set of process areas establishes a maturity level; each level builds a foundation for subsequent levels. [CMMI]
standard	Formal, possibly mandatory, set of requirements developed and used to prescribe consistent approaches to the way of working or to provide guidelines (e.g., ISO/IEC standards, IEEE standards, and organizational standards). [After CMMI]
state transition testing	A black box test design technique in which test cases are designed to execute valid and invalid state transitions.
statement coverage	The percentage of executable statements that have been exercised by a test suite.
statement testing	A white box test design technique in which test cases are designed to execute statements.
static analysis	Analysis of software artifacts, e.g., requirements or code, carried out without execution of these software artifacts.
static code analyzer	A tool that carries out static code analysis. The tool checks source code, for certain properties such as conformance to coding standards, quality metrics or data flow anomalies.
static testing	Testing of a component or system at specification or implementation level without execution of that software, e.g., reviews or static code analysis.
statistical process control	Statistically based analysis of a process and measurements of process performance, which will identify common and special causes of variation in the process performance, and maintain process performance within limits. [CMMI]
statistical technique	An analytical technique that employs statistical methods (e.g., statistical process control, confidence intervals, and prediction intervals). [CMMI]

statistical testing A test design technique in which a model of the statistical distribution of the input is used to construct representative test cases.

statistically managed process A process that is managed by a statistically based technique in which processes are analyzed, special causes of process variation are identified, and process performance is contained within well-defined limits. [CMMI]

status accounting An element of configuration management, consisting of the recording and reporting of information needed to manage a configuration effectively. This information includes a listing of the approved configuration identification, the status of proposed changes to the configuration, and the implementation status of the approved changes. [IEEE 610]

stub A skeletal or special-purpose implementation of a software component, used to develop or test a component that calls or is otherwise dependent on it. It replaces a called component. [After IEEE 610]

sub-practice An informative model component that provides guidance for interpreting and implementing a specific or generic practice. Sub-practices may be worded as if prescriptive, but are actually meant only to provide ideas that may be useful for process improvement. [CMMI]

suspension criteria The criteria used to (temporarily) stop all or a portion of the testing activities on the test items. [After IEEE 829]

syntax testing A black box test design technique in which test cases are designed based upon the definition of the input domain and/or output domain.

system A collection of components organized to accomplish a specific function or set of functions. [IEEE 610]

system integration testing Testing the integration of systems and packages; testing interfaces to external organizations (e.g., Electronic Data Interchange, Internet).

system testing The process of testing an integrated system to verify that it meets specified requirements. [Hetzel]

technical review A peer group discussion activity that focuses on achieving consensus on the technical approach to be taken. [Gilb and Graham, IEEE 1028] See also peer review.

test A set of one or more test cases. [IEEE 829]

test approach The implementation of the test strategy for a specific project. It typically includes the decisions made that consider the (test) project's goal and the risk assessment carried out, starting points regarding the test process, the test design techniques to be applied, exit criteria and test types to be performed.

test basis All documents from which the requirements of a component or system can be inferred. The documentation on which the test cases are based. If a document can be amended only by way of formal amendment procedure, then the test basis is called a frozen test basis. [After TMap]

test case A set of input values, execution preconditions, expected results and execution post conditions, developed for a particular objective or test condition, such as to exercise a particular program path or to verify compliance with a specific requirement. [After IEEE 610]

test case specification A document specifying a set of test cases (objective, inputs, test actions, expected results, and execution preconditions) for a test item. [After IEEE 829]

test charter A statement of test objectives, and possibly test ideas about how to test. Test charters are used in exploratory testing. See also exploratory testing.

test closure During the test closure phase of a test process data is collected from completed activities to consolidate experience, test ware, facts and numbers. The test closure phase consists of finalizing and archiving the test ware and evaluating the test process, including preparation of a test evaluation report. See also test process.

test comparator A test tool to perform automated test comparison of actual results with expected results.

test condition An item or event of a component or system that could be verified by one or more test cases, e.g., a function, transaction, feature, quality attribute, or structural element.

test control A test management task that deals with developing and applying a set of corrective actions to get a test project on track when monitoring shows a deviation from what was planned. See also test management.

test cycle Execution of the test process against a single identifiable release of the test object.

test data Data that exists (for example, in a database) before a test is executed, and that affects or is affected by the component or system under test.

test data preparation tool A type of test tool that enables data to be selected from existing databases or created, generated, manipulated and edited for use in testing.

test design (1) See test design specification.
(2) The process of transforming general testing objectives into tangible test conditions and test cases.

test design specification A document specifying the test conditions (coverage items) for a test item, the detailed test approach and identifying the associated high level test cases. [After IEEE 829]

test design technique Procedure used to derive and/or select test cases.

test design tool A tool that supports the test design activity by generating test inputs from a specification that may be held in a CASE tool repository, e.g., requirements management tool, from specified test conditions held in the tool itself, or from code.

test environment An environment containing hardware, instrumentation, simulators, software tools, and other support elements needed to conduct a test. [After IEEE 610]

test estimation The calculated approximation of a result (e.g., effort spent, completion date, costs involved, number of test cases, etc.) which is usable even if input data may be incomplete, uncertain, or noisy.

test evaluation report A document produced at the end of the test process summarizing all testing activities and results. It also contains an evaluation of the test process and lessons learned.

test execution The process of running a test on the component or system under test, producing actual result(s).

test execution phase The period of time in a software development lifecycle during which the components of a software product are executed, and the software product is evaluated to determine whether or not requirements have been satisfied. [IEEE 610]

test execution schedule A scheme for the execution of test procedures. The test procedures are included in the test execution schedule in their context and in the order in which they are to be executed.

test execution tool A type of test tool that is able to execute other software using an automated test script, e.g., capture/playback. [Fewster and Graham]

test harness A test environment comprised of stubs and drivers needed to execute a test.

test implementation The process of developing and prioritizing test procedures, creating test data and, optionally, preparing test harnesses and writing automated test scripts.

test improvement plan A plan for achieving organizational test process improvement objectives based on a thorough understanding of the current strengths and weaknesses of the organization's test processes and test process assets. [After CMMI]

test infrastructure The organizational artifacts needed to perform testing, consisting of test environments, test tools, office environment and procedures.

test input The data received from an external source by the test object during test execution. The external source can be hardware, software or human.

test item The individual element to be tested. There usually is one test object and many test items. See also test object.

test level A group of test activities that are organized and managed together. A test level is linked to the responsibilities in a project. Examples of test levels are component test, integration test, system test and acceptance test. [After TMap]

test log A chronological record of relevant details about the execution of tests. [IEEE 829]

test logging The process of recording information about tests executed into a test log.

test manager The person responsible for project management of testing activities and resources, and evaluation of a test object. The individual who directs, controls, administers, plans and regulates the evaluation of a test object.

test management The planning, estimating, monitoring and control of test activities, typically carried out by a test manager.

test management tool A tool that provides support to the test management and control part of a test process. It often has several capabilities, such as test ware management, scheduling of tests, the logging of results, progress tracking, incident management and test reporting.

Test Maturity Model (TMM) A five level staged framework for test process improvement, related to the Capability Maturity Model (CMM), which describes the key elements of an effective test process.

Test Maturity Model Integrated (TMMi) A five level staged framework for test process improvement, related to the Capability Maturity Model Integration (CMMI), which describes the key elements of an effective test process.

test monitoring A test management task that deals with the activities related to periodically checking the status of a test project. Reports are prepared that compare the actuals to that which was planned. See also test management.

test object The component or system to be tested. See also test item.

test objective A reason or purpose for designing and executing a test.

test performance indicator A high level metric of effectiveness and/or efficiency used to guide and control progressive test development, e.g., Defect Detection Percentage (DDP).

test phase A distinct set of test activities collected into a manageable phase of a project, e.g., the execution activities of a test level. [After Gerrard]

test plan A document describing the scope, approach, resources and schedule of intended test activities. It identifies amongst others test items, the features to be tested, the testing tasks, who will do each task, degree of tester independence, the test environment,

	the test design techniques and entry and exit criteria to be used, and the rationale for their choice, and any risks requiring contingency planning. It is a record of the test planning process. [After IEEE 829]
test planning	The activity of establishing or updating a test plan.
test policy	A high level document describing the principles, approach and major objectives of the organization regarding testing.
Test Point Analysis (TPA)	A formula based test estimation method based on function point analysis. [TMap]
test procedure specification	A document specifying a sequence of actions for the execution of a test. Also known as test script or manual test script. [After IEEE 829]
test process	The fundamental test process comprises test planning and control, test analysis and design, test implementation and execution, evaluating exit criteria and reporting, and test closure activities.
test process asset library	A collection of test process asset holdings that can be used by an organization or project. [CMMI]
Test Process Group (TPG)	A permanent or virtual entity in the organization responsible for test process related activities such as process definition, analysis and assessment, action planning and evaluation. Has the overall test process ownership as defined in an organization's test policy.
Test Process Improvement (TPI)	A continuous framework for test process improvement that describes the key elements of an effective test process, especially targeted at system testing and acceptance testing.
test progress report	A document summarizing testing activities and results, produced at regular intervals, to report progress of testing activities against a baseline (such as the original test plan) and to communicate risks and alternatives requiring a decision to management.
test run	Execution of a test on a specific version of the test object.
test schedule	A list of activities, tasks or events of the test process, identifying their intended start and finish dates and/or times, and interdependencies.

test script Commonly used to refer to a test procedure specification, especially an automated one.

test session An uninterrupted period of time spent in executing tests. In exploratory testing, each test session is focused on a charter, but testers can also explore new opportunities or issues during a session. The tester creates and executes test cases on the fly and records their progress. See also exploratory testing.

test specification A document that consists of a test design specification, test case specification and/or test procedure specification.

test strategy A high-level description of the test levels to be performed and the testing within those levels for an organization or program (one or more projects).

test suite A set of several test cases for a component or system under test, where the post condition of one test is often used as the precondition for the next one.

test summary report A document summarizing testing activities and results. It also contains an evaluation of the corresponding test items against exit criteria. [After IEEE 829]

test tool A software product that supports one or more test activities, such as planning and control, specification, building initial files and data, test execution and test analysis. [TMap]

test type A group of test activities aimed at testing a component or system focused on a specific test objective, i.e. functional test, usability test, regression test etc. A test type may take place on one or more test levels or test phases. [After TMap]

testability review A detailed check of the test basis to determine whether the test basis is at an adequate quality level to act as an input document for the test process. [After TMap]

tester A skilled professional who is involved in the testing of a component or system.

testing The process consisting of all lifecycle activities, both static and dynamic, concerned with planning, preparation and evaluation of software products and related work products to determine that they satisfy specified requirements, to demonstrate that they are fit for purpose and to detect defects.

test ware Artifacts produced during the test process required to plan, design, and execute tests, such as documentation, scripts, inputs, expected results, set-up and clear-up procedures, files, databases, environment, and any additional software or utilities used in testing. [After Fewster and Graham]

TPI Next A continuous business-driven framework for test process improvement that describes the key elements of an effective and efficient test process. TPI Next is the successor of TPI.

traceability The ability to identify related items in documentation and software, such as requirements with associated tests. See also horizontal traceability, vertical traceability.

trustworthiness The probability that there are no defects in the software that will cause the system to fail catastrophically. [Burnstein]

unit test See component test.

usability The capability of the software to be understood, learned, used and attractive to the user when used under specified conditions. [ISO 9126]

use case testing A black box test design technique in which test cases are designed to execute user scenarios.

V-model A framework to describe the software development lifecycle activities from requirements specification to maintenance. The V-model illustrates how testing activities can be integrated into each phase of the software development lifecycle.

validation Confirmation by examination and through provision of objective evidence that the requirements for a specific intended use or application have been fulfilled. [ISO 9000]

verification Confirmation by examination and through provision of objective evidence that specified requirements have been fulfilled. [ISO 9000]

vertical traceability The tracing of requirements through the layers of development documentation to components.

walkthrough A step-by-step presentation by the author of a document in order to gather information and to establish a common understanding of its content. [Freedman and Weinberg, IEEE 1028] See also peer review.

white-box test design technique Procedure to derive and/or select test cases based on an analysis of the internal structure of a component or system.

white-box testing Testing based on an analysis of the internal structure of the component or system.

Wide Band Delphi An expert based test estimation technique that aims at making an accurate estimation using the collective wisdom of the team members.

References

- [Bach] J. Bach (2004), Exploratory Testing, in: E. van Veenendaal, *The Testing Practitioner – 2nd edition*, UTN Publishing
- [Beizer] B. Beizer (1990), *Software Testing Techniques*, van Nostrand Reinhold
- [Boehm} B.W. Boehm (1981), Software Engineering Economics, Prentice Hall
- [BS7925-2] BS7925-2 (1998), *Standard for Software Component Testing*, British Standards Institution
- [Burnstein]. I. Burnstein (2002), *Practical Software Testing*, Springer Professional Computing
- [CMM] M. Paulk, C. Weber, B. Curtis and M.B. Chrissis (1995), *The Capability Maturity Model, Guidelines for Improving the Software Process*, Addison-Wesley
- [CMMI] M.B. Chrissis, M. Konrad and S. Shrum (2007), *CMMI Second Edition, Guidelines for Process Integration and Product Improvement*, Addison Wesley
- [DO-178b] DO-178 (1992). *Software Considerations in Airborne Systems and Equipment Certification, Requirements and Technical Concepts for Aviation* (RTCA SC167),
- [Fenton] N. Fenton (1991), *Software Metrics: a Rigorous Approach*, Chapman & Hall
- [Fewster and Graham] M. Fewster and D. Graham (1999), Software Test Automation, Effective use of test execution tools, Addison-Wesley
- [Freedman and Weinberg] D. Freedman and G. Weinberg (1990), *Walkthroughs, Inspections, and Technical Reviews*, Dorset House Publishing
- [Gelperin and Hetzel] D. Gelperin and B. Hetzel (1998), '*The Growth of Software Testing*', in: CACM, Vol. 31, No. 6, 1988, pp. 687-695
- [Gerrard] P. Gerrard and N. Thompson (2002), *Risk-Based E-Business Testing*, Artech House Publishers
- [Gilb] T. Gilb (1988), *Principles of Software Engineering Management*, Addison-Wesley
- [Gilb and Graham] T. Gilb and D. Graham (1993), *Software Inspection*, Addison-Wesley
- [Graham] D. Graham, E. van Veenendaal, I. Evans and R. Black (2007), *Foundations of Software Testing*, Thomson Learning
- [Grochtmann] M. Grochtmann (1994), Test Case Design Using Classification Trees, in: Conference Proceedings STAR 1994.
- [Hauser and Clausing] J.R. Hausing and D. Clausing (1988), The House of Quality, in: *Harvard Business Review*, Vol. 66, Nr. 3, 1988
- [Hetzel] W. Hetzel (1988), *The complete guide to software testing – 2nd edition*, QED Information Sciences
- [Hollenbach and Frakes] C. Hollenback and W. Frakes (1996), Software process re-use in an industrial setting, in: *Proceedings Fourth International Conference on Software-Reuse*, Orlando, April 1998, pp. 22-30
- [IDEAL] SEI (1997), *IDEAL: A Users Guide for Software Process Improvement*, Software Engineering Institute
- [IEEE 610] IEEE 610.12 (1990), *Standard Glossary for Software Engineering Terminology*, IEEE Standards Board
- [IEEE 829] IEEE 829 (1998), *Standard for Software Test Documentation*, IEEE Standards Board
- [IEEE 1008] IEEE 1008 (1993), *Standard for Software Unit Testing*, IEEE Standards Board
- [IEEE 1028] IEEE 1028 (1997), *Standard for Software Reviews and Audits*, IEEE Standards Board
- [IEEE 1044] IEEE 1044 (1993), *Standard Classification for Software Anomalies*, IEEE Standards Board

- [ISO 9000] ISO 9000 (2005), *Quality Management Systems – Fundamentals and Vocabulary*, International Organization of Standardization
- [ISO 9126] ISO/IEC 9126-1 (2001). *Software Engineering – Software Product Quality – Part 1: Quality characteristics and sub-characteristics*, International Organization of Standardization
- [ISO 12207] ISO/IEC 12207 (1995), *Information Technology – Software Lifecycle Processes*, International Organization of Standardization
- [ISO 14598] ISO/IEC 14598-1 (1999), *Information Technology – Software Product Evaluation - Part 1: General Overview*, International Organization of Standardization
- [ISO 155504] ISO 15504-9 (1998), Information Technology – Software Process Assessment – Part 9: Vocabulary, International Organization of Standardization
- [ISTQB] ISTQB – E. van Veenendaal (ed.) (2010), *Standard Glossary of Terms Used in Software Testing, V2.1*, International Software Testing Qualifications Board
- [Koomen and Pol] T. Koomen and M. Pol (1999), *Test Process Improvement*, Addison-Wesley
- [Musa] J. Musa (1998), *Software Reliability Engineering Testing*, McGraw-Hill Education
- [Musa and Ackerman] J. Musa and A. Ackerman (1989), Quantifying software validation: when to stop-testing, in: *IEEE Software,* Vol. 6, No. 3, May 1989
- [Pinster *et al*] I. Pinkster, B. van der Burgt, D. Janssen and E. van Veenendaal (2004), *Successful Test Management,* Springer
- [Sogeti] Sogeti (2009), *TPI Next - Business Driven Test Process Improvement,* UTN Publishing
- [TAMAR] A. Goslin (ed.) (2011), *TMMi Assessment Method Application Requirements V2.0*, TMMi Foundation
- [TMap] M. Pol, R. Teunissen, E. van Veenendaal (2002), *Software Testing, A guide to the TMap Approach*, Addison Wesley.
- [Trienekens and Van Veenendaal] J. Trienekens and E. van Veenendaal (1997), *Software Quality from a Business Perspective,* Kluwer Bedrijfsinformatie
- [V2M2] QualityHouse (2006), *V2M2; A Verification and Validation Maturity Model – Improving test practices and models*
- [Veenendaal] E. van Veenendaal (2004), *The Testing Practitioner – 2nd edition*, UTN Publishing
- [Veenendaal en Cannegieter] E. van Veenendaal and J.J. Cannegieter (2011), *The little TMMi – Objectives-Driven Test Process Improvement*, UTN Publishing
- [Van Solingen and Berghout] R. van Solingen and E. Berghout (1999), *The Goal/Question/Metric method*, McGrawHill

About the TMMi Foundation

A number of leading practitioners within the testing industry recognized there was a growing need to define an independent global model to be used to evaluate and measure test process maturity. Only limited attention is given to testing in the various software process improvement models such as the CMMI and the various 'test process capability models' that were available did not seem to satisfy the global requirement sufficiently. Out of these discussions, the TMMi Foundation was inaugurated in 2007 to support the development of TMMi. It was agreed that the model should be in the public domain and have no purely academic or commercial 'ownership'. The founding directors were Andrew Goslin, Fran O'Hara, Mac Miller, Klaus Olsen, Geoff Thompson, Erik van Veenendaal and Brian Wells. The TMMi Foundation is a 'not for profit' organization registered in Dublin, Ireland.

Since its inception, the Foundation has attracted interest from around the world and membership is growing all the time. In parallel, an increasing number of organizations are providing financial and other support to the work of the Foundation. These include organizations in Europe, India and South America.

In 2009, the Foundation expanded its organizational capability by creating a Management Executive committee. Membership of the Management Executive committee is open to all registered members of the Foundation and is determined by membership ballot at the Annual General Meeting. The Management Executive has responsibility for implementing the strategic objectives of the Foundation as set by the Board of Directors.

The stated objectives of the Foundation are the following:

- Identifying and securing the ownership of the TMMi Model standard and the ongoing intellectual property rights.
- Defining an international core TMMi Model standard and placing it in the public domain.
- Creating and managing an independent, unbiased central test maturity data repository.
- Provisioning an independent accreditation process for TMMi Assessment Methods based on the standard Model.
- Provisioning an independent mechanism to facilitate verification and formal ratification of TMMi Assessment Ratings.
- Defining and maintaining independent assessor training, accreditation, guidelines and examinations.
- Provisioning a public forum for interested parties to facilitate free interchange of information, education, ideas and usage of the public standard.

To satisfy these objectives, the TMMi Foundation aims to provide the following:

- A standard TMMi Model that can be used in isolation or in support of other process improvement models.
- An independently managed data repository to support TMMi assessment method accreditation, assessor and assessment certification/validation and validated assessment data and certificates.
- Assessment Method Accreditation/Audit Framework for TMMi in accordance with ISO15504 and the process to certify commercial assessment methods against the standard model.
- Certification and training/examination process, procedures and standards for formal, public accreditation of Assessors and Lead Assessors and the on-going management of these.

Through the Foundation, the testing community (via the technical drafting work groups and the extensive Review Panel membership) is assisting in creating and maintaining its improvement model: the Test Maturity Model Integration (TMMi). The TMMi model is a detailed model for test process capability measurement and the identification of improvements. It is complementary to CMMI but equally supports other software engineering models such as ITIL, ISO 9000 etc.

In 2008, the Foundation also published its TMMi Assessment Method Accreditation Requirements (TAMAR). These are based on ISO15504 and define the requirements of an assessment method package that, if satisfied, will allow the supplier to have the method certified (accredited) by the Foundation. Going forward, the Foundation is looking to provide its own assessment method package for use by organizations as well as providing training.

In parallel with the publication of TAMAR, the Foundation also published criteria and procedures for Assessors and Lead Assessors to be accredited with the Foundation as having the necessary knowledge, training and skills to undertake assessments.

The TMMI Foundation provides published requirements based on a common, global framework which comprises a standard to be used to evaluate and compare test processes. In addition to this standard reference model, the TMMi Foundation also provides services to publicly accredit methods and assessor resources. This makes it is easier for organizations to assess, measure and compare their processes against a public domain standard that is robust and widely accepted.

Full information on the activities, work, accredited TMMi assessment services providers, and publications of the Foundation can be found on the website www.tmmi.org.

About the Authors

Erik van Veenendaal

Drs. Erik van Veenendaal, CISA, has been working as a practitioner and manager in the IT-industry since 1987. After a career in software development, he transferred to the area of software quality. As a test analyst, test manager and test consultant, Erik has over 20 years of practical testing experience. He has implemented structured testing, formal reviews and requirements processes, and has carried out test process improvement activities based on TMMi in a large number of organizations in different industries. Erik has also been a senior lecturer at the Eindhoven University of Technology, Faculty of Technology Management for almost ten years.

Erik founded Improve Quality Services BV (www.improveqs.nl) back in 1998 as an independent organization that focuses on advanced high quality services. He has been the company director for over 12 years. Under his direction Improve Quality Services became a leading testing company in The Netherlands. Customers are especially to be found in the areas of embedded software (e.g. Philips, Océ en Assembléon) and in the finance domain (e.g. Rabobank, ING and Triodos Bank). Improve Quality Services offers international consultancy and training services with respect to testing (e.g., test process improvement using the TMMi framework), quality management and requirements engineering. Improve Quality Services BV was the second world-wide company to become accredited to perform TMMi assessments. They are a market leader for ISTQB Foundation and ISTQB Advanced training courses and a member of the International Requirements Engineering Board (IREB).

Erik is the (co-)author of numerous papers and a number of books on software quality and testing, including the best-sellers *The Testing Practitioner*, *Foundations of Software Testing*, *The Little TMMi* and *Testing according to TMap*. Erik was the first person to receive the ISEB Practitioner certificate with distinction, and is also a Certified Information Systems Auditor (CISA) and accredited TMMi lead-assessor. He is a regular speaker both at national and international testing conferences and a leading international trainer (ISTQB accredited) in the field of software testing. At EuroStar'99 (Usability testing), EuroStar'02 (Test Strategies and Planning) and EuroStar'05 (Inspection Leader), he received the best tutorial award.

He is a former vice president of the International Software Testing Qualification Board (ISTQB) (from 2005 – 2009). He is the editor of the ISTQB 'Standard Glossary of Terms Used in Software Testing' and vice-chair/chair of the ISTQB expert level working party since its inception in 2002. Erik is one of the founders of the TMMi Foundation and is currently the vice chair of the TMMi Foundation. He is the lead developer of the TMMi model. Erik is actively involved in various working parties of the International Requirements Engineering Board (IREB). For his outstanding contribution to the field of testing Erik received the 'European Testing Excellence Award' in December, 2007.

After having provided leadership to Improve Quality Services BV for over 12 years, Erik stepped down from that role in July 2010. Since that time he is living in Bonaire where Erik is involved in international test consultancy, training and international organizations (e.g., ISTQB, TMMi and IREB), publications and presentations. As a major shareholder, Erik remains to be involved in Improve Quality Services.

Erik can be contacted via e-mail at eve@improveqs.nl and through his website www.erikvanveenendaal.nl.

Brian Wells

Brian has specialized in all aspects of IT Test & Validation for over 20 years. Before becoming a consultant, he spent 16 years in HM Diplomatic Service. He has held many positions including senior test strategist/consultant and has worked with many blue chip companies in the UK, Europe and elsewhere. He provides comprehensive, flexible solutions for all aspects of Test & Validation to all levels of a corporation, which is targeted on priority/risk and achievability while remaining flexible in its approach.

Brian has presented at many of the industry's premier conferences such as EuroSTAR, UKSMA and Iqnite. He holds the ISEB/ISTQB (International Software Testing Qualifications Board) Foundation & Advanced Certificates in Software Testing and is a certified trainer of the ISTQB courses. He is also a qualified CMMI (Capability Maturity Model) Assessor and an active member of the UKSMA (UK Software Metrics Association).

He is an experienced TMMi Lead Assessor and has led many assessments across Europe and India as well as working with clients to realize process improvement programs derived from TMMi assessments which, when implemented, demonstrate tangible value to clients. He currently heads up the TMMi practice for his employer, Experimentus, Ltd, as well as being a leading (and founding) member of the TMMi Foundation. He is working closely with others to develop the Testing Maturity Model (TMMi) test process assessment model and method.

For Brian, effective interpretation and application of the TMMi standard reference model in operational scenarios works!

Index

Made in United States
Orlando, FL
04 November 2026

90201128R00195